HONOURING
HIGH
PLACES

HONOURING HIGH PLACES

THE MOUNTAIN LIFE OF JUNKO TABEI

Junko Tabei and Helen Y. Rolfe

Translated by Yumiko Hiraki and Rieko Holtved

RMB

RMB | Rocky Mountain Books Ltd.
rmbooks.com
@rmbooks
facebook.com/rmbooks

Cataloguing data available from Library and Archives Canada
ISBN 9781771602167 (hardcover)
ISBN 9781771602174 (electronic)

Printed and bound in Canada by Friesens

Cover photo courtesy of Eiko Tabe

Distributed in Canada by Heritage Group Distribution and in the U.S. by Publishers Group West

For information on purchasing bulk quantities of this book, or to obtain media excerpts or invite the author to speak at an event, please visit rmbooks.com and select the "Contact Us" tab.

We acknowledge the financial support of the Government of Canada through the Canada Book Fund and the Canada Council for the Arts, and of the province of British Columbia through the British Columbia Arts Council and the Book Publishing Tax Credit.

Contents

Author's Note

Honouring High Places is the memoir of Junko Tabei, the first woman to climb Mount Everest and complete the Seven Summits. The stories within are based on translated excerpts from several of Tabei's published Japanese books. Written in first person, each chapter represents experiences in Tabei's life that she felt were important to share in terms of mountaineering history; they also serve as invitations, encouraging people to go outside and to enjoy nature.

Mine was an enormous job to accurately interpret and express Tabei's disposition without having met her. I worked closely with Yumiko Hiraki, translator, and dear friend of Tabei, to be certain that every sentence, every word, reflected the era and person in Tabei's original books. Although challenging, it was a privilege to write about such an accomplished woman and tell her story in detail.

On October 20, 2016, when I was deep in the Annapurna chapter, Tabei succumbed to cancer and passed away. I was awash with emotion. Tabei was part of my daily life by then, and I was saddened that I would never have the chance to shake her hand in person. In addition, we had a book to complete with highlighted sections for Tabei to still comment on. Thankfully, in stepped her loving husband, Masanobu, and her good friend, Setsuko Kitamura, and, of course, Yumiko. Together, and miles apart, we filled in the blanks to unanswered questions. At that time, Yumiko and I, along with Rocky Mountain Books, sped up the process so we could present a finished publication to the Tabei family in fall 2017, marking one year since their beloved Junko had died.

To arrive at the final pages of this book was poignant for me, although I sensed more of a beginning than an end. My hope is that Tabei's story fulfills its main purpose, which is to offer inspiration and encouragement for people to push themselves in the direction of a challenging goal, whether it be a mountaintop or otherwise. As a certain female mountain-eer would have said, "*Ganbatte* – do your best."

– Helen Y. Rolfe

Introduction

by Setsuko Kitamura

Sometime in the early 1990s, Junko Tabei and I saw a pair of elderly ladies at the Nikko train station when we went skiing. Both of them had totally grey hair, and one was tall, the other one tiny. We quietly gazed at them for a while, admiring that they were caring for each other and still cheerfully marching off to somewhere. When they were gone, we giggled and looked at each other, "Haven't we just witnessed ourselves thirty years from now?"

Though we can never take our peaceful senior life for granted, as nobody knows what is around the corner in the aging years, I would love to become a granny who is as gentle and strong as Tabei has already been, with ice axe in hand (and let us not forget, the occasional application of lipstick, as well).

Elevation 5350 metres, the wave of dusk around the corner and a stabbing cold wind crossing over the glacier. On March 16, 1975, I was standing at Everest Base Camp on the Nepali side of the mountain. I had just arrived there, a few days ahead of the main party, as one of the Base Camp establishment members of the Japanese Women's Everest Expedition. When all the local porters, yaks and yak handlers left for home, as if being chased away by the impending dark of night, the world of rocks and ice quickly turned desolate. It was my first experience at that high of an altitude, and my job was to manage 15 tons of supplies. I was twenty-five years old at that time, and already I was exhausted. Having almost fallen forward into a temporarily pitched tent, and breathing hard with shaky shoulders, I was caught by the anxious thoughts of what was going to happen in the long stretch of mountaineering that lay ahead.

The very moment I began wallowing in the negative feeling, the tent door suddenly flapped open and a voice full of energy flew into the space.

"That's why kids are kids. Well, well, you stay lying down there and Mom will make tasty croquettes!"

After a short while, on a table in the mess tent, a plateful of perfectly fried crispy croquettes showed up. Dried mashed potato powder, tinned corned beef, half-frozen little onions and crushed biscuits (the stand-ins for crumbled, dried bread) were the modest ingredients used, and somehow, they turned out to be a dish of delicacy. The very taste of those hot croquettes I ate at the skirt of the highest mountain in the world became the symbol of Junko Tabei for me. She was good at managing groups, strong in high altitudes with great mountaineering skills. Always thinking positively, she both had a boyish sense of humour and a sensible nature that kept her grounded. Regardless of celebrity, she stayed an ordinary family woman, cherishing daily life, moment by moment.

The first woman to climb Mount Everest came from an interesting time in Japan, the Meiji era (1868-1912),[1] when the Japanese people were introduced to the idea of mountaineering for sport, of enjoying mountaineering in and of itself. Before then, mountaineering in Japan had only been pursued for the purpose of worship. Initially, the hobby, newly imported by Walter Weston and others, prevailed only among men.[2] Eventually, in the Taisho era (1912–1926), women of the intellectual class began to join in this European-style play. This is highlighted by Yoneko Murai on Hodaka in the Taisho era, Teru Nakamura on Mount Fuji in the early Showa era (1926–1989), and Hatsuko Kuroda and Kimiko Imai's climbing on Hodaka, just to list a few.

After the Second World War, the sport of mountaineering expanded beyond a few upper-class women and opened its doors to the broader

1   Most of Japanese history is divided into conventional eras that are based on the reigns of the emperors. The modern eras from 1868 are:

1868–1912	Meiji	Emperor Mitsuhito
1912–1926	Taisho	Emperor Yoshihito
1926–1989	Showa	Emperor Hirohito
1989–present	Heisei	Emperor Akihito

2   Walter Weston was an English clergyman and Anglican missionary who helped popularize recreational mountaineering in Japan at the turn of the twentieth century.

population. Under the newer "gender equality" philosophy, local mountaineering clubs gradually started to welcome women, and eventually, women-only mountaineering clubs were being born.

In 1949 the long-established Japanese Alpine Club wasted no time in creating the Ladies Section in its Tokyo branch, and in the mid-1950s, Edelweiss Club (1955) and Bush Mountaineering Club (1956) were initiated. The university mountaineering clubs at Waseda and Nihon also began to accept female students, and Tokyo Women's Medical University established its own mountaineering club.

This era of mountaineering in Japan encouraged and appealed to women who were full of curiosity and the spirit of challenge.

It was also during that time when, in 1956, the Japanese Manaslu Expedition succeeded in the first ascent of that 8156-metre giant. "Not the post-war-era anymore," and "Japan will revive," were the general social confidences that resulted from the success on Manaslu. This same sentiment was also applied at the time to the Japanese ship *Sōya* that was first used during the war and then was refitted as an Antarctic icebreaker. She became famous for her rescue work in the late 1950s, served for a long time, and is now a museum in Tokyo.

Surfing on top of the booming economy was the enormous youthful energy that spilled out of students and workers who sought to live in the big cities. Also, women were receiving a higher level of education than before, albeit at a more gradual rate. It was no wonder that the interests of men and women alike naturally shifted overseas.

In 1960 Bush Mountaineering Club sent an expedition to India, where members summitted a 6000-metre peak. In 1966 Edelweiss Club travelled to the Peruvian Andes. And in 1965, a women's mountaineering club called Jungfrau was established in the Kansai region,[3] with the concrete aim of "overseas expeditions by women." They kept their word and reached the summit of Pakistan's Istor-O-Nal (7403 metres) in 1968. In addition, the Ladies Section of the Japanese Alpine Club had a joint venture with the women's team of India.

Tabei, who had moved to Tokyo for her university education in 1958,

---

3   Kansai is a region in the south of Honshu, Japan's main island. In its centre is the
      city of Kyoto, Japan's capital from 794 to 1869.

was exactly in the right place at the right time for climbing. Numerous pieces of mountaineering equipment, lighter than before, were invented one after the other, and alpinism was flourishing as a popular sport for ordinary people, including women. There was no doubt that Ryoho, the climbing club she joined after university, was ripe with the spirit behind the slogans "man or woman – it does not matter," and "next, to the mountains overseas!" In this context, it was natural for Tabei to dream about the Himalayas. At the time, she was seriously into rock climbing in Tanigawa-dake and Hodaka-dake, and so she helped establish the Ladies Climbing Club in Tokyo with the clear purpose of "going to the Himalayas by women alone."

I first met Tabei in 1973 when I was a rookie reporter for a Japanese newspaper. I was assigned to research the Ladies Climbing Club, which had received a climbing permit for Mount Everest – the first-ever women's team to go there. Subsequently I shared several expeditions with her, admiring her (ten years my senior) and calling myself her disciple (without her permission). During the time I spent with Tabei, I often saw in her the qualities that make a person a successful, high-mountain climber.

First, she was physically strong, period, particularly in terms of cardiovascular strength. Only once did I witness her suffer from high-altitude sickness, and that was on Shishapangma (8013 metres) in 1981, which she climbed without supplemental oxygen.

Second, Tabei had a high level of practical business skills. The speed at which she typed, in English, the customs documents required for the Everest expedition was impressive; it was as if she were shooting a semi-automatic gun. The image of her typing like that has never left my memory. Then there was her trouble-shooting capability. Her way of finding a solution for complicated problems in prioritized order along with the right judgment call for each issue was breathtaking.

Despite the above descriptions that make Tabei sound like a superwoman, fittingly, she was also unexpectedly a "person of worries." There was something almost timid in her personality in that she was known to care too much about how others felt. For instance, so far as I know, she cried two times on the Everest expedition alone. First, as we trekked to Base Camp and our team leader surprised us with a sudden departure.

Tabei stood forever in the garden of the Tengboche temple where our tents were pitched, looking up at Everest in the distance, her right elbow held high as she wiped her eyes on the back of her hand. The other occasion was after the success on Everest, at a celebration with locals in Namche Bazaar where the Sherpas were based. On the way back to our tent site, slightly removed from the village, after having drunk a bit too much *chhaang*, she cried hard, like a waterfall.[4] She lamented the negative attitude and distorted passion of the teammates who felt they had "missed the limelight of grabbing the summit." Tabei cried, "Why, we have come here together...."

Tabei was also a sensitive mother who did not forget to draw a picture of a birthday cake with coloured pencils on a postcard and send it, from Everest High Camp, for Noriko, her daughter, turning three years old at the time.

It was probably due to her compassionate personality that Japanese society adopted Junko Tabei as a "star of the mountaineering community" and "role model for Japanese women," which certainly reflected the era's shifting values from submissive women to active ones. At the same time, while welcoming "women full of energy," Japanese society was not ready to accept radical feminists as it was still attached to traditional women figures: good wives, perfect mothers and modest behaviour.

Thus, it was reasonable that Tabei's brand of conservatism, claiming she was "merely a housewife," even long after her Everest success, made people feel comfortable. They loved the story of a strong mother, with a young child, courageously conquering the highest mountain in the world.

But a few times *I* criticized Tabei and her modest proclamations of "Because I am a housewife...," or "...since it's me being selfish going mountaineering...." Once I told her straight up: "Hey, there are countless women who wish to pursue their own interests as much as you do. If you continue acting like an elite mom, they would hesitate, like, 'Oh, I'm not that superwoman like Junko Tabei,' and the bunch of husbands

4   *Chhaang* is a relative of beer. Barley, millet (finger-millet) or rice grains are used to brew the drink. Semi-fermented seeds of millet are served, stuffed in a barrel of bamboo called a *dhungro*.

would take advantage of it, and say, 'See, she doesn't sabotage her domestic duties. Can't you be as perfect as she is?' In the first place, you don't want to make a false claim as 'housewife' while you make money from mountaineering and presenting speeches, et cetera. You are an authentic professional. You do pay taxes, right?"

My opinion might have had some effect on her, or she herself naturally came to realize her social role as an established commentator in the mountaineering community, because I noticed that in later years when we went on mountain trips together, she started to write "mountaineer" in the "occupation" blanks of hotel check-in forms. Those socially accepted images of her – as a housewife, an established mountaineer or both – were continuously overtaken by her own new activities, much to my pleasure.

Tabei's new ventures included the start-up of numerous mountain-related social activities and organizations. The establishment of the Himalayan Adventure Trust of Japan in 1990, the International Symposium on Conservation of Mountain Environments (held in cooperation with Sir Edmund Hillary and Reinhold Messner) in Tokyo in 1991, and the Mount Everest Women's Summit 1995, also in Tokyo, were all initiated by Tabei. These events and their organization gradually revealed Tabei's ability as "mountaineer and businessperson," though in a way still faithfully reflecting the ideal woman role model that the new generation had been weaving.

Then, something else – Tabei was not going to sit satisfied in the comfortable chair of the rock star for the mountaineering community or celebrity for the TV screen. In the summer of 1999, she climbed Pobeda Peak (7439 metres) in Kyrgyzstan. Towering on the border of China, this mountain is infamous for its frequent avalanches, a danger Tabei experienced when she was first there in 1986 (on the Chinese side of the mountain, called Mount Tomur). She almost lost her life on Tomur, tumbling down in the throes of an avalanche. Having survived that close call, and then having summitted the peak in 1999, she was honoured to receive the Snow Leopard award for her achievements on all five of the 7000-metre peaks in the Pamir-Tian Shan mountains (in 1985, Ismoil Somoni Peak [7495 metres], formerly named Communism Peak, and Lenin Peak [7134 metres]; and in 1994, Korzhenevskaya Peak [7105 metres] and Khan

Tengri [7010 metres]). Tabei received the award a month shy of turning sixty.[5]

Tabei poured her passion into these lesser-known mountains, out of the public eye compared to the highest in the world or the Seven Summits. Yet, they were still demanding peaks that required more physical power and technical skill than some of the "easier" 8000ers. Her tenacity on these peaks demonstrated her purely personal goal, which had nothing to do with basking in social popularity.

The same was true in her continuous climbing of several 5000-plus-metre peaks in South America, starting with Tocllaraju (6032 metres) in the Peruvian Andes with youngster Dr. Shiori Hashimoto. Tabei was almost obsessed, again faithfully, with those summits, even though she did not have to prove anything – she was already in the hall of fame.

"Oh, I was pretty nervous, ha, ha!" She laughed as we talked about how an appearance of hers went. While I was writing this article in mid-February 2000, Tabei had just finished a presentation of her thesis – "Study Regarding the Mountaineering Waste at Everest Base Camp" – for a postgraduate course at the University of Kyushu. In 1999 she visited Base Camp, twenty-five years after her summit, and completed detailed research at and around the camp where conditions had been drastically altered by the increased number of climbing teams from all over the world.

By the end of the twentieth century, Himalayan mountaineering had become quite a popular sport. Also, the Japanese yen has been a strong international currency since the 1985 Plaza Accord.[6] Familiar with the attitude that "one must keep working no matter what" through the economy's high-growth period (1960s to 1980s), the Japanese middle-senior age group that had been dreaming about the Himalayas started to apply the same go-getter spirit to peaks in Nepal and China once they reached

5   The Snow Leopard award was a Soviet mountaineering award given to experienced climbers who summitted the five peaks of 7000-plus metres in the former Soviet Union.

6   The Plaza Accord was signed in 1985 by the governments of France, West Germany, Japan, the United States of America and the United Kingdom. It aimed to depreciate the US dollar in relation to Japanese and German currencies by intervening in currency markets.

retirement. Tabei was interested in the mountain pollution that resulted from this trend. Along with her involvement in the Himalayan Adventure Trust of Japan, she became very pro-environment.

After Tabei's early successes, the forefront of female mountaineers who followed her path and kept pushing their own limits achieved such astonishing goals as climbing the Himalayan high peaks without supplemental oxygen. In 1995 British climber Alison Hargreaves had an amazing success reaching the summit of Everest without oxygen, and solo.[7] In 1994 Taeko Nagao and Yuka Endo from Japan displayed their high spirits by climbing a difficult route on the Southwest Face of Cho Oyu.[8] In other words, Junko Tabei has become "old school" in the history of mountaineering.

However, in the midst of the intense game of chase, where new generations of young women climbers caught up with Tabei's accomplishments and surpassed her with their impressive feats, Tabei continued to sail into her own new world, business as usual.

From the era of Showa to Heisei (1926-present),[9] from the twentieth to twenty-first century, in the period when Japanese women finally gained small wings, a woman less than 153 centimetres in height flapped her wings big time and became an important figure in mountaineering history.

7   In May 1995 Alison Hargreaves took on the North Face of Everest, the route pioneered by George Mallory and his companions in the 1920s. Hargreaves insisted on carrying all her own gear, pitching her own tent and surviving without the aid of supplementary oxygen.

8   Taeko Nagao (leader) and Yuka Endo, both with three 8000ers to their credit, and male partner Yasushi Yamanoi, with two 8000ers, climbed Cho Oyu's Southwest Face, in pure alpine style. At the time, this route had been scaled only once before by Swiss climbers Erhard Loretan and Jean Troillet, and Poland's Voytek Kurtyka in 1990.

9   Most of Japanese history is divided into conventional eras that are based on the reigns of the emperors. The modern eras from 1868 are:

1868–1912	Meiji	Emperor Mitsuhito
1912–1926	Taisho	Emperor Yoshihito
1926–1989	Showa	Emperor Hirohito
1926–present	Heisei	Emperor Akihito

I wish I could enjoy again the hot croquettes that Tabei cooked for me in the past, while I see how things turn out in the next chapter of mountaineering that follows my friend's footprints to the summit.

(Originally written in February 2000; adapted for the 2017 publication of Honouring High Places.*)*

CHAPTER 1

Avalanche!

May 4, 1975

We were a month and a half on Mount Everest, no more than a week from the summit, with our route fixed as high as Camp 5 at the South Col. In an unusual combination of logistics, several of us had descended to Camp 2 for the night. There, our group of expedition tents was pitched along the broad knoll that marked the camp on the Western Cwm Glacier, positioned away from the threat of falling cornices off nearby Nuptse. We considered ourselves to be in a safe spot – a welcomed event on Everest, and enough to let me sleep. I surrendered to the silence. Then, at half-past midnight, vibration, a deafening noise and – WHAM – impact.

With no warning and in the frigid hours of darkness, several tons of snow and ice had suddenly released from the flank of Nuptse and exploded downwards a thousand metres. Non-stop, the thunderous mass of snow pushed up and over the knoll where we slept and barrelled directly across the glacier of our camp. Earlier, there was a mix-up in ferrying loads, and we arrived at Camp 2 short one sleeping bag. Watanabe and I shared a bag with our legs stuffed in together for warmth, our upper bodies wrapped in down coats. When the avalanche hit, I was forced upright, yanking at Watanabe by way of our proximity as the immense blow shook me to my core. Within seconds I could hardly breathe as an enormous pressure bore down on me. Confusion set in as I was tossed and turned upside down, the tent whipping around in somersaults amongst the churning ice. I thought for a moment I was dead.

An instant later, the avalanche stopped. The entire camp was frozen in place, crushed between unyielding chunks of ice blocks, myself included. I was unable to move an inch. Any attempt to flex a muscle or shift my position was met with defeat. All effort was in vain while our tent, with my teammates inside, was buried in a mound of avalanche debris.

"Everybody OK?" I yelled at the top of my voice, startled by its loudness. There was no response. I realized then that someone was on top of me. It was Mihara, her hair smothering my face. Our noses touched. Neither of us could properly breathe.

Instinct told me I needed a knife. I reached for the cord around my neck and yanked at the hidden tool with my right hand but I was unable to free it, my arm rendered useless. With urgency, I bit at the knife with my teeth and pulled the blade from its sheath. "Mihara-*san*, cut the tent open!" My breath was short.

"I can't do it," she said. The cord of her sleeping bag was wrapped around her neck, her hands and feet unable to move. "Tabei-*san*, I'm suffering." I could feel her pain exhaled on my face as she spoke.

As if in fast-forward, I realized there were too many of us at Camp 2. Usually a dozen or so climbers based themselves there, but we were a party more than twice that size. My mind filled with newspaper headlines: "Worst accident ever in the climbing history of Mount Everest – seven climbers, three journalists, 18 Sherpas – a total of 28 killed in an avalanche." I was convinced that everyone had been buried. My thoughts rushed to family and friends at home and how they would feel when they read such a thing.

I was shocked back to reality as my breathing continued to fail. Coloured lights of red, yellow and purple started to flash in front of my eyes. Mihara was gasping, too. My mind flitted to Noriko, my three-year-old daughter; she would be devastated if I died. I was determined to hang on, to stay alive. As soon as I processed that thought, I slipped into unconsciousness.

No sooner had I felt a strong physical pull on my body than I was thrown from the tent and on to the snow. Beside me was Mihara, kneeling and mumbling in a barely audible voice, her hands in prayer position. In the sheer darkness, I could vaguely see the feet of the person leaning over me, someone I failed to recognize, but in that moment, I knew I had been saved. "Everybody alive?" I instinctively asked.

Although I spoke in Japanese, a response came in English. "Yes, all members safe." No fatalities. Relief flooded over me, which allowed my mind to slip into unconsciousness once more.

The loud voice of cameraman Akamatsu jolted me awake. "She could die from hypothermia if left out here for too long! Where is Ang Tsering? Clear out a Sherpa tent and bring all the climbers in!" I heard the goings-on around me, but my body was unable to respond to my own orders to move. The Sherpas ran to help me, and I was carried inside a tent. My teammates were already lying there: Naka, with assisted oxygen, and Mihara, Nasu, Manita and Arayama. I was placed on the ground right in the middle of them.

As I joined my teammates, I could see in each climber's face the fear and shock caused by the mayhem of the avalanche. Frantic voices of the journalists and Sherpas filled the nighttime air that hovered around −20°c outside the tent. The feel of a disaster zone seeped through the thin nylon wall that separated us from the chaos. Orders were yelled back and forth, everyone uncertain of exactly how things should unfold next.

"Fix the kitchen tent then brew tea for everybody!"

"Lights! What happened to the lights?"

"Where's the first-aid kit? One of the Sherpas has a serious cut on his forehead and the bleeding hasn't stopped."

"Pitch an extra tent! We'll get frostbite in this condition. Put on proper clothes to stay warm!"

"Is there any further danger of avalanche? We should be on watch all night."

"Where are the oxygen bottles? Find the masks, as many as possible!"

"Where's the radio? We need to let Base Camp know as soon as possible."

"We're unable to call in the middle of the night."

"Then send the mail runners to Camp 3, Camp 1 and Base Camp right away. Look for a note pad to write on. We can't wait for the regular radio call tomorrow morning."

Akamatsu, who had previous expedition experience, entered the tent. He checked my neck, hands and feet, and then shifted me onto my belly and surveyed my back and trunk. As abruptly as he had arrived, he concluded, "No part of your body seems broken. Don't move; we'll get oxygen right away." I heeded his words, stunned by the severity of the situation.

As I lay there, I counted and recounted the number of us in the tent, each time ending up with six, including myself. This bothered me to no end. Someone was missing, but I was unable to fathom which team member was not present. Again, I asked if everyone was safe. Akamatsu said, "Watanabe is all right in the other Sherpa tent." At first, I doubted his answer, certain he was meaning to console me. Judging by our positions in the tent prior to the avalanche, I was sure that Watanabe had been badly hurt (or worse), as she would have likely been the one to end up underneath the pile of climbers when the snow hit and we were sent into a mad tumble. But it turned out that Watanabe was safe. She had been thrown from the tent and trapped between ice blocks that kept her unscathed rather than pummelled by the debris and the weight of four women, all of which landed on me instead. In our jumbled state, I was buried by Nasu and Manita, large-sized climbers by Japanese standards at 60 kilograms each, and Mihara. Once the three of them were dug out, there was only one pair of feet and ankles still visible above the mass of snow: mine. It took the strength of four Sherpas to pull me out, an action that left me unable to walk for a while afterwards since my ankle and hip joints had been completely stretched loose. This was a small price to pay for their quick response – if the Sherpas had taken another four or five minutes to rescue us, several climbers, including me, would have died from suffocation.

When Akamatsu left the tent, cameraman Kitagawa stepped in to reassure us. "Everybody is all right. Stay calm. We're brewing tea for you right now," he said, but his voice depicted distress instead of the reassurance he had intended.

Someone beside me moaned, "I'm sick, Tabei-*san*, I'm very sick." I immediately tried to turn towards the voice, to see who had spoken, but my attempt was futile as my body remained immobile. The shock of this realization, that I was potentially impaired, ran right up my spine. I felt like a slow-motion mime, only able to carefully shift my neck to the side.

Naka was the source of the anguish beside me. The day before, she had been on her way down from Camp 3 to Base Camp via Camp 2 for one night due to altitude sickness. Now she lay in total distress. The six of us were arranged in alternating headfirst and foot-first positions in the tent, so it took a concentrated effort for me to sit upright to look at her. I immediately saw the problem. The flow of oxygen from the bottle to her mask had been cut off by weight on the tube. I properly adjusted the oxygen so Naka could breathe easier, and then Mihara groaned in a weakened voice. Her chest hurt. In total darkness, Kitagawa managed to set up a second oxygen bottle for Mihara to use. With that in place, a third person spoke up. Nasu complained of an extreme chill. Mihara and I tried to help by doubling up sleeping bags on Nasu's feet and switching Mihara's oxygen mask to Nasu. Meanwhile, I was in excruciating pain; it felt like my body was being crushed with every movement I made, yet I had to continue to help my teammates.

"I'm bleeding," Nasu cried. My head began to swim. She must have cut her finger when she slit the tent open with her knife. Mihara gently wrapped Nasu's hands with her own, and soothingly said, "It's OK, it's OK." Manita also complained – her chill was incessant – but I was too far away to assist. Arayama sat nearest to the entranceway in a squatted position without uttering a word. Our team was as far from the summit of Everest as we had ever been.

Ang Tsering finally came in to check on our condition, his face strained with worry. In answer to my immediate question about what the journalists were doing, he said they were about to discuss the necessary next steps. Despite my hopes of joining them, my body lay non-responsive. Then bit by bit, my chest began to hurt, and pain seeped into my back. I wondered what was wrong with me. My lower body felt stick-like – a useless segment that I had no control over. Next, somebody put an oxygen mask on my face, which eased the pain, but my irritation grew. I knew what was happening outside the tent, and I was unable to participate. As overall trip assistant and leader of the climbing party, I was supposed to take charge, yet I was helpless due to injury. My futile state was excruciating to me.

Camp 2 had been established weeks earlier, on April 8, at which time the Sherpas pitched their tent to the west of where we pitched ours, a slight distance apart. At the time of avalanche, one of the Sherpas was up to use the toilet and noticed the start of the slide. He knew it would escalate and, acting quickly, he woke the rest of the Sherpas. They braced themselves for impact, gripping onto the tent poles as if to make an impenetrable wall. Later they would speak of wild sparks of electricity shooting through their hands when the huge blocks of snow and ice flew over their tent with an unbelievable roar. Once the avalanche stopped, the six of them escaped from their tent by slamming against the mass of snow that barricaded the entranceway. A look towards where our tent had originally stood confirmed what they feared, that it had disappeared. In a panic, they began to search for us without even pulling on their climbing boots. Bulldozed 10 metres downslope from its initial site, our tent was found buried under the frozen debris. The Sherpas dug and pushed their way through blocks of ice, shredding the tent into pieces so they could extract us one after the other.

Three of the expedition's seven journalists were also at Camp 2 that night. Their tent was located higher than ours and managed to stand its ground amidst the moving snow. Although Akamatsu, Kitagawa and Emoto were knocked over and piled up at the doorway, they were able to crawl out themselves by cutting the tent fabric open.

It was evident that all the tents, including the Sherpas', would have been completely buried, with no chance for our survival, had we set them up in the same spot as the Spanish team did the previous year.

In the pre-dawn hours at Camp 1, Kitamura, the manager of ferrying equipment on the mountain, was asleep alongside Hirashima and Fujiwara. In a dreamlike state, she heard the approach of crampons crunching on snow. Knowing it was too early for the first ferry load to arrive from Base Camp, she tried to tune in to what else she could hear outside the tent. Then, in alarm, a voice in broken English bellowed: "*Memsahib, memsahib*! Avalanche, avalanche! But nobody is die." Kitamura was instantly awake and out of her sleeping bag. *Nobody is die?* She struggled to open the tent and take in the scene of confusion thrown at her by two Sherpas panting and yelling at the doorway. They thrust the note sent from the journalists into her hands in hopes that she could quickly comprehend what had unfolded only hours ago at Camp 2.

After the Sherpas recovered from their hasty descent to Camp 1, they readied themselves to continue to Base Camp to further convey news of the avalanche. Knowing that team leader Hisano would soon be informed of the night's events allowed Kitamura to focus on the task at hand in preparation for what was to come. She and her teammates fired up the stove and began the painstaking process of melting snow to brew litres of tea for the sick and injured climbers who would ultimately arrive back at her camp.

To Kitamura's surprise, the Sherpas returned within an hour of leaving Camp 1 and reported that the icefall below had collapsed. They were unable to find the ladder to continue down. Their only solution was to notify by radio the Sherpas at Base Camp and have them climb up, find the ladder and fix the route; but this was communication that would have to wait for the scheduled morning call. Kitamura grew more anxious by the minute at the delay in contact with Hisano, but she was able to reach her teammates at Camp 2. One after the other, their wound-up voices described the incident: "Incredible disaster … tents buried under ice blocks … food and equipment also buried in avalanche debris." The words that counted the most though, the ones that reassured her long enough to wait for interaction with Hisano, were these: "…no fatalities."

By dawn, several other Sherpas arrived to help at Camp 2 after notification from the Sherpas who had run to Camps 1 and 3 with news of the avalanche. Among them were teammates Taneya and Shioura from Camp 3.

At 6 a.m., the scheduled radio call broke the silence as climbers nervously waited to communicate the disaster to Base Camp. Reporter Emoto from *The Yomiuri Shimbun* was the spokesperson from Camp 2. "Base Camp from Camp 2," he said. "Leader Hisano, are you there?" Once contact was confirmed, he began: "Please calmly listen to me. Last night, at 12:30, Camp 2 was caught in an avalanche. Fortunately, nobody was killed. But the scale of the avalanche was huge. Quite an amount of our food, equipment and oxygen bottles have been buried. To my regret, we have no choice other than to give up this expedition."

Shocked, Hisano said, "Everybody alive? All of them alive?! Confirm again, please."

"Yes," said Emoto, "everybody survived; however, there are a few injured Sherpas, and Naka has altitude sickness. We will send them to

Base Camp right away. Please have the doctor prepared to treat them immediately."

"All right, all right. Tell me more about the avalanche." The leader's unease and concern were clear despite the heavy static of the radio. Then Kitamura at Camp 1 interjected.

"This is Kitamura at Camp 1. I hear you. At dawn, two Sherpas from Camp 2 came down here with a letter reporting that Camp 2 was caught in an avalanche. They tried to continue to Base Camp; however, they couldn't due to the collapse of the icefall right below Camp 1 at the ladder, which disappeared into the crevasse. Send Sherpas and high porters as soon as possible to fix it, otherwise it's impossible to get back to Base Camp."

Hisano said, "All right. I will arrange Sherpas and high porters to go up there. Let the injured Sherpas and Naka descend to Camp 1 for now, and have them wait there so they can reach Base Camp as soon as the route is fixed."

Once that exchange had ended, Emoto spoke again. "There's more. The most badly injured is Tabei-*san*. Although she seems to have no broken bones, the contusion appears critical, so she needs to be the first one to be evacuated. A rescue helicopter should be arranged."

Me? In the worst shape of everyone? Fly me out from here? I could hardly absorb what Emoto had said. There was no way I would leave the mountain. Why were they fussing over these trivial injuries? Neither broken bones nor internal bleeding. A contusion and some pressure on my chest, and lingering pain from being pulled out from the avalanche debris – that was all. "I'm OK!" I yelled. "NO! I won't go down. Don't call a helicopter for me!" Uncontrollably, I continued to shout from inside the tent to put a stop to their nonsense. Our climb would be over if we broke up the team and descended for any duration. There was not enough time to start over and attempt a second expedition. The monsoon season would begin in a few weeks. We had ten days to reach the summit, and we would not deny ourselves the fighting chance to try. If I was the most badly injured, then I knew the other climbers could still make it. They were young and strong. If anything, I was more concerned about their mental wellness after the distress of the avalanche. If they could work through that, the summit was still within the team's grasp.

Ang Tsering returned to the tent to check on me. "*Daijyobu?*" he asked in Japanese. "Are you all right? Would you like some drink?" I told him I was fine and inquired about everyone else. To my relief, there were no other serious reports except for Naka's condition and the injuries of the few Sherpas, one with a pronounced cut on his forehead and the others not so bad. In light of the situation, Ang Tsering asked if I would fly out. A simple no escaped my lips. I explained my stance, suggesting that since there were no fatalities, then only Naka and the Sherpa with the cut needed to go down. Also, I said it would be riskier to descend the icefall in a panicked state rather than regroup and continue to climb. He understood. "We'll stay as long as you *memsahibs* stay," he said, providing me with great encouragement.

As we remained in our tent, cocooned in sleeping bags, sipping milk tea and slowly coming to terms with what had happened, I was more at ease in conversation with Nasu, Manita, Mihara, Watanabe and Arayama. We spoke about our disbelief of the avalanche, our survival and our desire to continue up the mountain. When I explained that I would not descend to Base Camp, each one of them replied, "If Tabei-*san* isn't going down, neither are we." Teammates who were uninjured or only mildly hurt would start to dig out our equipment from under the debris right away. Despite my feeble state, I could not have been happier.

As the morning progressed, it became obvious, even to me, that I was unwell. The other climbers were able to tend to themselves, but I was incapable of positioning myself upright. My stubborn attitude and refusal to abide by Emoto's suggestion to return to Base Camp drove him to impatience. He pushed for a scheduled call with Hisano once the injured Sherpa and Naka, with oxygen and carried on the back of another Sherpa, were on their way down to Camp 1. By 10 a.m. the radio discussion between Camp 2 and Base Camp began.

"Tabei-*san*, Tabei-*san*, can you hear me?" said Hisano.

"Yes," I said. "Thanks for your concern. I'm all right."

Hisano wasted no time in making her point. "In detail, I've heard from the reporters about what happened at Camp 2. Please come down to Camp 1 today. I think it's a good idea for you to come down now, take a good rest and rethink what to do next. Would you agree?"

My heart sank. "No, I don't. I'll be totally recovered in two days. It would be much harder for me to recover and be ready to climb again if I go down today. I'm serious. I'm the one who knows what's best for my body, and that is I stay at Camp 2."

The team doctor spoke next. "Tabei-*san*, you speak this way likely due to the tension of the situation right now. It's obvious that your whole body will be in significant pain by tomorrow. We insist. Go down to Camp 1. If you still say no, we'll have to ask our sirdar to drag you down."

"I know these are sensible words of advice from you, Dr. Sakaguchi, but I can't follow them. This is about *our* climbing team; it's not just about me. I'm OK. I'll be able to walk in two days."

Taking a different approach, Hisano asked, "How about you, Watanabe-*san*?"

"I'm totally fine," Watanabe said. "As doctor and team leader at Base Camp, you don't know the topography of this area. Up here, I would like to follow the advice of our climbing leader, Tabei-*san*."

Hisano pushed again, "One more time, I'm asking, only once more, would you come down to Base Camp?"

"Sorry for talking back to you," I said, "but I won't go down. Though we are mentally distraught right now, physically, we're all fine. I'd be more concerned about climbing down through the icefall with a distressed mind than taking a few days to recover at Camp 2."

She finally conceded. "Understood, Tabei-*san*. Can I hear from everybody as well?"

Each climber alongside me in the tent with me replied one by one with the same answer: "I don't want to go down, but would rather stay here with our climbing leader." With that, our chance for the summit of Everest was solidified.

The next discussion that occurred was between our liaison officer Lhakpa Tenzing and the Sherpas, of whom Ang Tsering, as sirdar, was the spokesperson. In the case of our expedition, Lhakpa Tenzing was more like a sirdar than the government watchdog the liaison role usually denoted. Their conversation was a sensitive one. The Sherpas could easily have opted to go home based on their respectful fear of avalanches, which in their culture represents a raging god. Instead, they stood by the original statement Ang Tsering shared with me earlier: if we stayed, they stayed.

The journalists had a different reaction. In their mind, knowing the damage that Camp 2 had incurred, in particular the burial of oxygen bottles and food, the continuation of the expedition was impossible. In addition, based on previous Himalayan expeditions where Sherpas quit after serious avalanches, they were convinced our situation was a simple matter of calling off the climb and radioing for a helicopter. With that assumption, the journalists announced among their crew that the climb was defunct, and they readied their cameras and film equipment to descend the mountain. They planned to leave immediately.

I fought their negative attitude in my head. This was *our* climb. The decision to continue was up to us and our team leader, not the journalists. To me the climb was not over, but I had no way of voicing my opinion to them from where I lay. Wrapped in my sleeping bag as I tried to recover, I was not not prepared to argue. Thankfully, Hisano stepped in. She submitted to our persistent ways and announced that she would no longer force us to descend from Camp 2, but the summit was still in question.

Once we had permission to stay, our tents were moved to a higher location within the area of Camp 2, as we were fearful of another avalanche. Shioura and Taneya and the three Sherpas who had descended from Camp 3 re-pitched the tents. I was carried to my new resting spot on the back of one of the Sherpas, feeling miles away from my usual ability to climb. Right then I knew I had to remain positive and keep Everest reachable in segments: first we clean up from the avalanche and allow injured party members to recover; then we continue to build the route upwards and acclimatize until we are ready and in a good position for an assault on the summit.

The true state of Camp 2 was realized by midday. The place was a disaster. The spread of avalanche debris was several hundred metres across the glacier. Food cartons and propane and oxygen bottles were strewn, half-buried, amidst the vastness of ice blocks. It was difficult to know where to begin to salvage equipment.

Our relationship with the journalists began to sour when our differing opinions on whether to descend or not became obvious. But what intrigued me was that despite their desire to leave camp in a hurry, they began to film the avalanche site with added interest as soon as they had dug their camera equipment from the snow. My regard for their professionalism improved with each piece of footage they shot. They had found their story.

May 5

The onslaught of repair began. One stitch at a time we sewed torn tents back together, and item by item, we resurrected everything we could from under the swath of debris that filled the camp.

All our food had been buried in the avalanche, and we ate only boiled potatoes that were brought to us from Base Camp. We sprinkled them with salt, which seemed gracefully simple on Everest and reminded me of when I was a child, digging up potatoes from the field and enjoying the sensation of being barefoot in the soil. There at Camp 2, amidst disarray, memories suddenly became vivid to me: a little girl pulling thick stalks from the ground with half a dozen or more potatoes falling about; their thin skins slipping off with the touch of rinse water; boiling them in a large pot until they surfaced and broke open, ready for my family to enjoy. All I could picture was my mother's fields, our stone stove and me sitting on a straw mat eating the freshly boiled, piping-hot potatoes. When I shook myself from the daydream, I was met with the view of a half kilometre filled with giant-sized blocks of ice. I had to remind myself of our luck that no one had died in the avalanche, and that we could attempt the climb again.

Much like me as a child surprised with each potato nugget I pulled from my mother's garden, the Sherpas delighted in every item they rescued from the snow. "I found it!" they yelled as though on a treasure hunt. One after the other, reports flooded into the tent where I lay: four oxygen bottles had been found; food remained intact, despite crushed boxes; tents would be durable enough with stitching and duct tape. Their excitement was welcomed, and the renewed hopefulness of the team fuelled my own determination to persevere. I would ask Hisano to join us at Camp 2 to prepare the team for the summit assault. The next day I would begin all efforts to stand on my feet and walk. I was convinced that anything was possible, whatever it took, and that we would reach the top of the mountain.

May 6

Another day of restoration took place on all fronts, in terms of health, supplies and resolve. It was notable that the urgency from the avalanche had dissipated and was replaced by clear thought and determination. The team's willpower was paying off. Although at Camp 2 we already felt certain we could continue, it was tremendous news when Hisano officially announced on the scheduled radio call that the climb would go on. Each of us felt our entire being pulsate when she said, "Let's try climbing to the top of Everest, for one last chance."

May 7

I was bothered by the delay of me spending two full days in bed and was in need of a sign that my condition would improve. Slowly, the chest pain I felt with each breath settled, but the instability in my hip joints and the pain that radiated from ankles to thighs had me worried. Somehow, on the second night, my teammates helped me from the tent – the first time I had been outside since the avalanche – and I managed to walk. My few steps were enough to re-convince me that a descent to Base Camp was unnecessary, and that the team should focus only on the summit.

By the third day, I could walk on my own.

May 8

Five days after the avalanche, Hisano finally climbed up to Camp 2 accompanied by two Sherpas. By then I was recovered well enough to hike down with Shioura and Ang Tsering and meet her partway. My body was wrapped with cooling pads on my neck, back and hips, emitting a therapeutic mint odour all around me, which I quite liked. I must have very much looked the character of the patient.

Stunned at the sight of us and at the avalanche debris spread in front of her, Hisano spoke in a quiet voice. "How could you have survived this disaster?"

As she continued to survey the land, her eyes fell upon the renovated Camp 2 and her heart lifted. There stood a *koinobori* made by the climbers and journalists: a giant white cloth, like a windsock, with the shapes of two carp painted on it in red and black, joyfully flapping from a log pole high in the Everest breeze. This was the resolute symbol of the team's unyielding mindset to resume and pursue what mountaineers desired – to climb.

May 10

On May 10, Hisano called us all into an overcrowded six-person tent. The only few missing from the meeting were Naka and Naganuma, who were still at Base Camp suffering from altitude sickness, in the care of Dr. Sakaguchi. After we paid our respects to our sick friends, Hisano announced her plan for the summit.

Chapter 2

The Meaning of Mountains

When people meet me for the first time, they are surprised by my size. They expect me to be bigger than I am, more strapping, robust, like a wrestler, for example. As I am the first woman to climb Mount Everest and the Seven Summits, they equate a certain body type to my accomplishments. I grin whenever I am first overlooked then greeted at a train station or a speaking engagement. "Are you really Tabei-san?" they ask. At a height of five feet, and weighing 49 kilograms, I throw newcomers for a loop. Questions like how do I carry such a heavy pack, or how large is my lung capacity are the usual conversation openers. I was always puzzled by this, by people's obsession with the physical appearance of a mountaineer.

Once, I presented a lecture at a private university in a coliseum-style classroom full of mostly young male students. During the question period, one of the students from the middle of the room vigorously stood up and said, "All women mountaineers are not good looking. Is that true?" He had based his question on a quote from a popular Japanese novelist.

"If you look at me," I said, "then you know that isn't the case." That shut him up. So many questions and assumptions about body, looks, appearance – I was baffled at people's inability to dig deeper in their inquiries about mountaineering, and especially about the female mountaineer. There is more to us; we all come from somewhere.

Country Girl

I was born in 1939, in a small town called Miharu, in the Fukushima area. *Miharu* means "three spring," as in the season, for the three flowers – plum, peach and cherry – that bloom together come springtime. It was a pretty place surrounded by green mountains laden with cherry blossoms and terraced fields of vegetables. In the middle of the townsite was a hill with the remaining old stone walls from a historic castle. As children, we called the hill Castle Mountain since it was high enough to see the vista of the entire town from its top.

Miharu had a population of nearly 10,000 people, and was adorned with eleven temples, all of which grew cherry and plum trees in their gardens. In mid-April the entire town was full of pink flowers, creating a hue of colour that evoked nature's exquisite beauty.

In the front of my house lay the Sakura-gawa (*sakura* for cherry blossom; *gawa* for river), and a trip across its bridge and up a hill led to the trailhead of Fudo-*yama* (mountain).

Fudo-yama was a playground for children. I remember its hillside being covered with trees – crepe myrtles and maples – and we played Tarzan on rope swings and hung hammocks from their branches. The south slope of the mountain was covered with azaleas, adding more shades of pink to the surrounding area in spring. I ate those flower petals from time to time to quench my thirst. From the high point of Fudo-yama, we could see a palace-like building in the distance, an image I had only seen in picture books, and I used to believe it was the home of the Emperor of Japan. In reality, it was one of the many temples that dotted the countryside. Nonetheless, standing on that small summit was enough to show me what lay beyond my hometown, a moment when the flicker of aspiration ignited.

My family ran a printing company. My father, Morinobu Ishibashi, and my mother, Kiyo, were the parents of seven children, five of whom were girls, including me, the youngest. I can only assume my father was hoping for a boy when I was born because I later learned that he had said, "A girl again…" and failed to name me for many days after my birth.

The printing factory was on the street side of our property and the house was at its back, so I grew up listening the noise of machinery. Four factory workers lived in our home, along with two housekeepers. At mealtime, we pulled out a long table and everyone ate together. We were a fairly close-knit family, but there was such an age difference between me and my oldest brother and sister that I rarely saw them.

I grew up during the Second World War yet have little memory of the war itself. I remember having to wear a *boku-zukin*, a cotton-padded air-raid hood, designed especially for wartime, and running to the air-raid shelter, sirens blaring in the background. As only a child would imagine, the gatherings in the shelter seemed festive since everyone from the neighbourhood was there. More clearly than any war stories though, I recall the fire at the elementary school two years post-war. The entire town shone abnormally bright as my dreams of schooling went up in flames and my father and brothers sprinted to it to help. The destruction of the school, in combination with societal confusion after the war, had me miss kindergarten. Eventually, classes were set up in a gym, with dividers as walls, for morning and afternoon school groups. I quickly fell into the routine of being greeted with "Jun-*chan*!" each morning by a neighbouring friend, Hideo-*chan*. We walked hand in hand along the Sakura-gawa, later joined by another friend, Kazuo-*chan*. The three of us entered the classroom every day together. As an adult reflecting on that time, I realized how lucky I was to be protected by two boys en route to school, and the importance of long-term friendships.

As a child, I had always been small in stature and considered weak. I was often struck with a high fever and had pneumonia several times. My siblings were similar, and when the doctor was called to visit our home, as he was on numerous occasions, he would say, "Which one this time?" Years later, when people who knew me from my childhood heard that I had climbed Mount Everest, they would be lost for words and then say, "How could *that* tiny Junko possibly have done such a thing?"

I performed poorly in physical education classes, too, unable to succeed at a kip or vault until the end of Grade 6. In elementary and middle schools, the so-called popular kids, the ones other classmates looked up to, were those who were good at sports, not grades. Sadly, I felt I had nothing to be proud of in that regard, but I did love to sing. My older sisters sang in a choir, and in support, my father bought us an old organ. After supper, we had little else to do but sing songs together while one of us played at the organ's worn keys.

Although my sisters were in high school at the time and were given parts to sing in soprano or alto, I was told by my own music teacher that my singing voice was beyond the years of a young child, and I was invited to sing solo on a Japanese public radio program. I could have become a professional singer. Instead, I recognized my calling when my fourth-grade teacher, Watanabe-Shuntaro-*sensei* introduced me to the wonders of the mountains. Who knows which life pursuit – mountains or music – would have been more advantageous to me.

Watanabe-*sensei* was much like the popular kids – everyone looked up to him. When students caught sight of him walking to school, with his *furoshiki* bag in one hand and his unkempt long hair being combed by the other, everyone raced towards him, hanging from his arms in order to get even closer.

Children two or three layers deep would surround him as he neared the schoolyard. Despite his strict nature when necessary, he was constantly encircled by students. On the evenings when he was on night duty as a security guard, I would return to school with some friends to listen to his stories about the mountains while I practiced calligraphy or edited my essay booklet. If the weather was nice in the daytime, he would invite us to eat lunch at Castle Mountain – no sooner would he announce the idea than everyone was running outside, delighted by it. Under the cherry trees, he told us about books like *Jiro's Story*, *The Diary of Anne Frank*, *The Broken Commandment* and *Before the Dawn*. Those were difficult stories for young children to understand, but we listened intently with tears running down our cheeks. Inspired by Watanabe-*sensei's* storytelling, I started to read countless books from wherever I could find them – my sisters' bookshelves, the public library. Sometimes I read sitting on the cart that my mother pulled into the farm fields in the evenings, anything for a good story. Looking back, I remember more about the times I spent outdoors rather than learning from textbooks inside the classroom.

In a less stringent manner than the way current-day school trips are planned, Watanabe-*sensei* casually asked my Grade 4 class, "Who wants to go to the mountains this summer?" My parents agreed to the excursion provided a teacher was present. A handful of us – a few boys, two girls, Watanabe-*sensei*, his brother and a female teacher – headed to Nasu-*dake* (peak), one of the hundred famous mountains in Japan, in Nikko National Park in Tochigi Prefecture north of Tokyo. The adventure included transport by train, bus and foot. Accommodations were set up for self-catering, so we carried our own food (miso, rice, vegetables) and cooking pots. In our small backpacks we also stuffed blankets and extra clothing. When the hiking portion began at Yumoto hot springs, we crisscrossed our way along the trail, passing each other back and forth in conversation with the teachers.

"The ground is somehow warm," one of us commented, and everyone reached for the moistened soil beneath our feet.

"Yes, this is a volcanic area, so hot water is running underneath the ground," said Watanabe-*sensei*. Nasu-dake is one of the hundred-plus volcanoes in Japan.

"Hot water?" We could hardly believe it. We pressed our hands into the ground, stunned at the temperature that was emitted. Until that moment, I believed that only cool water ran in rivers, but right in front of us flowed steaming water. A hot spring had formed where the river was blocked with rocks. "It's a river bath! A running hot-water river!" I was in awe that such a feature existed. So went my introduction to the natural *onsen* of Japan that peppered the country, the beauty and warmth of which I would crave some twenty-five years later when camped on Mount Everest.

At night, we peeled and chopped potatoes and carrots to make curry, and fried eggplant and diced tomatoes. Although I never helped my mother in the kitchen at home, to prepare food with my friends and cook for our teachers enraptured me. After dinner, we went for a soak in the hot spring, and then, under lamplight, listened to stories from Watanabe-*sensei* as we fell asleep.

The next day, in a dress and running shoes, I hiked up Nasu-dake and Asahi-dake (*asahi* meaning morning sun). There, I was treated to a view from the top that was unlike anything I had ever seen. I was much higher up than the mountains that surrounded my home. These were not the green hills covered with grasses and trees that I was used to; this was a setting where everything was new: the foliage, the landscape, the scent in the air. I loved every element.

All around us, sulphur-stained holes in the ground sizzled where natural *onsen* came to life at our feet. I admired the juxtaposition of the heat from the springs and the cold temperatures (despite it being summer) on the mountain. The impact this had on me, the effect on my body and skin, was unforgettable. It triggered an awareness that there were many things in the world for me to discover. When we reached the summit that day, I felt a joy of achievement that I had never experienced before.

After that, I thought more about mountaineering. My initial sense was that it was not competitive, unlike other sports, at least not in a team-like manner. No matter how slow a person walked, they could reach the summit, one step at a time. On the other hand, I also understood that in mountain climbing, no matter how hard the struggle became, there would be no substitutions, no switch of players. One had to complete the task themselves. I learned those lessons on Nasu-dake, at age nine, and applied them to the rest of my life.

There is no doubt that I became an accomplished climber due to having met my Grade 4 teacher.

In 1994, when Watanabe-Shuntaro-*sensei* turned seventy years old, he had one remaining wish: to see the Mount Everest that I had climbed. In full appreciation for his contribution to my life, I invited him, my brother and a few of my earlier classmates to Nepal. We chartered a helicopter, and after thirty minutes in the air, we were blessed with the grand view of the Himalayas. When Everest came into sight, there sat my teacher, arms spread in disbelief of the mountain's immensity, face pressed against the window like a child in wonder, eyes filled with tears. I had come full circle in my life as a mountaineer, from beginner to beyond, and it all started with my grade-school teacher, a person willing to share his passion for adventure with me.

City Life

The girls-only students' dorm at university in Tokyo had an etiquette all its own. Upon entering, we knelt in front of the room and greeted everyone with "Gomen asobase," a very feminine, polite, upper-class way of saying excuse me. These ways were foreign to me. Six girls, from first to fourth year of study, lived together in a ten-tatami room, a size that was considered large in Japan. We woke at 6 a.m., lights out by 10 p.m., and the only days we were permitted to leave the campus were Wednesdays, Saturdays and Sundays – with a curfew of 7 p.m. We required our parents' permission to receive letters from men, and only parents or siblings could pick us up to spend a night away from school. We brought our own chopsticks to the dining room for every meal, arranged ourselves in assigned seating based on room number, waited for the music to

end after prayer, and began to eat. The strictness of our communal living never
waned. The year was 1959.

The enforced quiet in the dorm extended to the classroom, and rarely was
there a peep heard from student or teacher. It was a stern environment, one
that exuded self-control and discipline. Later, on high mountain peaks, I
would be grateful for my mastery of these qualities, but at twenty, the stress of
the place unnerved me.

As my attention to detail intensified while living in the dorm, small things,
like a dirty tatami mat or a roommate's tea cup left on the table, began to
bother me. The anxiety of daily life had me worried around the clock about
tiny infractions, like making a slight noise when turning a page as I completed
homework before bedtime. I was no longer able to sleep, my heart felt as though
it was being squeezed tight, I lost my appetite, my eyes grew dark and my
skin showed signs of distress. I was having a breakdown. Ultimately, I was
prescribed extended rest.

Chikako (less formally, Chika), my sister closest to me in age and friendship, became ill when I was in Grade 6. She was diagnosed with leuk-
emia, which shifted our life from playful to serious. While daily chores
were maintained in our household, my mother spent all her time by my
sister's bedside in the hospital. My father sold his farm estates to pay for
treatment, and he diligently prayed for her each morning by way of a
traditional ice-cold shower with buckets of water from the well. Hun-
dreds of Chika's fellow schoolmates from high school donated blood for
her transfusions. She was well-loved and supported, but sadly died at
age eighteen, the year I began Grade 7, middle school. My attachment
to Chika had me visit her grave every day, and without fail, whenever
I arrived there, I laid fresh flowers, *orizurus* (paper cranes) and written
poetry on slips of paper. Her spirit certainly lived on amongst her friends
and loved ones.

Something changed in me after my sister's death. I turned from a
cheerful, relaxed child to a problematic girl, marked by a newly found rebellious behaviour. My antics were very unladylike: I told a few boys from
class to catch a frog and hide it in the teacher's desk drawer, knowing
they would be blamed, not me; I squeezed a bag full of ash between the
sliding door and the wall so it would fall upon the teacher as he entered

the room; I looked elsewhere, blankly into the distance, when the teacher addressed the class.

I developed a particular disdain for my English teacher. Even though my high marks were easy to attain in elementary school, I found Grade 7 difficult. I elected to not study at home because I had no desk, and the negative result of that choice was obvious on my first English exam. The low mark I received was enough for me to switch gears, and I began to study each night at the dining-room table with my brother, who was in Grade 9. When I produced a better mark on my next test, the teacher accused me of cheating. After that, I completely ignored him but continued to study with my brother. My marks remained high, which was my intention – to show the teacher I could succeed without him. Looking back, it was foolish to play tough, but the experience taught me perseverance. Once again, with no athletic ability, thus no sports to partake in, and still grieving for my sister, I turned to reading books to get me through the middle-school years. I longed for something more in my life but was unable to identify what that could possibly be.

While friends of mine applied for jobs after middle school, I was expected to continue my education. My father was a proponent of higher learning, in a variety of ways. When one sibling showed interest in photography, my father bought a camera and converted a backyard shed into a dark room; he purchased a radio for one of my brothers to listen to on-the-air classes. I took it for granted that I would pursue high school and likely university. What surprised me was the lack of interest teachers had in female students attending post-secondary institutions. Information on options was scarce, and it was up to the individual to make it happen. I bargained with my father, because by that point in my schooling, I had my hopes set on university in Tokyo. He would rather I attended a school closer to home, but I was greatly inspired by my sisters having been there, by their stories about cafés and concerts and the theatre. I made it clear that if I completed four years of university, I would need nothing from my father after I graduated and married. Consequently, I applied to Showa Women's University in Tokyo, with the picture-perfect image of how the female student life would be. I could see myself as an independent, intelligent and popular woman, able to debate and philosophize about plays and such, and meet a nice man who is attracted to her. I believed that was how the next stage of my life would unfold.

Instead, when I arrived in Tokyo, I found it an uncomfortable place to be. I was shocked by the number of war veterans who begged for money at train stations. I was embarrassed about my rural background, not believing it was good enough for city life. I simply could not fit in. I was deeply aware of my dialect being different from others, and I worried that everyone was better than me. I was shy and nervous and could hardly speak to a soul, much to my own detriment. I failed to adjust at school, and ultimately, my father came to see me and helped me seek the medical attention I needed. The doctor prescribed time away from the city, so I went to stay at Dake hot springs, near Miharu. Every day, I hiked in the forest by myself and wrote in my diary. I dug deep to figure out what I wanted in life and to decide how important schooling was to me. In the end, I returned to Tokyo to finish university. I remained forever grateful to my father for providing the time and environment I needed to answer those questions for myself.

It was the middle of second semester when I returned to school, and I rented a room in a house rather than succumb to the restrictive dorm life again. I still struggled with a feeling of despair, but no one seemed to notice, and classmates thought I was much better after my time away. Life felt more positive, and when some friends invited me to join them on a hike, I rediscovered my love for the outdoors. I was thrilled to learn that there were mountains in the Tokyo area. As we stepped beyond the trailhead to Mitake-yama, deep in the forest, my body quivered with the cool air of nature and the scent of the earth. I felt instantly alive as I found my pace and relaxed into each forward stride. I began to open up again.

Persimmons were dark orange with ripeness in the nearby village, and the sight of farmers carrying their equipment on carts reminded me of Miharu. I was transfixed by the scenery, the growth of the trees, and how the foggy summits were like a black and white photograph – everything was so varied from the mountains I had known all my life. As on Nasu-dake in Grade 4, I had the same realization that there were many more destinations in the world for me to realize.

On my way home that day, I stopped downtown and bought a guide book called *Mountains Around Tokyo*. That evening, I read the section on where I had hiked. It was glorious to be able to identify the trail that I had completed, and that, yes, there was a shrine on the route, and that the mountain I could see in the distance from the summit was called Kumotori-yama. Flipping through the pages and reading each climbing description, I found that there were countless mountains near Mitake-yama, and that single-day ascents were possible if one travelled to the area the night before. This catapulted me into a whole new way of seeing things – mountain hikes no longer meant leaving home in the morning and returning the same day.

I became excited – happy – with planning my next climb, and then the next and the next, one after the other. Tanzawa-yama, Haruna-yama, Yatsugatake, Tanigawa-dake and Kumotori-yama, the highest peak in Tokyo Prefecture. Each trip had a purpose, and what elated me most was the fact that if I kept walking, no matter how fast, or slow, I would arrive at a place I had never been before.

I knew that not many of my university friends could relate to how I felt in the mountains, that the release I had there was nothing like what they experienced in their fashionable world of shopping. I could hardly explain how much I needed to climb and to be among the peaks. The rocky landscape had become a part of me.

I constantly wrote to my father about the adventures I went on. He replied in letters attached to an allowance he sent me each month. In his six- or seven-line responses, he would say, "Hiking is good for your health," and then he would always add, "Take care of your health." He understood me.

Even though I was absorbed by mountain life, and school, I was able to create room for another passion of mine: music. I chose to play the *koto* (Japanese harp) in university, and quickly advanced under the guidance of maestro Ms. Ando. I gravitated towards her strict lessons, given twice a week, and was amazed at how the more I practiced, the more there was to learn.

I worked hard at my grades in order to maintain my dedication to music and the mountains, and my health was better for it. Still, at times, I could feel my mood shift downwards, and I would behave excessively cheerfully so friends were unable to sense my decline.

During one of those periods, a telegram arrived for me. With no warning, I read the words: "Father passed away; come home immediately. Mother." Neither my parents nor I had a telephone, so I promptly left rather than attempt a convoluted stream of communication with family. My host mother had told me to go, she would inform the university, and I headed to my sister Fuchi and her husband's house in Tokyo. They were yet to receive the news and at first thought it could be a mistake. My brother-in-law rushed to a neighbour's house to use their phone only to return with a nod, that yes, my father was dead. The three of us boarded the night train to return to Miharu to be with our family.

My father had died in a work accident, such a sudden occurrence that my entire family was in indescribable grief. Despite the pain we felt, my mother and brother (who had worked for my father) told me to remain at university, to finish my two years until graduation. They would send me money. This brought more tears to my eyes – I had caused my father a lot of worry in his years, and now I could do nothing more to ease his concern for me. He was gone.

That first time I travelled to Tokyo, a few years before my father died, I arrived there by train with him, and we walked the streets to my school together. He was a dilettante and a hard worker. He rode a Harley-David-son motorcycle and played the violin. He absolutely loved new things (a trait I inherited). But he lived by a very cautious philosophy: "Put your cane on the ground before you fall, as it's too late once you're hurt."

The city was traced with our time together, my father supporting me as I found my way in the world. I always felt safe with him. How I would transfer that sense of protection to the heights I was yet to climb was hardly imaginable. Yet, my father's teachings seeped into my mountain-eering years and offered a lifetime of great guidance. "Prepare yourself for whatever you do," he always said.

White Mountains

The relentlessness of the winter mountain environment surprised me – the gusts of wind that almost lifted my body from the ground, the freezing temperatures that numbed my fingers and toes and face, the challenge of the polished, icy surfaces we climbed – and I enjoyed every bit of it. I was like a child discovering cool, running water for the first time. It was exhilarating to know what cold and scared really felt like.

As graduation from university neared, my life expanded in front of me. I had yet to confirm a job, but I felt hopeful with opportunity. When I saw an ad for the position of editor with the Physical Society of Japan, in the science faculty at the University of Tokyo, I hastily applied for one of three available spots. Of the two hundred applicants, I was chosen for the job and started immediately. I continued to live in the house I had called home for the past several years, under the guidance of the host mother, and was pleased that I could stay in Tokyo.

The University of Tokyo is a beautiful location with open space and lots of greenery. It is one of the highest-level government-funded universities in Japan. My job, although not too exciting, was to edit English papers for a 250-page monthly magazine called *Journal*, without being familiar with much of its content. I shared the small office with another woman, and I worked hard in appreciation of the rare benefits of equal (and decent) pay among female and male employees, half-day Saturdays and twenty paid days of leave a year. I was happy there.

As I settled into my role, I began to think of winter climbing. The lofty peaks were pulling at me. Since I no longer qualified to be a member in the student mountaineering club, I sought out other options and finally found a club that would accept women. It was called Hakurei-*kai* (club), and most of the members were rock climbers. They spoke in terms unfamiliar to me: piton, carabiner, belay. I learned that there were a variety of climbing and mountaineering styles, not just the one I had envisioned, which was to climb a singular route to the summit and descend the same way or traverse to a different descent. It was news to me that, generally, there were multiple routes up a mountain, and that climbers constantly challenged the more difficult lines.

After attending my first club meeting, I felt the adrenalin from the night's discussion rush through me on the way home. I was unused to climbing with men, having mainly joined female groups of friends in the mountains during my university years, and I was certain in thinking that I was part of this new club to climb, not to meet a man. My dedication to mountaineering was clear to me.

My inaugural trip with the club was to Harutake-*sawa* (creek) in the Tanzawa area, southwest of Tokyo. That was the first time I used a climbing rope, and I was energized when I placed my hands and feet on the rock and climbed the face. The experience solidified my passion for the mountains. "Next Sunday, we'll hike up the creek to the south face of Tanigawa-dake, and after that, snow training on Mount Fuji," the club announced.

Mount Fuji was cold and conditions were tough, and that introduction to on-snow training resulted in numerous scars on my face from being hit by brittle ice. But it fuelled me, and afterwards, I sought out my first winter mountaineering trip, a traverse from Toumi Ridge on Goryu-dake. As the novice of that excursion, I followed the more experienced climbers by way of food and gear preparation.

I was excited that my dream to climb in what I called the white mountains (snow-covered peaks) had come true, but I lost a bit of my shine when I donned my backpack at the trailhead. I had never carried such a weight – 27 kilograms strapped to my small frame. It was already a struggle to walk the short distance from Kamishiro Station to the trailhead. Then I reached the snow, an altogether new battle with the load on my back. This trip was a debut of sorts as I was one of four new members to the Hakurei club, and I was determined to prove my worth despite the stress and nervousness I felt. I was steadfast about not giving up.

I must admit, although I was in the mountains I had dreamt about for years, I hardly remembered anything about them. Head down, I was completely absorbed by chasing the footsteps of the others in front of me. I felt relief when one of the new members gave up from exhaustion; I was not the only one who found the climb to be an enormous struggle. Then, as the snow-covered summit of Kashimayari came into view to the south, I was awash with renewed excitement. I was proud of myself, that I had made it to the white mountains and that I was in the throes of winter mountaineering.

Invitations to various outings continued, and I wanted to be a part of every one of them. But I needed proper equipment to continue winter climbing on snow and ice. My paycheck, reasonable at 15,000 yen per month, was only enough to cover rent and food, with a bit left over for train travel. I had to save money week by week to slowly acquire what I needed for mountaineering. When a friend gave me a second-hand pair of overboots to use, I cherished them. Just saying the word "overboots" made me feel like a true mountaineer.

Even my insufficient equipment, and the political atmosphere of Japan at the time, could not stop me from going to the mountains. Demonstrations took place on the streets and people were active in voicing their objections about national alliances with the United States, yet I spent most of my weekends climbing. I felt peace in the mountains and could sense my father watching over me. As time passed, I became more comfortable among men and could easily climb with either male or female partners. Eventually, I even felt at ease sharing a tent with men – it seemed like the natural thing to do in the mountains, but the rumours that resulted bothered me to no end. I had no time for assumptions that so and so were dating because they had climbed together. Still, I had come far in my dreams of the white mountains, and I could endure such gossip if it meant continuing to climb.

Mountain Mentor

We were an odd pair, me so very small in size, and Yoko-o-san, a tall, advanced climber, but we shared the rope many times. Yoko-o had become my mentor. He would always encourage me to lead a pitch somewhere along the route, constantly pushing my skills. His repeated words of simple advice made me a better climber – lean out; don't climb with your arms; use your feet – and he took me everywhere, even though a woman climber was a rare sight in Tanigawa. I ignored the rumours that began to spread about us. After three years of climbing together, I was capable of mastering quite difficult routes. One day he turned to me and said, "Go to 8000 metres. You're ready to lead with female partners. Try that from now on."

As I progressed in climbing, my days at Hakurei became numbered. I was bothered by the club's strict rules and the constant gossip. I had heard that a fellow member, reputably a superb mountaineer, was starting a new club with a focus on cutting-edge climbing. So I left Hakurei and joined Ryoho-Toko-kai (Ryoho Climbing Club, Ryoho for short). There were seven members in total, and it was in that group that I met my soon-to-be mentor, Koichi Yoko-o. We all have encounters in life that either brighten our future or dampen a dream. For me, meeting Yoko-o was entirely about positive steps forward.

Yoko-o, the youngest member of Ryoho, opened the doors for me to the 8000-metre peaks of the world. I knew of his name when I first joined Hakurei, for his climbing ability but also because of a fall he and a climbing partner had taken on the first attempt of Direct-Cante, on the wall to the right of Tsuitate-*iwa* (rock). They were a teenage pair attempting the route a year after Tsuitate-iwa was first climbed in 1959. Not that anyone wished to be remembered for this, but their story became legend. They had slipped near the pinnacle of Direct-Cante and plummeted to the rock slabs of Tsuitate-iwa. Yoko-o somehow leapt into the bush alongside the slab, saving his life, but his friend later succumbed to injuries sustained from hitting the rock below.

Stories about Yoko-o were ample, about his hermit lifestyle, and his vitality and will power during his recovery from the accident, and his continued strong sense of balance in climbing. I tried to picture him from those stories and looked forward to meeting him, having joined Ryoho partly for that honour. At my first club event, there he stood at the café exit, very tall, with long tousled hair and a somewhat cynical expression on his face. I mistook him for a hard person to get to know.

I was surprised to be so easily accepted as a fellow climber by the Ryoho club. At that first meeting, I made plans with Yajima, another club member, to climb Yunosawa in Tanigawa-dake the following week. The trip was an experience of firsts for me: new mountain, new partner, the use of etriers, and lead climbing on a difficult route. We made a route-finding mistake near the top and had to ascend a grassy section, which taught me that it can be more dangerous to climb wet grass than rock, a lesson I would tuck in my back pocket for future scenarios.

Upon returning from Yunosawa, I received a call from Yoko-o. "Let's go to the Back Wall at Ichinokura-sawa next week," he said.

"The Back Wall? No way," I said, not feeling ready for such a climb. "That's my ultimate goal."

"The Back Wall is your final target? Come on! Don't be silly. Just bring your personal gear. We'll take the 10:12 night train as usual. Got it?" He was persistent and I was unsure. I was also committed to play the *koto* in a concert that next Saturday. My mind was conflicted with two different thoughts. Mountains or music?

I went back and forth between "No, I'm not joining him on that climb," and "It's a great chance. Why not?" I was unable to choose. In the end, my desire to climb was immense and I could not withstand missing the opportunity. So, Yoko-o's persistence paid off and that next Saturday night, after the concert, I changed from *kimono* to climbing attire and headed for Ueno Station.

At the station, I realized Yajima would be joining the trip. Neither he nor I knew that the other had been invited by Yoko-o. Our surprise was difficult to hide. "Oh, you're coming, too?" asked Yajima with doubt in his voice. "Yoko-o, is she OK to climb The Flanke?" I had no idea our intended route was the steep rock face that its name denoted. The South Ridge Flanke was the back wall of the Back Wall and had never seen a first ascent. Yet, standing there at the train station, I trusted Yoko-o and Yajima, even though we had spent little time together. It felt strange, this new trust, but I believed we would succeed as a team, even on The Flanke.

Climbing with Yoko-o was like watching a person dance on rock. He was an amazing climber, and his elegant movement from one hold to another showed no signs of the terrible accident he had endured years ago. From the base of the route, he climbed directly up Tsuitate Slab with perfect balance, ignoring the ridge as a possible option. We climbed as a threesome with me roped in between the two men. In a mist-like rain that heightened the darkness of the wet Back Wall, we started up, the rope smoothly uncoiling between Yoko-o and me as he stepped forth. I followed, thinking nothing of fear, and instead giving my best. Being in sync with Yoko-o's moves increased my confidence and made me feel like I could easily climb this route, until Yajima spoke up. "You'd be killed just following him like that," he said, even though he was copying the same movements from lower on the rock.

Unfortunately, the misty rain gave way to a downpour. It became impossible to climb above the chimney section, and we decided to back off with barely the second pitch complete. I had practiced rappelling before in Tanzawa at the small cliffs of Momiso-iwa, but this was, again, a first for me – rappelling off a multi-pitch route where a mistake would be costly. The hemp rope tied to us became rough as it soaked up the heavy rain, and my spirits felt heavy, too, as we switched from going up the route to going down.

Although we failed in our attempt on The Flanke, it was the test that Yoko-o used to measure me as a climber, and I had passed. From then on, he made me his climbing partner no matter who else joined the trip. I was never sure if it was a matter of course for the most experienced climber to partner up with a novice, but I greatly benefitted from the arrangement as we climbed together nearly every weekend. Although Yoko-o never gave me detailed instructions, I gained specific skills and knowledge from him over time, like tying ropes, placing anchors and setting routes. I absorbed everything climbing-related from this person, and as nice as it was to climb a new route, I came to realize the importance of a climbing partner and how great an impact that partner has on the route itself. Most important of all, what I learned from Yoko-o was to embrace the entirety of climbing and the resulting joy that it evokes.

My small stature made it difficult for me follow Yoko-o on approaches and climbs. His height and strength, along with his mantra "I don't climb with anyone weak," forced me to conserve my energy levels whenever possible, for instance sleeping on the train, so that I could keep up to him. Still, he offered help when I needed it and shared the lead on pitches, fuelling my elation of accomplishment. His confidence, decision-making skills and sense of balance in the mountains, and his care and compassion for his climbing partner, added together to make me feel like I could climb anywhere with him. Maybe he was frustrated with not having a partner equal to his ability, hence his efforts in training me to that level, but if that was the case, I was unaware of it. He seemed happy enough to focus solely on climbing with me.

I thought this was the relationship I craved. I revelled in the simplicity of experiencing the mountains with a male partner, yet with no other expectations. On hikes to and from the base of a route or along ridgetops, or during breaks at a belay, Yoko-o spoke of his childhood, his journey back from China after the war, his marriage, and the novel he was writing at the time. The fact that we were connected by a deep trust, not by romance, in a dangerous environment where a mistake could cost a life, pleased me. Despite my assurance of our relationship and my hard-earned competency in the mountains, I sometimes felt other male climbers gave me the once over at the crags while saying, "This is no place for women." It was an era of few female climbers, but none of that mattered to me. My commitment was to climb, and I loathed the idea of having to spend a Sunday sitting idle rather than being on a mountain.

Up to that point in my adult life, the only other event that I thoroughly looked forward to was a visit from my mother and brother, who would travel from Miharu to see me. I could hardly wait for their arrival – until I became obsessed with climbing. After that, I would silently pray that they would choose any other day than a Sunday to visit. Often, while on a small ledge partway up a climb, I would imagine my mother's reaction, her blood pressure jumping sky high if she saw where I stood.

Her daughter scaling a rock wall was not the picture she had of me. By remaining silent about my climbing pursuits, I left her content to believe that I had stayed in Tokyo after university to continue practice of the *koto* and to gain work experience in the city. My family was adamant in stating, "Easy hiking is OK, but no winter mountaineering or rock climbing."

Little did they know, the very activities my family had wished for me to ignore had become everything to me. In my mind, the only choice I had was to pursue my love for the mountains.

Female Climber

"I've met my match," I thought to myself, "and she's different, beyond ordinary." I knew this as soon as I was told that Sasou travelled to the crags after work on weekdays to climb a few routes, and then took the train back to Tokyo first thing the morning to not be late for her job. All this because she was impatient for the weekend to climb.

One day, out of the blue, I received a phone call at work. "My name is Rumie Sasou. I'd love to climb with you. Could you meet me sometime?" I was immediately drawn in, partially because Yoko-o had already suggested it was time for me to climb with female partners. We decided to meet at Shibuya Station, near the entrance to the Inokashira train line. I was slightly nervous to make her acquaintance, wondering what she would be like. Then someone in the crowd called out to me, "Jun-*chan!*" Only fellow club members and a few others identified me with that name. "Sorry for catching you off guard. I'm Sasou. I've seen you around in the trains on my way to the mountains, and at Tanigawa, too. All of your buddies call you 'Jun-*chan,*' so I just said it with no thought." She was very friendly, and I relaxed with her welcoming manner.

Sasou stood an inch taller than my five feet. She was stockier and fit, with short hair and a sun tan. We immediately hit it off and made plans to climb Inago-dake in the Yatsugatake area the next week. Despite her spoken old-Tokyo accent, which had a rougher enunciation compared to modern Japanese, I found her to be quite precise. Attention to detail was foremost in her actions, highlighted by her well-organized backpack that looked more like the perfect picture in a climbing magazine. Even the handle of her umbrella was removed to reduce the weight in her pack, so exact was she. As a graduate, then employee of the Tokyo Woman's Christian University, Sasou enjoyed long summer vacations that enabled her to spend a month climbing at Tsurugi-dake. She also climbed at the crags as often as possible. I had finally met someone who shared my same desire for the mountains. Behold, my new female climbing partner!

I visited the home where Sasou lived with her mother and brother on a big lot in Hamada-yama of greater downtown Tokyo. The family also owned an apartment that was rented by a fellow climbing club member. During my stay there, we were completely dedicated to the mountains – all we did was climb and discuss the next route for summer training. "My mom tells me this and that," Sasou explained, "but I just have to tell her that climbing is an absolute priority for me." And so, our climbing together increased. We were fully satisfied when we had completed the Central Ridge of Ichinokura-sawa, a success that made us determined to climb the ice wall on that same mountain in winter.

Routes took longer to climb with a female partner, but somehow, I felt more rewarded by the accomplishment. Being physically more equal to one another seemed fairer to me, and this made me happy to climb with a woman. Sasou played an additional role in my life too – she had become my closest friend. And when I moved to my sister Fuchi's house in downtown Tokyo (at my mother's insistence), Sasou enabled me to sneak away to the mountains *and* to date (against my mother's wishes) the man who would ultimately become my husband. "Hello," she would say on the phone. "This is Sasou. How are you? I wondered if Junko-*san* has left already. We planned to do some editing work on a mountaineering report together at my house, and she's staying overnight with us." Her voice was polished every time, unlike her usual course accent, and easily misled my family regarding my whereabouts. "I'm very convincing," she bragged.

The downside to where we climbed in Tanigawa-dake was the countless number of climbing accidents that occurred in those days. It was a mixed blessing to get to know the rescue crew of that area. On occasion, we helped them carry bodies back into town after a serious fall. In turn, they were kind to us and welcomed us into their homes for a brief meal or hot bath before catching the train home. Repeatedly they said to us, "Please, please do not become number 365," referring to the toll of climbing fatalities that had reached 364 at the time, a number too high to imagine.

Despite the tally of accidents, we climbed there almost every week.

Life Partner

Each time Masanobu informed my family of the news that I had reached the summit of a significant mountain, like Annapurna or Everest, my brother whole-heartedly thanked him. "It's all because of you," he would say. "She is so lucky to have you." It almost made Masanobu cry with joy to hear my brother's words. Thinking back, marrying Masanobu was the most important turning point of my life.

In 1964, around the same time that Sasou and I were introduced, I also met Masanobu Tabei. I recognized his name because he was well-known among climbers. People always gawked at him at train stations or at the crags, saying things like "There goes the Tabei party; they're awesome," or "They never fall," and so on. I ignored the talk, but I had noticed that he always sat in the top car of the midnight train. This was a luxury reserved for high-end climbers that allowed them to exit the station ahead of everyone else in order to arrive first at the climbing area and have their choice of routes.

We met on a Sunday after the Golden Week holidays in May in Tanigawa-dake. Usually on Sundays, the routes were full and we had to wait our turn to climb. But on that particular day, the place was quiet. There were only two parties of two: Masanobu and his friend from the Honda Climbing Club, and Tatsuo Ishii and me from Ryoho. Of all the routes to climb that day, my partner and I picked the same one as Masanobu, the South Ridge of Ichinokura-sawa. I was surprised to make his acquaintance when I crested the snowy flat top of the route, but there was Masanobu eating an improvised dessert of sorbet made from snow and laden with sweet azuki (red beans). He had it ready to serve to us as we finished the climb. At first, I was amazed that Masanobu would carry something as heavy as a can of beans on a route. Yet, it was the sweetness of the wild sorbet and azuki that became etched in my heart's memory as the meeting of my life partner.

Come mid-winter, Sasou and I were breaking trail through deep snow from the Doai Station to Deai for a female-only attempt on the Central Ridge of Ichinokura-sawa. Masanobu and Ishii were also there to climb Cup Rock on Ichinokura-sawa, which had seen only one previous winter ascent. The danger of both routes was understood, and we accepted that both parties were entering terrain that could end one's life by way of avalanche or a simple slip. Hence, we wished each other well and hoped that with luck and in good time the two teams would meet again.

Sasou and I were bogged down with trail breaking to the base of the climb, which delayed our start up the route to noon. There was no way we would reach the top in a day, so we decided to bivouac on the wall. It began to snow that evening, and there was no space at the bivy for us to sit together. Instead we stood slightly apart on the narrow-terraced staircase of rock. I wondered how Masanobu and Ishii were succeeding on the more difficult Cup Rock route. Their demeanor was calm that morning when we said goodbye, unlike the nervousness I felt, and likely Sasou too, before a winter ascent.

For our night's perch, Sasou and I placed two anchors each, one for a self-belay and the other to secure our equipment. A series of carabiners rattled with the slightest of our movements. Eventually I relaxed, and even smiled, once I was warmly wrapped in a space blanket and tiny flames came to life on the camp stove that balanced on my lap. Somehow, I found that to be peaceful.

Avalanches were not a worry at the height and steepness of where we bivied, but the remaining three legs of the route were still of concern. We had the rock section to complete, and a steep snow slope and knifepoint ridge to the summit. Difficult trail breaking lay ahead, and I had the fleeting thought that we might not finish the climb by the end of the next day. Nonetheless, we remained optimistic and cheerfully chatted throughout the night. Sasou showed me a boiled egg with a face drawn on it. "Someone gave this to me," she said. Although she disclosed no more information, I knew exactly who had given it to her. Sasou had several admirers, but they all hesitated to confess their feelings to her. The egg was a good sign.

As we stood there, anchored to the wall, the hearty aroma of grilled meat filled the space around us as I cooked slices of salami over the flame of the stove. As I tried to cut one more piece, my hand slipped and knocked a chunk of the blue-flamed lard-like fuel, causing it to jump from the burner and fall into the darkness below. The persistent flame caught on a bush that clung to the side of the ridge and continued to burn as it swayed on the branch. Sasou giggled, "It'd be funny if we started a fire on the Central Ridge in the middle of winter." Her giggles were a reliable gauge of her good mood.

The next morning came with no sleep. Carefully, we moved our stiff bodies after a long night and slowly put on our climbing gear. As we completed two more pitches, we heard Ishii's voice echo from above: "Hello! Sasou-*san*, Jun-*chan!*" We returned his greeting, stunned to see the pair casually snapping photos of us on the final traverse. They had climbed the more challenging Cup Rock route faster than we had finished the Central Ridge.

It was a snowy dull day, an observation easily overlooked with the excitement of both teams on the summit of Ichinokura-sawa, having arrived there via two significant winter routes. Our success felt wondrous as we stood together with no one else around for miles.

Then the descent. We took turns breaking trail in the deep snow, still full of energy. The routine movement became automatic: raise the ice axe overhead, place it horizontal to the steep slope and push the snow away, clearing a path in front of us as we pressed forward with our knees. We were almost crawling rather than stepping forward, but even the tediousness of those tiring efforts could not dampen our spirits that day. I was particularly pleased with Sasou and me having been the first female pair to complete the Central Ridge route in winter.

After that exuberant experience on Ichinokura-sawa, I often ran into Masanobu in various places. Though these meetings were unplanned, I wondered if fate was at work. One time I bumped into him on the bus and took advantage of the moment by offering him a candy. It was wrapped in *oblaat*, a thin starchy edible paper also used to encase powdered medicine to ease swallowing. As he peeled the *oblaat*, Masanobu said, "I've eaten many kilograms of these." I asked him what he meant and was shocked to learn that he had spent four of his middle-school years bedridden with tuberculosis. I was amazed at his climbing ability after having had such an illness. This was an eye-opener for me. Having listened to his story, I felt humbled by his calm nature and matter-of-fact approach. As I was becoming a more accomplished climber, I ran the risk of developing a bit of arrogance; I might have come to think less of those who climbed easier routes than me. But Masanobu's pleasant way, despite the hard routes he was capable of, kept me in check. I learned modesty that day on the bus.

Since we were members of different mountaineering clubs, Masanobu and I never had the chance to climb together. It was expected that trips were planned among members of the same club – Sasou even quit her club and joined Ryoho so we could climb together without issue. Even though I relied on this protocol to access the mountains, it meant that climbing with Masanobu was unlikely. Then one day he said to me, "Maku-iwa on the south face of Tanigawa-dake is great in fall colour." Rules be darned, our first climbing date was arranged. On the rock, I observed how he moved at the same stable pace he walked on flat trail. As he climbed an overhang with ease and moved onto a grassy area, he said, "It's more dangerous on grass." I had learned this on Yunosawa in the past, but again took it to heart as coming from an expert. Even having said that, Masanobu moved without effort over the grass and continued on his way. After I heard the distant tap of him placing a piton, his voice reverberated down to me: "OK, climb up."

The surrounding view was beautiful. Autumn leaves painted red blurred in the distance as we climbed higher onto the ridge that braced the blue sky above. The cool breeze offered relief to my sweating skin. As I climbed towards Masanobu, I enjoyed the comfortable feel of this partnership. It was the kind that would make anyone feel good.

Opposite to the enjoyment I had discovered with Masanobu, my mother relentlessly tried to persuade me to consider an arranged marriage. "You are already twenty-six and not married," she said. Her deep disappointment was evident. Although not enforced, an arranged marriage was a common occurrence in Japan. Adding fuel to fire were the invitations I received from former schoolmates, informing me of their pending marriages. Solely committed to climbing, I turned down every invite to a wedding. But there remained a slight doubt in my mind. Was I all right with living like this forever, unmarried? The question popped up every time I saw a nice couple sharing an intimate conversation on the train.

I was conflicted. It certainly would have been easier to accept one of my mother's many proposed arrangements. My sisters had done so and they seemed happy enough. But then I would ask myself again, "Do I really want that?" I tried to picture myself as a traditional Japanese wife who followed her husband. The idea never sat well with me, and I began to conclude that a healthy marriage was one that allowed people to do things they would otherwise not accomplish alone, hence enriching the lives of both partners.

As expected, my mother was deeply upset when I told her about Masanobu. She considered him an insignificant man without a university degree. I was tempted to argue but remained silent, hopeful that patience on my part would prevail. But she persisted: "It's not good for you to live on your own in the city. Come back home to Miharu and learn to cook to become a good wife. That or move in with your sister." I endured her lack of understanding of me, as she was a feisty woman of an earlier generation, and I wondered how different my father's input might have been if he had still been alive.

To temporarily appease my mother, and for my own peace of mind, I moved in with Fuchi and her family. Still, I refused to give in to my mother's objection to my choice of husband. Masanobu knew she was not in favour of our union and suggested that, with time, she would come around to our proposed marriage. He even arranged for his parents to travel to Miharu with us to speak to my mother. In the meantime, my mother demonstrated her non-forgiving ways whenever I spent time with her. She would refuse to drink the tea I brewed or to accept the rice I served, dumping it back in the pot to serve herself. Yes, it would have been easy to declare enough was enough and walk out on my mother, but she was my only surviving parent and I respected her. I again chose to remain patient in hopes that some day she would recognize my marriage choice as being right for me.

I remained in that limbo of hope for nearly two years as, slowly, my mother's degree of objection began to ease. Although she never officially permitted our marriage, she appeared to finally admit, "I may have to give in as my daughter never changes her mind." Overnight, she suddenly demanded a big traditional wedding so as not to be embarrassed by anything less. We had to laugh at my mother's about-face, and in Masanobu's words, we just did "whatever we could to make her happy."

Since we had limited funds to spend on our wedding, we had to consider other options. At the time, TV weddings were popular – essentially, the event, if interesting enough, was filmed and broadcasted at the expense of the television company. That idea would not fly with me. Instead, with Sasou's input, we decided upon a collect-fee style of wedding, where guests (except parents) would each pay 1,000 yen to attend. More than one hundred guests joined us in celebration, with my mother proudly dressed in her formal *kurotome* (black silk) kimono. Each guest was given a beautiful cut-glass salad bowl as a gift from Masanobu and me. I still use mine, and each time I do, I am pleasantly reminded of my mother and my friend Sasou. As simplistic as we tried to be with wedding arrangements, we spent almost our entire savings on this one-time event.

Our new home was a tiny single room in Shiinamachi, the first stop from downtown Tokyo on the Seibu train line. We outfitted the place with old furniture, a desk, futons and books. I had nothing fancy like what Fuchi had received for her wedding, but I indulged in one bridal item, a mirror stand, which allowed me to get rid of some of the cardboard boxes I had used as a table when I was single.

To us, our honeymoon was a big deal, the trip of a lifetime. We planned to hike Miyanoura-dake on Yakushima (*shima* meaning island), in the very south of Japan. As airline tickets were clearly unaffordable, we travelled by train and boat to get there. On Yakushima, we required permission from the forest service to take a tram to Kosugidani (*dani* meaning valley). The tram ride remained memorable to me for years afterwards: huge cedar branches sweeping down so close to the rails that they brushed my face as we passed by; monkeys jumping from one tree to another, all within our grasp. It was bliss.

Quite the opposite to the spacious outdoors of our honeymoon, our single-room home could barely hold our small kitchen. There was no bath in our unit, and we shared a common toilet room with other residents of the apartment. We used an outside wash basin for laundry and relied on a public bathhouse a five-minute walk away to get clean, except it closed at 11 p.m., often before we returned from a day of climbing. Our neighbours became used to us bathing in the apartment's outside basin, or bent over our tiny kitchen sink.

We had no telephone; a phone was for emergencies only and could be used at the landlord's house if needed (with a 10-yen fee each time). Despite being impossible to reach by phone, and regardless of the limited size of our place, we always had mountaineering friends there to visit, rarely leaving my husband and me to dine alone. A knock on the wall from our neighbour would remind us to quiet things down when our friends visited, followed by another knock a little while later as our voices began to escalate again. Basically, that pattern repeated itself many times on multiple occasions.

Four months into our marriage, a gift arrived from my mother. To our surprise, in item and in gesture, it was a refrigerator. After all her years of objection, we received this as a sign of acceptance. Even though we spent most of our weekends in the mountains, we made sure to visit my mother in Miharu at least once every three months to maintain progress with her. Oddly, once in our company, she would order Masanobu to complete chores for her, like chopping wood or moving items into storage. My sisters' husbands would never have been asked to do such work, but Masanobu never complained and diligently fulfilled every demand made on him. Gradually, the relationship with my mother improved. She even joined us on a trip. Another time she chose to stay with us at our tiny residence in Shiinamachi. Masanobu and I could hardly believe it.

In September 1967, I was twenty-eight years old and happy. I had married the man of my choice and we shared a deeply satisfying mountain life together. Then, while I was on a trip home to Miharu to honour the seventh anniversary of my father's death, Sasou, my dear friend and climbing partner, was killed in an accident on Tanigawa-dake.

Farewell Friend

A report by Morie Yamazaki, one of the two other climbers with Sasou on Ichinokura-sawa, and who would later climb Annapurna III with me, provided some understanding of what had happened to my friend.

Got up to the col of the Fifth Runse, 2 p.m. "It was fun!" "My first time to climb Runse, I'm freaking happy up here today." So, we cheered and shook hands to celebrate the successful climb. Feeling a bit chilly with the autumn breeze, we left there quickly. Yoshimura asked about roping up, and I answered no. "Careful, it's not over yet," said Sasou.

Yoshimura went first, myself next, and then Sasou. I found it a bit sketchy when I got close to the bottom of the rocky ridge. All the spots for possible footholds were covered by thick red dirt and looked slippery. That was why the party ahead of us took their route to the left. We also went to a dry white rock on the left. It was good for the first five to six metres, but got worse, and I kept traversing to the left looking for a stable foot placement. Yoshimura, ahead of me, asked again about roping up. "No, I'm fine," I declined for the second time. Sasou also caught up to me on my right and suggested getting the rope out, but I continued traversing to the left bit by bit as I couldn't find a stable foothold. I started to feel like I might not be able to make it, but a need for the rope hadn't really occurred to me.

Yamazaki had held onto the loose rock and lost her balance, falling as her foothold also gave way. Sasou stood to the right about a metre below and tried to stop Yamazaki by grabbing her but was instead pulled off the mountainside and fell as well. By a miracle, Yamazaki was stopped short after falling 80 metres when her backpack caught on a tree root. Sadly, Sasou fell out of sight.

Before that trip, I suggested to Sasou that she not go since I was unable to join her due to my father's memorial in Miharu. Ever the climber, she went anyway, but she hardly knew Yamazaki and Yoshimura. The lure of the Fifth Runse on Ichinokura-sawa was too much for her to resist.

I had returned home from Miharu to an urgent telegram that read: "Sasou is missing in Tanigawa-dake. Come as soon as possible." Masanobu and I lost no time changing clothes, packing ropes and climbing gear, calling all our climbing friends, and leaving for Tanigawa-dake. It was the responsibility of each climbing club to help rescue its own members in the event of an accident. The club would assist the professional rescue team, an offshoot of the police department. By the time we arrived at Doai Mountain Centre, Sasou's mother was already there. Sasou had not yet been found. Masanobu went straight to the rock wall, and I waited with her mother.

"You know, it's Sasou, a good climber; she must have bivouacked somewhere. She's the kind of person who can easily spend a night or two out on her own." Hopeful comments like these were spoken amongst the group as we waited, but it caused me angst, and I was unsure of what to do, what to think. I would have felt better if had I gone with Masanobu, but I dared not risk slowing them down as they sped to the area where Sasou had fallen. So, I waited at the rescue centre and catered to colleagues and friends of Sasou who arrived burdened with concern for her.

More than six hours later, we were informed that Sasou's body had been found and that our friend was dead. It was Koichi Yoko-o who found her, jammed tight like a wedge, face down, between two rocks in the upper part of the Third Runse. Yoko-o was terribly distraught as his relationship with Sasou had become strained earlier that year at a summer climbing camp when a mutual friend, Ito, died in a fall. Yoko-o was Ito's climbing partner and Sasou was camp leader; both parties took responsibility for the accident at the expense of their own friendship. At news of Sasou's accident, Yoko-o was quickest to the scene in hopes of rescuing her and ending past bygones.

Sasou looked unusually small when her body was carried down the mountain in a yellow sleeping bag, surrounded by leaves turning to the shades of autumn. Against the white rock slab, an array of colourful ropes was tied to lower her body. Saying goodbye to the many rock routes she had poured her passion into – Cup Rock, Tsuitate-iwa, Back Wall, Takizawa Slab – Sasou made her final descent, quietly embraced by the silent prayers of her many climber friends. I could still hear her cheerful voice saying, "Hurry up, let's go!"

Sasou's mother and brother were waiting at Doai. I lacked the words to express my sadness, anger and pain when I saw her mother look at Sasou still tied in the climbing rope. "You must have been so cold…" her mother said as she touched her daughter's face and combed Sasou's hair, which was matted with blood. Later, as we dressed Sasou in her favourite navy blue *kasuri kimono* with a bright yellow sash, we noticed that her bones were broken throughout.

As I helped prepare Sasou's body, I noted that only forty-nine days had passed since she and I had put a *kimono* on Ito, the friend who had died in the earlier climbing accident. I was shaken to the core with loss. I brushed Sasou's lips with lipstick, placed her hands together on her chest and shook her hand for the last time. Her face was calm, as always.

She was put into a coffin with the flowers and chocolates that she loved, surrounded by the beauty of trees, rocks and creeks, and the sadness of tears. We said farewell at the crematorium in Numata, at the foot of the mountains. When I saw the blue-white smoke rise into the sky, I began to cry inconsolably, like a waterfall, my mind churning: why Sasou-*san*? My climbing partner, at thirty-one years of age, was gone.

Although I had experienced grief for my sister and father, Sasou's death came as a shock to me. She was a person I spoke with every day to make plans to climb, and her voice stayed with me long after she died. I can still picture how she glanced upwards from her shyly tilted head as she spoke gruffly to men.

When Ito died at the summer climbing camp, Sasou could not rid herself of responsibility. We spoke many times about that accident, especially with it being the first fatality for our club. Sasou was extremely exhausted from the stress of the incident, so we decided to take a break together and go on a driving trip around the Tohoku area to gain some mental clarity.

Our plan was to travel to Sendai, then Matsushima via the scenic coastline of Rikuchu-kaigan, and to Aomori, Akita and Niigata before heading home. En route we camped at the seaside, barbecued the fish we caught and played on the beach, but it was not enough to put Sasou at peace. The thick coastal fog gave a spooky feel to the place, and at times I watched her stare into the horizon. She was as unmoving as the Sanzu-no-kawa of Osorezan, an imaginary river in Buddhism that represents the in-between of this world and the afterlife. Sasou stood there in her usual style of short pants and a scarf on her head, looking lonely and serious. I was unable to reach her. The sight of my friend that way, and comments she made like, "My life may be done in its thirties anyway," left a sorrowful impression on my mind, yet I never once thought she would succumb to a fatal accident so soon afterwards.

Sasou's death made me face the reality that everyone, including me, would eventually die and return to the soil of the earth. I become contemplative, questioning if I was fully living the life I wanted. Simultaneously, I felt such confusion and disappointment that the world around me could continue in its day-to-day manner, business as usual. There was only one solution for me: I had to embrace the sadness and emptiness in my heart and begin to climb again.

Life Continues

"What does a climber think in mid-air as they fall?" I asked Masanobu.

"Suddenly your body is afloat and you see the sky, and then you see the wall coming at you. You realize you'll crash into it unless you do something, and you panic, looking for anything to grab onto. It feels like quite a long time passes while you are actually falling," he said. He had fallen once, having been pulled off by a second climber on the Third Slab.

I appreciated his honesty, and I wondered if Sasou had felt the same way as she fell. Since her death, I climbed more with my husband.

In those years of climbing, people spoke mainly of first ascents on a wall or in the winter season, but the Himalayas remained largely undiscussed. Climbing there was only a dream or a story in a book. One day, however, Yoko-o visited us in Shiinamachi, asking Masanobu to join him to climb in Europe the coming summer. Yoko-o would be the trip leader, with the goal of climbing the North Faces of the three big walls – the Grandes Jorasses, the Eiger and the Matterhorn – in one season. Masanobu had never climbed outside of Japan in all his life. I was thrilled at this opportunity for him, and knowing I would slow them down if I joined them, I wholeheartedly encouraged the male-only expedition.

Masanobu and I both had jobs, so we knew we could afford the trip, and by luck, Honda, the company he worked for and that we had assumed was strict, agreed to more than a month's holiday. I was elated, as my approach was one of not worrying about the loss of a job or missing out on a promotion – I felt it was more important to live a life we would never regret. In that instance, Masanobu had the benefit of both, the dream climbing trip and keeping his job.

In June 1969, three of them, Masanobu, Yoshimura and Yoko-o, left Yokohama, southwest of Tokyo, on a ship to Nakhodka, in the very western part of the former Soviet Union. A fourth member, Noguchi, would join the party later. It had been about a year since Sasou's death, and as I bid farewell to the ship leaving the harbour, I recalled her words when we bivouacked at the top of a route in Japan's Northern Alps: "Let's go climb K2 if we ever go to the Himalayas." Even then, I could hardly imagine myself on a mountain overseas.

"We've been waiting for good weather at the Eiger for ten days, but it's not happening, so we'll try the North Face of the Grandes Jorasses first." That was the first communication I received from Masanobu on their trip. Shortly after, the second telegram arrived: "We did it!" Since I had no doubt of their potential success from the start, I felt more satisfied than overjoyed about their news. Then the next update arrived. They had also climbed the North Face of the Matterhorn but were caught in a snowstorm and had to bivouac on the route. Masanobu's toes were frostbitten and he was admitted to hospital as soon as they finished their descent. In his letter, he sounded almost happy, as if he was staying in a fancy hotel with great food. In comparison to the cold and uncomfortable night on the mountain face, maybe that was the case, but he was yet to inform me of his condition, or his plans for coming home. What was I to think?

Another ten days passed before I finally received a telegram that stated he was on his way back to Japan by airplane. I had no idea what to expect when I went to meet him at the Haneda Airport. I watched Masanobu step off the plane and relief washed over me. Though his toes were bandaged, my husband could walk. He seemed more excited about the first-class seat he had flown in and the luxury of the Swiss hospital than the joy I expressed at seeing him standing upright. But once we were settled in our tiny home, and I asked to see how badly damaged his toes were, the truth surfaced. His account made me cringe: "We were caught in a snow storm on the North Face of the Matterhorn and stuck on the wall for two full days. I was worried about getting frostbite since there was no space in the bivy sac for my feet. The ledge was small, and Noguchi and I had to sit with our legs dangling over the edge. Noguchi also suffered from frostbite on his toes, and we were together in the hospital. He's supposed to come back in three days. We had injections and intravenous. To be honest, it doesn't hurt anymore."

He removed the bandage and showed me his toes. A third of two of his toes were black, and his big toes and middle toes were shrunken. "It doesn't look good," I thought. There was no doubt in my mind that we had to see a doctor the next day. Frostbite was a rare condition in Japan back then, and we had no idea which hospital would be best to care for Masanobu. We first tried the hospital close to our apartment, but the doctor said he knew nothing about treating frostbite. We ended up at the university hospital near my office, where Masanobu was immediately admitted.

Home alone, I wrote in my diary for consolation: "September 22, it's my birthday and my husband is in the hospital. I'm so busy and exhausted. It was only Sasou whom I could talk to in hard times. Today, instead, we're having the memorial climb for the first anniversary since her death at Tanigawa. We always walked together along the paved trail to Ichinokura-sawa. I can still see us walking there when I close my eyes. Sasou-*san*, I'm so tired. I feel sad and lonely to my core, not having someone to talk to, and for not having my good climbing partner."

By autumn, Masanobu accepted that his toes were to be amputated at the second joint. There was no other choice despite the efforts made to save them. I tried to cheer him up. "It'll be just fine. You'll still be able to walk after," I said, but I could feel his uncertainty. Noguchi was admitted to the same hospital when he arrived back to Japan, and sadly, he also lost his toes. Five for him, four for Masanobu.

The surgery sites were wrapped and tucked with skin that used to cover bone. Although the stitched areas recovered well, the doctor explained that it would take a long time for the wounds to toughen up. So, to and from our local public bath house, Masanobu wore *geta*, wooden sandals like flip flops with a middle and back heel, to challenge his balance. A month after the amputations, ready to try more, he was out there on a training hike to Futago-yama. The daytrip was difficult, he said, especially on the descent as the tender joints touched the front of his boots. Noguchi also spoke of how his socks were stained with blood when he first tried to hike. These trials marked the true beginning of their recovery.

I was not in the position to say anything to Masanobu as I knew he was suffering from the fact that he lost his toes due to his own mistake. All I could do was remain positive and encourage him back to health with rehabilitation and training, to be as strong and able as he was before the incident. His family remained quiet, too, and the silence became harder for him than the expected fuss over what had happened.

One day, he suddenly announced that we should buy a piece of land and build a house. Although my first choice was to not live in a one-room apartment for the rest of my life, I had never dreamed of buying land. Neither Masanobu nor I earned that sort of money. At the same time, the thought of having our own *castle* sooner rather than later was nice. I could suddenly imagine myself playing *koto* and enjoying the scent of flowers in a room that overlooked a yard full of osmanthus, roses and daffodils in bloom.

Masanobu presented his case to convince me about the land. He explained that although he no longer had the same physical base to stand on, having lost several toes, he believed that owning a piece of real estate would provide the base we needed to move forward in our life, that it would put us in a good position for the future. He planned to borrow money from Honda for a down payment. The selling point for me was how such a purchase would finally put my mother's mind to rest about my stability with Masanobu.

We began to spend Sundays searching different areas of Tokyo for possible locations to buy land. In doing so, we realized that it was the first time we had travelled by train on a Sunday for anything other than climbing. We had one requirement for our purchase: it had to be easy to reach. In hindsight, we should have considered other factors like the surrounding environment, schools, hospitals and various other facilities, not to mention the availability of a sewage system. In truth, we could not afford anything near a train station that had a sewage system in place and offered a little bit of space. Everything that fell into our budget was too small, so we shifted our mindset to that of hikers – we could walk any distance to a train station. The world of real estate suddenly opened, and we could buy a moderate-sized lot in the middle of a silvery grass field. We were land owners.

Our new acreage was a mile from the nearest train station, and we were a bit skeptical of how we could live there with not much else nearby. Rather than being happy about our decision, we became slightly nervous. Also, we only had enough money to buy the lot, which alone extended our comfort level in affordability – building a house would have to wait. And there was climbing. Despite all our savings and bonuses and any extra money we could scrounge being put towards the land purchase, we never gave up climbing. To us, climbing remained central to our life together and no land or house would be worth pushing that aside.

It was ironic that Masanobu losing his toes to frostbite was the impetus for us to buy a piece of property and ultimately build a house away from the city. Every time we saw the remaining stubs on his feet, we laughed in appreciation: "The purchasing of land all happened because of those toes!" In a sense, our move allowed me to come full circle from country to city and back again, all the while evolving as a climber and nourishing my quest for the mountains.

I had no idea what I was yet to discover about the high places of the world.

CHAPTER 3

Annapurna III

The Annapurna Range in the Himalayas, a 60-kilometre stretch of mountains that runs east–west across north-central Nepal, is a gateway to expedition climbing. The massif's skyline is dotted with more than a dozen 7000-metre giants, including Annapurna I through IV. At 8078 metres, Annapurna I is the tallest of the range, and the tenth tallest in the world, and is well-known as the first-ever successfully climbed 8000-metre peak, by Maurice Herzog from France in 1950.

Annapurna III (7555 metres) has its own history. Also first climbed in 1950, by Captain Manmohan Singh Kohli of India, the mountain saw its second ascent twenty years later, on May 19, 1970, by the Japanese Women's Annapurna Expedition, led by Eiko Miyazaki as leader and me as assistant leader. We added two firsts to the mountain: a route up the unclimbed South Face, and an ascent by an all-women's team. Both accomplishments stirred the pot from the start.

Mountaineering expeditions take planning and finances, which for us added up to a lengthy pre-trip process, and big last-minute decisions are best avoided. Yet, a mere two weeks prior to our departure to Nepal, the final nine members of the climbing team were only just being declared. Concern amongst the group had begun to brew a month earlier, so the eleventh-hour timing of the team announcement was no surprise, even though it had been more than a year since the trip was first proposed. Nevertheless, we were mountaineers driven by a similar single-mindedness to climb. We were focused on the expedition slogan that promised us this: "Go climb the Himalayas, by all means, by women alone."

Annapurna III Route Map, Japan Women's Annapurna Expedition, 1970
COURTESY OF TABEI KIKAKU/ LADIES CLIMBING CLUB

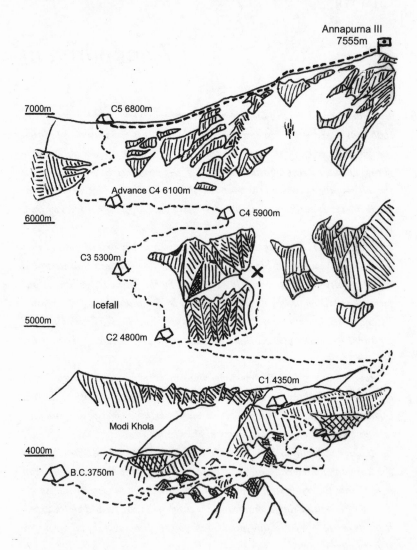

I had recently returned to the mountains after having lost Sasou, my dear friend and climbing partner. My husband, facing his own challenges with newly amputated toes, roped up with me more often than usual, and we climbed multiple winter routes on Tanigawa-dake. That same season, I completed multiple mountain traverses and joined several women-only climbing camps with members from the Ryoho Climbing Club. My intensity for climbing was back, and it was then that Yoshiko Wakayama gave me a call.

Wakayama was an important person in the history of female mountaineering. Along with partner Michiko Imai, she made the first female ascent on the North Face of the Matterhorn in 1967, a mountain she later died on during her honeymoon in 1973. It was in 1969 that I made her acquaintance, when she asked me to meet her, along with two others from the Japanese Alpine Club, to discuss a women-only expedition to the Himalayas. She instantly had my complete attention.

The planned get-together would be a meeting of the minds. The two other climbers were Eiko Miyazaki, the Japanese leader of a previous (and first) India–Japan co-mountaineering trip, and Michiko Sekita, an experienced mountaineer who had summitted Huayna Potosi in the Andes, and later, North America's Denali. Sadly, Sekita was killed in the Japanese Alps in 1976.

I was nervous to introduce myself to these three great women, as I was the only one who had never climbed overseas. And although I was already a member of the Japanese Alpine Club, thanks to a colleague at my workplace, my impression of the club was that it was no place for layperson climbers like me. In retrospect, my club connection and the resulting meeting were the well-fated threshold that pushed me into the world of the Himalayas.

Hence, on March 5, 1969, the four of us met at a coffee shop in the mall of the Tokyo subway station. The premise of the meeting was straightforward, delivered by Miyazaki: "Let's go to the Nepali Himalaya as a women-only team. Women climbers from just one club won't be enough to make an expedition party. So, let's each talk with friends and climbers that we know and meet again with an update." I was surprised at the quiet tone in which she spoke, given the excitement of the subject, but I would come to learn that Miyazaki always remained unruffled. Sekita amazed me with her familiarity with mountain names, as in how she easily suggested the unclimbed Lamjung Himal for our list of potential goals. I had never even heard of the peak let alone know where it was located. By the end of the night, we agreed that our trip would occur the next spring or fall, but the mountain of choice was yet to be determined. We would see each other again in two weeks, with more women climbers as part of the group. For me, the experience of meeting Miyazaki turned out to be one of destiny.

That night, I could barely sleep. Prior to the meeting, I was somewhat familiar with Wakayama as we often ran into each other climbing at Tanigawa-dake, but Miyazaki and Sekita were completely unknown to me, as though from a different world altogether. I knew I had to join this trip to the Himalayas, that it was a rare opportunity and one that might not present itself again. A year had passed since Sasou had died, and it was time for me to push myself beyond the challenging routes of Japan. I had to see past my membership with the Ryoho club and reach farther than what it could offer me. Was I truly considering a visit to the mountains overseas, the very ones that I had thought of as not for me even though I wished they could be? Yes, and now they were within reach. During that sleepless night, I made up my mind – I would do whatever it took to pursue my dream; I would cooperate with whomever necessary to make this a reality. Otherwise, I might as well live the rest of my life like a frog in a well, as we say in Japan.

As Miyazaki said, it was impossible to form a team of women from a single mountaineering club. While numerous clubs existed throughout Japan, they often only had two or three female members, not all of whom were winter climbers. Some of the clubs still maintained a "no women allowed" mentality, restricting the populace to draw from even more. We had to branch out, despite loyalty to our respective clubs. I felt a bit unsure about this until my husband encouraged me in the right direction. "It would be nice if you could gain such experience from within Ryoho, but you can't. And for the future of the Ryoho club, it's crucial to bear as many overseas-experienced climbers as possible. You don't have to leave Ryoho while a group of you establish a ladies' climbing club for the expedition," he said. His open-mindedness made sense and allowed me to embrace my Himalayan opportunity without question.

We gathered again, on March 19, this time at a different coffee shop in downtown Tokyo. Thirteen mountain women, threaded together by friendship and various club connections, were about to formulate the basis for the first Japanese all-women's Himalayan climbing team. In her gentle fashion, discussion began with Miyazaki: "Personally, I'm not aiming for an 8000er this time, but I certainly will in the future. So, I'd like to pick a suitable mountain to test the water."

Sekita said, "Women's plans often dissipate after just one talk. This time, I'd like to develop a plan even more escalated from the original idea. As I proposed in our first meeting, I have Lamjung Himal in mind."

Wakayama was less specific. "I don't mind if the targeted mountains are small and rather low in height. I'd like to climb as many interesting and fun mountains as possible."

Then I spoke. "I'd like to climb Annapurna I," I said, "and hopefully by the Herzog route." Everyone responded with a surprised "wow." Miyazaki, Wakayama, Sekita and Naoko Nakaseko suggested a 7000-metre peak, but most of the group seemed drawn to the idea of 8000 metres, if not now, at least in the future. Morie Yamazaki immediately agreed to do her best to support the team but said she would not be part of the summit assault. My heart broke because I knew the reason for this. She had been injured in the fall that led to my friend Sasou's death. Big mountains were no longer achievable for her.

The four of us from the initial meeting – Miyazaki, Sekita, Wakayama and I – formed a committee to sift through ideas, begin research and figure out the next steps. Our objective evolved to Annapurna III, with the intention to expose as many female mountaineers on our team as possible to high-altitude climbing for other future endeavours we had in mind. The mountain of choice was in our favour: travel days to the base were relatively short in distance, and at 7555 metres in elevation, Annapurna III was the ideal precursor to anything above 8000 metres.

The conditions to which each team member would have to agree were strict but necessary: three months off work, a personal contribution to the expedition of 700,000 yen per person (a lot of money in those days), and attendance at meetings and mountaineering camps. No other specific requirements were in order at that time. Regular meetings would be held the last Thursday of every month at the Mita Public Library in downtown Tokyo. Specific groups were established to be in charge of food and equipment. Extensive research began on the Annapurna area, and we all tried to learn the Nepali language.

Even though we had a basic structure to our team, we were merely a group of colleagues that would not meet the status of an organized association required for a Himalayan expedition. Back then, prior to the era of commercial expeditions, the Nepali government chose one climbing party per mountain per season. We had no idea what the selection process was based on, but we knew there were multiple applications already submitted and that to apply we had to establish our own proper organization. Hence, the Ladies Climbing Club came into existence, and the Japanese Women's Annapurna Expedition (JWAE) was formed.

JAPANESE WOMEN'S ANNAPURNA III
EXPEDITION TEAM MEMBERS

Miyazaki, Eiko, 36	Leader
Tabei, Junko, 30	Assistant Leader
Hirakawa, Hiroko, 30	Report/Records
Manita, Michiko, 28	Food
Sato, Reiko, 25	Equipment
Yamazaki, Morie, 28	Equipment
Hirano, Eiko, 37	Treasurer
Urushibara, Chieko, 31	Photographer
O-no, Dr. Kyoko, 31	Medical Doctor

Team training began on April 29 on Mount Fuji in Japan. Although not technically difficult, the climb was perfect for familiarizing ourselves with one another. Sekita, Hirano, Wakayama, Sato, Nobue Yajima, Setsuko Watanabe and I travelled from Tokyo, and Kyoko Endo and Nakaseko came from Nagoya to meet us. Endo and Nakaseko would later become part of the first women's team to summit Manaslu in 1974, on the descent of which a teammate fell to her death. But on that day on Mount Fuji, we were all pumped up and a bit arrogant, mountaineering together for the first time and reaching the summit in record time. Each of us was out to prove she was ready for the Himalayas.

Then, Wakayama quit the team. She felt the large-scale style expedition was not to her taste. Two others followed for various reasons. The team was down to thirteen members. Lucky thirteen, perhaps.

The process for the Ladies Climbing Club to be recognized by the Tokyo Prefectural Mountaineering Association took a frustrating three and half months. This was due to Japanese bureaucracy questioning countless elements of an all-female organization, including the small number in our party. Despite that delay, our application to climb Annapurna III was accepted by the Nepali government, and a permit was on its way within thirty-seven days of our team's initial request. The express nature of our permit was likely due to the rarity of such applications but also to help end the dearth of women's teams on Nepali soil. Our excitement soared; we knew we were the second-ever women-only expedition to be granted permission to climb in Nepal. The first expedition was led by Claude Kogan of France on Cho Oyu in 1959. Sadly, that trip ended in tragedy with four members (Kogan, a Belgian climber and two Sherpas) killed in an avalanche. Their goal of the summit remained unfulfilled. Our trip to Annapurna certainly brought thoughts of Kogan's team to the surface.

Even as plans unfolded, we still had one outstanding matter to address – we needed a group leader for our trip.

Miyazaki was unanimously nominated for the position at a meeting on October 20, but she was hesitant to accept. Without this role secured, we were limited in the trip details we could provide to the media or have printed in the expedition plan. A leader was critical to the final organization of the trip, and in Japanese style, we were reluctant to publicly share trip information while specifics were incomplete. So, the search for a leader continued, extending far and wide, and including requests made to Teru Sato, Hatsuko Kuroda, Kimiko Imai and Sachiko Kawamori – all considered to be the pioneering women of mountaineering in Japan. Unfortunately for us, they declined our invitation. (Each of them would go on to live long lives; Sato, for example, retired from mountaineering decades later at age eighty.)

Finally, Miyazaki conceded to the role, but she insisted that her expectations must be met. Fellow cooperation and open communication were fully required, and decisions were to be made on a team basis, not for personal gain. She acknowledged her simple nature and explained that she preferred no fuss. "It took me more than a week to make this decision," she said. "I've imagined so many negative things that could go wrong that I didn't want to be leader. But then I realized that it isn't only me. I have eleven of you to make it work. I was afraid, but now I'm not." By the end of her acceptance speech, she warmed up enough to say, "I hope we can make it together and feel satisfied at the end of the day." With that, she nominated Sekita and me as assistant leaders, and Hirano as manager and treasurer, and everyone applauded. I had no idea why I was chosen as assistant but felt it must have been my presence on the start-up committee. I disregarded my lack of experience in climbing abroad and figured the job would be doable with the experienced Sekita by my side.

Unfortunately, I felt an uneasiness about Miyazaki that became difficult to suppress. Curt interactions, such as meetings that were announced without checking teammate availability, and phone messages that were left in an abrupt and unemotional tone, highlighted her forewarned direct nature more than I liked. Nevertheless, I began to sense that she might be less domineering than I initially thought. In my first visit to her apartment, her kitchen showed no trace of activity; the rice-cooker was desert dry with traces of old grains stuck to it. She grinned, confessing, "Oh, I eat outside most of the time." I felt like I had discovered her simple personality.

Sekita was also different. She carried a daunting energy around her, and her sturdy body type and height strengthened her intimidating presence. My heart always beat faster when she made her thoughts known, like when she said, "A group of climbers isn't reliable without knowing what everybody's skills are. I can't automatically trust someone on this team to belay me. We should have our skills tested." Of course, she was right, but her delivery of the idea unsettled me. I had to remind myself of an earlier commitment I had made if it meant climbing overseas: cooperate with everyone and avoid any drama.

My life snowballed into chaos as soon as the Ladies Climbing Club was established, an experience I learned was directly connected to being part of an expedition. Commitments to my other club, Ryoho, were still important to maintain, as were meetings and training for Annapurna III.

Through it all, Masanobu stood by me without complaint, continuing his own climbing and caring for me with suppers ready for my arrival home (albeit, his menu was always the same). Sometimes I went a week without cooking my share of dinners, yet this seemed to work easily between us, even as I became more exhausted and consumed by trip logistics.

In the early days of planning Annapurna, Masanobu and I would stay up late after a meeting to talk about every trip detail, but eventually the meetings became too complicated and their frequency too much to share. Instead, I would fall asleep while my husband never gave up figuring out how to squeeze money from our savings to pay for the expedition. The fact that we remained married despite a demanding lifestyle of mountain madness, and without as much as an apology from me during times when I was fixated on a climb, amazed me. I always knew that I was fortunate to have Masanobu as my partner and that his support was the true base to my continued success in the mountains.

In early November, winter training began with a two-day traverse of Sennokura, part of the Tanigawa-dake range. The bushwhacking was horrible, and we lost our way multiple times on the descent, even with red markers in place to follow. Our group had been split in two, and it was with great pleasure for my team that the other party arrived at the base first – a curry dinner had been simmering for hours by the time we showed up. Once we were together and relaxed that night, conversation revolved around what to wear in the Himalayas. The most pressing question was whether or not to each bring a *kimono*.

By that point in team development, we had reached the stage where we felt we knew one another, for better or for worse, and everyone's characters and expectations had been fully disclosed. Despite the label that we were simply a collection of female climbers from several different mountaineering clubs, we were all very active members, which meant that each of us had unique ideas and strong personalities. For instance, when it came to equipment choice, there were arguments over brands and shapes of ice axes and pitons, and lengths and diameters of ropes, as if no one suggestion was good enough. Any chance of compromise seemed impossible. Hushed voices began to converse behind the backs of fellow teammates. Comments like "I think it's an issue that she only rock climbs," or "she's never even touched real rock before," were said with an attitude of one-upmanship, in order to appear to be the strongest player on the team. In the New Year, less than two months before we were to depart for Annapurna, an inevitable and irreversible battle began to brew, one not to be underestimated when female temperaments ultimately collided.

Trouble

We united on Sennokura again, this time for our New Year's training camp. The weather was stellar and the trail breaking manageable, and we cheerfully shared a much-exaggerated handshake at the top, pretending it was the summit of Annapurna III.

Our playful attitude came to a halt on the way home from Sennokura when the team's doctor, Dr. O-no, informed Miyazaki of the seriousness of a medical condition Yajima had, to the extent that Yajima might have to forgo the expedition. Earlier, at the team's first mandatory medical check-up in August, Yajima's blood work showed red blood cells in her urine, enough of a concern to warrant follow-up. The test was repeated at the end of December and disclosed the same results. A serious discussion ensued. Miyazaki disagreed with bringing a sick climber to the Himalayas; Sekita strongly insisted we do so and that she would take responsibility for Yajima. "We've come this far together; let her try," said Sekita, pleading her case. Sekita and Yajima were housemates and climbing partners; together, they had even established the Ryosetsu club for climbers. It would be unfair to leave her behind. Unsurprisingly, no decision was made that day, and we went home feeling somewhat deflated.

Dr. O-no's explanation and opinion would lend itself to the final verdict. Meanwhile, we were deep into packing boxes, using Sekita's house as the base for pre-trip organization. Sato was also a housemate to Sekita and Yajima, and other team members lived there short-term prior to departure for Nepal. Friends and acquaintances joined in to help, causing neighbours to question our packing activities, which continued past midnight. Finally, we were asked to lower the noise level. Once, the mail delivery man inquired if we were in the dried-food business, such was the volume of food stacked a mile high in the rooms of Sekita's home. Eventually, the entire house was overtaken by the expedition, with gear and boxes and bags covering every inch of bare floor, turning the place into one giant tripping hazard.

There were days when I would go straight to Sekita's house from work, run around the city to shop, pack (sometimes all night), and then return to work the next morning with only five minutes of sleep on the train. That was our routine, and I accepted it as what it took to travel abroad, to climb the highest peaks, to be a successful women-only team. But the strain of Yajima's position, possibly having to quit the team, added enormous stress for each of us. We looked like zombies, with dark circles under our eyes and unkempt hair, the result of our mixed emotions about losing Yajima.

January 16

The day came when we bid farewell to the countless boxes that quantified our trip. After feverishly packing for weeks, the boxes were suddenly gone, driven away in the back of a six-ton truck, to be met by stormy winds, pushing them ever forward to our destination. The disoriented look on the faces of my teammates, unsure of what to do next, stayed with me forever after.

The team was torn and time was running out to decide about Yajima. The pressure of the situation was causing friendships to unravel and fingers to be pointed. Accusations of not caring enough for Yajima's health to make her step down from the team were countered with caring too much about her desire to climb. From the start, I strongly opposed the idea of a sick team member joining us in the Himalayas, and I would not back down. Miyazaki was of a similar vein until she conceded to pressure from Sekita, but then she had to revert to her original stance on the subject. As a last resort, Dr. O-no made a final request at one of our meetings: "Let Yajima sign a waiver that clarifies it's neither medically safe nor is her life guaranteed in expedition activities." The evening was adjourned in total silence.

With further discussion pointless, we held a vote on February 2. Four members opted for Yajima's position on the team; seven opted against. Sekita announced her withdrawal from the expedition immediately after the vote, as did three others a few days later, all of whom claimed varied personal reasons for their resignation.

The date for departure to Annapurna was twenty-five days away.

February 14

Another climber, Chieko Urushibara, who had been helping with expedition preparation all along even though there was no space for her on the team, was unanimously approved to join. She had less than a month to raise money and gather the necessary personal equipment to be part of the trip, and she succeeded. In addition to her vigorous passion to be the official camerawoman for the expedition, her hobby as a photographer and her job with Nikon paid off. Urushibara was going to Annapurna.

In regard to my job, I was surprisingly granted an eight-month leave from work. I had already decided to quit if my request was denied, but not having to do so was a great relief. Masanobu and I were in the midst of drawing up blueprints to build a house, and construction was soon to begin. For me to have employment to return to was a good thing, even though Masanobu had put my mind at rest about our financial state. "Trust me with the goings-on in Japan, and you focus on climbing at your best," he said.

Departure

February 27

Reiko Sato and Hiroko Hirakawa were the first two to leave Japan, the initial party that would get our expedition under way. They were to reunite with the equipment and food boxes that had been shipped to Calcutta, India, and transfer all supplies to land travel for the remainder of the journey to Nepal. Right up to the last minute, as our friends were about to board the plane, I offered advice about drinking only boiled water in India. "I know, I know," said Hirakawa as she disappeared through the gate, nervously studying a piece of paper dotted with a selection of quotes from *Easy English for Travellers*.

> Going to the Himalayas, my dream is finally coming true today, regardless of how odd it feels. I'm on an airplane for the first time ever. I also feel more burdened as part of the headstart party rather than being purely excited to go to climb a big mountain overseas. I'll wear jeans and put on a sun hat in India for the much-concerned business of the overland transportation of our boxes from India to Nepal. What if the

driver is a scary guy? In these circumstances, I had almost forgotten that I was going mountain climbing because of the newness of everything I would have to do first. Actually, we had some difficulty going through customs and learned a big lesson about how far away the Himalayas are!

– Hirakawa's diary

▲

Having cleared the procedure to get the boarding pass quicker than expected, I had time to have tea with my boyfriend. He switched his ring from his right to his left ring finger, re-marking that he was now cheat-proof. His commitment to me was steadfast. In later days, he confessed that he had ex-pected a romantic comment back from me, but I was too full of anxiety about whether or not the 50,000 yen, which was to be brought to me by my sister-in-law for personal spending, would arrive in time for my departure. I had no room for ro-manticism. When she finally showed up, I firmly grabbed the money, still talking with members of the main party about important logistics and being interviewed by news reporters.

Time flew like a second, and before I knew it I was pushed towards customs. When the plane started moving forward, I realized we were actually leaving Japan and I wouldn't see my beloved for a long time. I thought to myself, "So long every-body," and watched my boyfriend and others become smaller and smaller in the distance. It made me a bit sentimental, but not a single tear fell. Why not? Because I'll be able to sleep well now that the trip has started. I genuinely felt relief, in particular by watching the countless lights of Tokyo in the night that reminded me of the limitless numbers of stars I would soon see under the mountain sky.

– Sato's diary

March 2

The main expedition party, made up of Eiko Miyazaki, Eiko Hirano, Morie Yamazaki and me, left Japan. Any gear that failed to make it in the earlier-sent boxes was left for us to carry onto the plane – down jackets, ice axes, cameras (including a 16-millimetre movie camera) and binoculars were stuffed into our arms as we bid farewell to our families and friends. There they stood, fervently waving to us in the cold wind on the outside deck of the airport, in the dark of night. We waved, too, passionately, until we could no longer see them as we lifted off from our homeland.

We were on our way to the Himalayas.

In the whirlwind of final preparation before we actually left Japan, I asked my husband to do a last-minute shop for the trip while I went to the hairdresser. My perpetually uncared-for hair needed slight attention before months away. The appointment stopped me long enough to realize I had not allowed enough time to speak with Masanobu that day, or, once I thought about it, for the past several months. I had failed to return the favour of him cooking for me all those times, and I suddenly felt awful about his obvious recent weight loss. I wished I could have prepared a hot meal of miso soup and rice for him instead of the tea and toast we shared at lunch. As I sat stationary for a moment, hair trimmed and tidy, I readied myself for the approaching departure to Annapurna. Despite the emotions of the day, I was certain about my goals in the mountains.

My mother travelled the long distance from Miharu to say goodbye. Surprisingly, she shook my hands, a gesture considered highly sophisticated behaviour for a Japanese woman of her age. That was the first time my mother had ever engaged in this form of acknowledgement – the handshake – with me. Funny, as she did so, she looked at Masanobu and asked, "Annapurna is higher than Aizu Bandai, right?" Aizu Bandai, a volcanic mountain in Japan, stood a quarter of the elevation of Annapurna III. My mother's topography may have been limited to her home country, but I appreciated her interest nonetheless.

Then came the moment when there was nothing else to say. The time had come to board the plane. Despite a two-hour flight delay, our entourage of family and friends remained on the deck in the cold and dark, continuing to wave until the plane began to move forward at 7 p.m. I saw Masanobu smile at me. "Yes," I said to him, regretful that my sentiments would not be heard, "I'm going now and I will do my best." To myself, I added, "Please let me land here again, back on the ground of Haneda." I was frozen in emotion and could not utter another word to anyone for a while as I settled into my seat and the new world of big-mountain expeditions.

Miyazaki sat beside me, and as she put a handkerchief to her eyes, my eyes also sprang tears. I was stunned at my reaction to her subtle yet profound affection, and my heart stirred even more. "Don't cry," I thought, making a point of swallowing my tears. "We've made it this far despite all the events up till now. Stay strong." Still, the faces of the ones I loved, their hands frantically waving, remained imprinted on my mind.

"Oh, no, I left the bag!" bellowed Yamazaki from the other side of me. I instantly panicked – what could we possibly have left behind? "The bag with rice cakes and puddings, to snack on. A friend had given it to me." ok, not urgent. Amusingly, Yamazaki's outburst was exactly what each of us needed. It brought us back to the whereabouts of our trip and abruptly the four of us opened conversation like never before. The dam of tension had been released and we were truly on our way.

> Tabei's husband sent her off, coming all the way to the customs gate. He, the one who had climbed two of the three biggest faces of Europe, knows mountains. His inner wish radiated strong enough to ring in me when I saw him smiling. My heart filled with a powerful sense of mission to bring his wife back to him intact and by all means possible. And not just Tabei, but everyone. The most important thing is that each of us must stand on Japanese soil again. That's it.
>
> – Miyazaki's diary

March 16

The last three of the expedition members, Dr. Kyoko O-no, Chieko Urushibara and Michiko Manita, left Japan. Due to political upheaval in Calcutta, their flight had to change route via Karachi, Pakistan, and New Delhi, India, to eventually land in Kathmandu, Nepal. This was an immediate eye-opener to travelling in foreign countries and added an element of concern to the trip. Nonetheless, everyone safely arrived, and we were a team once again.

The torrential rain that started this morning has ceased. My fellow teachers and beloved students, mountain buddies and family – I was very glad to have such a surprising number of people send me off at the airport. I must come back in good shape. I hope that Ken-*chan* passes his exam to be admitted to university; the result will be out tomorrow. After all he strived for in the last two years for that. He may be worried inside even though he put a good smile on his face for me. Don't give up, Ken-*chan*, even if the result is undesirable. Look, my dream to go to the Himalayas came true ten years after my longing for mountains began.

– Manita's diary

▲

There is pleasure in going to an unknown world, liberated from all the annoyances and routine chores of life; although the downside exists, such as my family that doesn't fully approve, in particular my old and ailing dad, and my colleagues who carry some burden during my absence at the hospital, for whom I certainly feel bad. Somehow, it still makes me grin. It also confirms that I don't have anybody, at the moment, who tries to stop me with worry, like "It's dangerous and I'm concerned." I take this as positive, even a happy and clean way to leave Japan behind for a while.

I had fleeting thoughts about the possible hardships that may be waiting to happen over there, or that we may not come back alive, but my own answer to this, and my normal way of seeing things, quickly kicked in. "Whatever my fate is, let it be."

The flight took off on time as my face brushed pink with excitement.

– Dr. O-no's diary

To the Mountains

March 5

With three days of travel and changeovers behind us, we were on the final stretch to Nepal. As the small plane approached, I wondered how long I had been sitting there in awe, my forehead pressed hard against the window that provided a glimpse into another world – the majestic Himalayas.

Yamazaki, also inhaling the view of the giant peaks that pierced the navy-blue and purple sky, announced, as though in a trance, "It's Kathmandu." A brown path of pavement scraped into a field of green became visible, and the plane began to descend towards the primitive runway.

We disembarked into folds of fresh air and bright sunlight so different from the dull and sticky feel of Calcutta. Our landing spot was barely large enough to be considered an airport; a pair of compact, two-storey, white concrete buildings was all that stood there.

Yamazaki and I had flown to Kathmandu earlier than the rest of the team due to an urgent issue that arose in Calcutta. Our group had been told that in order to have the expedition boxes officially land in Kathmandu, a trip leader's signature was required on every single document related to each box. Miyazaki and company stayed back to accommodate said signatures while Yamazaki and I flew ahead to Kathmandu to address other matters that needed attention. This was a new flavour of big-expedition bureaucracy beyond what we had first experienced in Japan.

With our obvious lack of overseas travel experience, Yamazaki and I followed closely behind the few Japanese parties that arrived on the same flight: prominent artist Hisao Yamazato, and two climbing teams – the Kansai University team headed to Annapurna IV and the Kansai Climbing Club going to Dhaulagiri. While we tried to gain our footing in the airport, as small as it was, we were quickly surrounded by four approaching strangers. By their onslaught of questions, we knew they were reporters.

"Are you ladies the members of Annapurna III expedition?"

"How many of you are there overall?"

"Are you going to use oxygen?"

"When do you plan to get the summit?"

"Are you confident of success?"

"Is your doctor a female, too?"

Their letter r was pronounced with a rolled tongue, and the sound lingered in my ear. I was lost in translation, and Yamazaki and I were like deer in the headlights, our answers dazed and confused. They took note of every word we said, and to be honest, I was unsure of how successful that interview was rated in the long run.

"Women alone? Wow! That's big work. Take heart, ladies," remarked a nearby Japanese man, offering us little in the way of a mutual conversation. He was Shintaro Ishihara, who in future years would be known for two major accomplishments: as commander-in-chief of the 1970 ski descent of Mount Everest by Yuichiro Miura and as premier of Tokyo Prefecture from 1999 to 2012. After the impromptu interview we had just endured, Ishihara's words were flattering enough to make us feel that our trip had generated some sort of interest. It was obvious that the arrival of an all-women's expedition in Nepal was an unusual sight. As such, we were certainly the cause of a large fuss at the airport.

The population of Tokyo Prefecture equalled the whole of Nepal at 10 million people. The size of Nepal was twice that of Hokkaido, Japan's second largest main island, and the area of snow-covered mountainous terrain was incredibly vast, unlike anything I had seen before. Its capital city, Kathmandu, sat at 1400 metres above sea level, at a similar latitude to Japan's tropical Okinawa Islands. These combined features made us want to stay in Kathmandu that March day as it reminded us of midsummer in Kamikochi in the Northern Japanese Alps. It felt a bit like home.

A fifteen-minute drive delivered us from airport to townsite, during which the view of the landscape remained much like that of the Japanese countryside – very pastoral. Children ran around barefoot, the curious stare of an old woman sitting on the ground followed our taxi as it drove by, and cows crisscrossed the road. The dark atmosphere of Calcutta had faded away, and I felt a level of relaxation settle in, as though I were in my own country surrounded by a familiar language.

We passed what I guessed to be a college for girls, judging by the group of young women in brown uniform saris. I turned my head to look back at them and was completely taken by their deeply sculpted faces and mysterious eyes. No wonder most of the expeditions to Nepal had been all male up until our trip; these women were beautiful. The royal palace stood out with its large green lawns and mature trees that marked its grounds. An easy ten-minute walk from there led to the New Road, where makeshift shops were jammed up beside one another in the form of a bazaar. The smell of mutton hit my nostrils as I walked past the vendors who sold vegetables and fruits in the square. Nostalgia washed over me when I saw carrots, spinach, cucumbers, oranges and onions piled up on the ground. The array of differences and similarities to Japan made me agreeable to my new surroundings.

Yamazaki and I settled in at the Hotel Laligurans, named after Nepal's national flower, a vibrant red variety of rhododendron, which, when in bloom, fills the countryside. Our accommodation was owned by a friendly local who put us at ease with his generosity and welcoming nature. This enabled us to immediately set off to our tasks in Kathmandu, where we quickly lost all the comfort from the hotel. It was evident we had no idea what to do first, or how to even begin. Much to our relief, we were rapidly taken under the wing of Ishikawa, the correspondent for the Japanese Everest party, and Takeo, Teramoto and Ichijima, all of whom had been staying in Kathmandu since January as the first members of the Kansai University party to arrive. Compared to these expedition experts, Yamazaki and I knew nothing. Our newly found friends directed us to the Ministry of Foreign Affairs to clear paperwork and then to the Himalayan Society to hire Sherpas. The showed us how internal airlines worked and where the post office was located. They kindly escorted us on our first shopping experience, as we had no understanding of the Nepali rupee. Still, even with all their help, the initial five days in this foreign land had me in survival mode. We were busy from dawn until dusk, and into the night with practicing English to the point that my brain was on overload. My tidy pre-trip haircut was a dishevelled mess as I ran around trying to gain footing for our expedition. Each obstacle, like closed offices in celebration of the marriage of Nepal's prince, had me in a lather. I was never quite able to attain the laid-back nature of the employees who took more than two days to find our trip documents that required signatures. My mind raced and my energy was spent on irritation. I was exhausted, so I took it upon myself to recognize that when in Nepal, do as the Nepalis – relax.

The Himalayan Society was a type of Sherpas' guild. We used the guild to hire Sherpas for our trip and draw up a contract for each of them. Nine Sherpas, including a cook, plus two high-elevation porters, two mail runners and a kitchen boy – fourteen in all – became part of our team. Every hired individual was as important as the next, for either their past climbing experience or their unique personality. Tenzing Girmi, for example, at fifty-one, had worked on previous Japanese expeditions; Phurba Kitar, thirty-nine, was part of a German team on Gangapurna in 1965 and had first-hand knowledge of the South Face of Annapurna III; and Pasang Nima, thirty-eight, had climbed on Makalu with a French team in 1960. Others, like Mingma Norbu, thirty-five, a quiet person, essentially discovered mountaineering on our trip; we taught him how to put on crampons.

Then there was Mr. Gopal, our trip liaison officer. He was quite a character, literally as an actor on Nepali television, but also as a comedy writer and a police officer. In 1961 he had spent five months in Japan working with the Japanese national broadcasting company, and was able to greet us in our own language. "My name is Gopal of Nepal. Lady mountaineers are all beautiful. Did you bring *oishii-mono?*" We had no such Japanese delicacy to share, but we quickly fell into stride with his humour and appreciated his previous Himalayan expedition experience (seven times as a liaison officer since his first trip in 1958 on Himalchuli, six of which were with Japanese parties). He was yet to enjoy the glory of a team reaching the summit, so his sights were set on us for success. His contribution to our trip was to be invaluable, and due to his understanding of Japanese, our leader, Miyazaki, managed to complete the entire expedition without speaking any other language while in Nepal. I, on the other hand, struggled with English and disjointed Nepali for the duration of the trip.

March 19

In two chartered planes, we flew 200 kilometres west from Kathmandu to Pokhara, another of Nepal's major cities, and in proximity to three of the ten highest summits in the world. No sooner had the plane taken off than Miyazaki announced, "Mountains on the right side." As if on cue, the team sirdar, Girmi, yelled for the Sherpas who sat on the right to move aside so we could see the spectacular scene. Ganesh Himal and the three peaks of the Manaslu Himal (Manaslu, Himalchuli and Ngadi Chuli) came into view. In the far distance, there stood one outstandingly high, black peak, but I had no idea of its name. I strained to find our objective amongst the sea of mountains. Miyazaki, her forehead pressed against the window, her tea turned cold with neglect, finally said, "Wow! Isn't that Machapuchare? Yes, it's part of the Annapurna Range!"

Thoughts flooded my mind: "We're here. We've come a long way and we're finally seeing Annapurna with our very eyes. It's no longer a fantasy mountain in my imagination; it's real." I wanted to shout, "It's been a long journey!"

The plane touched down and jolted to a stop on the runway that only seconds ago I had caught a glimpse of from the sky. On the ground, a dust storm engulfed the aircraft and our surroundings were briefly concealed. This gave me a chance to catch my breath from a flight that had me in a mix of emotions. I was rattled by both excitement and nerves on a plane crammed with team members and Sherpas, oxygen bottles and fuel, altogether sharing one fate, in the hands of our pilot. While the Sherpas chanted their prayers from the moment we took off until we landed, I, too, desperately prayed for an uneventful voyage. To safely land was to exhale my nervousness. Kathmandu was now behind us.

As we disembarked, the reality of the airport's setting sunk in. It was more like a grassland ranch, with Machapuchare and Annapurna II and III magnificently standing on the outskirts. Stunned by the place's beauty and unable to contain myself any longer, I ran laps around the meadow/airport with a feeling I can only express as pure joy.

March 20

Our main purpose in Pokhara was to buy food and hire more porters to help transport supplies to Base Camp. Back in Japan, we had already secured one hundred porters through the Himalayan Society, but once in Nepal, we realized we needed forty more. Circumstance was against us. The Kansai Climbing Club had already departed for Dhaulagiri, as had the Kansai University party towards Annapurna IV; and a British party, lead by Chris Bonington, who stayed at the same hotel as us, was to leave for the South Face of Annapurna I. A joint party of the British and Nepalese Armies were also en route to the North Face of Annapurna I. From my understanding, the combination of these expeditions required at least 450 porters. I thought forty more would be impossible to find, but we were reassured that porters would come from other villages only a few days' hike away in order to work. The wait turned out to be painless.

Mr. Gopal, who took it upon himself to solve the problem, hired forty-four porters, all Tibetan, from one of the British teams. There was mention about the manager of the British team not wanting Tibetan porters for some reason, so, as luck would have it, they became part of our group instead. In the end, we found them to be the hardest working of all the porters, and everyone benefitted from the exchange.

Another surprise reared its head just as we thought we were fully organized. At our place of accommodation in the Snow View Hotel right across from the Pokhara Airport, I ran into a Japanese man speaking with Mr. Gopal. He was a doctor at the local medical clinic and was involved in researching the spread of typhoid along the Modi Khola River basin. He advised our entire team to receive the inoculation against the disease. So, Dr. O-no purchased the vaccine from the British-run Shining Hospital in Pokhara Bazaar, and all of us, Sherpas and porters included, received the shot. Just another day in preparation for the Annapurna III expedition.

March 23

One-hundred-and-forty porters were gathered in the courtyard of the hotel, among them a ten-year-old boy, a stumbling senior citizen and half a dozen clever-looking middle-aged women, to mention a few. All walks of life were amidst this colourful tribe, and I was certain our hike to Base Camp would be nothing less than interesting.

Miyazaki, Dr. O-no and Mr. Gopal left by Jeep from the long line of porters to finalize a few details in Pokhara Bazaar. They had to pay for the typhoid vaccines and arrange for a local man to be a correspondent during our expedition. The correspondent's role would include communication between Base Camp and mail runners, and established contacts in Japan. In the case of an emergency, he would oversee initiating a rescue operation. When their jobs were finished, they waited at a tea house for the rest of the team to arrive, and slowly but steadily, we appeared on foot in the distance. First, a porter came into view, the trip name – JWAE – vivid on his backpack. Then another and another. Porters, Sherpas and women team members formed a snaking line of 168 people moving forward with 4.5 tons of supplies. Spectacular. And like a theatre troupe, we continued this way for eight days, northwest from Pokhara to

Lumle, then north–northeast to Base Camp. We transitioned from a hot and humid climate at 1000 metres in elevation to temperatures near 0°c at 3750 metres.

At one point, no sooner had I felt a huge drop of rain slap my face than a torrential downpour began. I was soaked within the time it took to pull my umbrella from my pack. The storm only lasted ten minutes, lengthy enough to put a dent in our comfort level, but for the cracked dry path we walked along, it was merely a drip on a burning boulder, a momentary sizzle of moisture. The porters, with no hint of protection from the rain, felt the effects for a while, as the water streamed down their faces long after the clouds closed overhead.

The peaks unfolded to new heights as we made our way from Pokhara. We passed through a Tibetan village and the ground transformed into a large grassland, the vast mountains beyond spreading like an ocean dotted with giant white caps. The unmistakable range of Ganesh appeared, and Machapuchare pierced the skyline like the Matterhorn. Soon the Annapurna Range would be in front of us.

March 25

After two more days of walking, there she was, the South Face of Annapurna III. From Chandrakot Pass at 1550 metres, I recognized the crux of the mountain where it reached the col shared by two routes that gained access to Annapurna III and Gangapurna. If we could navigate that section, we would reach the summit. My body tightened with positive tension as I considered the ascent.

March 26

We divided the group into three. The first of the pack was led by Hirakawa and Dr. O-no, the middle by Sato and Manita, and the tail by Hirano, Yamazaki, Miyazaki and me. Mr. Gopal fit somewhere in between.

Hirakawa was both climber and nurse, which kept her busy with Dr. O-no as there was no shortage of medical concerns to address. Every day, as soon as we arrived at a new location, porters and local villagers gathered around the two of them. Abdominal pain, achy legs and endless coughs were attended to time and again, and the team of doctor and nurse worked efficiently to manage the stream of patients in line.

Hirakawa, from Osaka, spoke with a dialect that was permanently rich with laughter, no matter how serious she tried to seem. She had strived hard to be on this expedition, training with 30-kilogram loads on her back after midnight shifts of work. She was the tallest of the group and had a monstrous appetite. Her appearance was one of immense strength. Accordingly, we nicknamed her Sherpani.

A similar air surrounded Dr. O-no. Despite her lack of mountaineering experience, she always hiked ahead of the group with fresh energy and zeal. Her will power was stoutly positive and unhindered, which unleashed an added confidence in all of us. The only time teammates were hesitant to approach her was at the dinner table, where, like Hirakawa, she displayed her large appetite. Only Dr. O-no could get excited about canned Pacific *saury* as a meal. There was no surprise when we established the doctor as being the best – and Hirakawa as second best – when it came to resilience in drinking.

In the middle of our meandering convoy was Sato, the tiniest of the team members, and Manita, who stood as tall as Hirakawa at 5-foot-5 but with a stockier frame. Hiking together, Sato and Manita made a comical pair in regard to their size differences. Sato was popular among the Sherpas and porters because she was cute, and she was the only smoker among the women. When she ran out of her Japanese-made cigarettes, the Sherpas and porters were quick to offer their local stash. Her posture when she smoked – left hand casually placed in pants' pocket and a gentle lean forward while she inhaled – was the subject of much mimicking by our comedian, Mr. Gopal.

Manita was a high-school science teacher. She was meticulous in her ways, as one would expect from a scientist, and cleanliness was of utmost importance – to the point of washing her hair every third day on our trip if water was available. At Camp 3, she even collected droplets of water from ice, in order not to waste fuel, so she could brush her teeth.

Manita's passion for expression came out in her diary, with detailed and precise illustrations and descriptions of our journey. Sadly, her diary was lost deep in a crevasse on Annapurna when she tried to throw her backpack across the giant crack in the ice. Sherpas managed to rescue the pack by lowering themselves into the crevasse, but the diary had slipped out and was gone. Words could not express the regret Manita felt for a long time afterwards. Everyone was upset by her loss of personal communication.

Miyazaki and Mr. Gopal often hiked together. They usually departed early and arrived late at the next location. Having caught up to them one day at a spot that overlooked the village of Ghandrung, our routine banter began: "Wow, here you are, Mr. Gopal!" we announced. "Yes, we see each other again!" he replied as we started to hike as a small group. His jokes continued along the way as he pointed to himself and Miyazaki. "We're an example of *before* and *after*. Do you understand?" he asked, making fun of how a diet works – Miyazaki being so skinny that we called her Ms. Bone, and Mr. Gopal overshadowing her with his large size. Finally, I said, "See you after the expedition!" and I sifted my way to the back of the line to check on the Sherpas and porters.

One night, as we were about to crawl into our sleeping bags, begging for rest, one of the Sherpas explained that the villagers wanted to dance with us to display their welcome. It was an odd request since we had heard that the very next village, Chomrong, was "no country for women." Nevertheless, we rose to the occasion and attended the party. There, dancing, was a boy disguised as a girl. To our amusement, a closer look disclosed that he was one of our porters. No one would believe that this finely dressed-up maiden could be such a hard worker on the trail. Another porter lent himself to the band as he cheerfully sang for his audience. All the entertainers were men, a garish show, indeed, and at the end, the villagers stepped up with fresh leis to place around the necks of the team members and Sherpas. Sirdar Girmi shouted out, "Success for Annapurna III!" Whether it was his enthusiasm for the climb or his allotment of locally brewed whisky that fuelled his outburst, one will never know.

For the remainder of the night, under a crisp moon, I hung on to those words: success for Annapurna III.

March 27

Chomrong, the women-forbidden village, sat at the headwaters of the Modi Khola River. Our mood abruptly changed from excitement at the joyous welcome of the night before to concern for what lay ahead in Chomrong. A Japanese mountaineering party in 1964 and a German party in 1965 both had their female porters stopped and pushed away from entering this village. The restriction was based on the belief that the area beyond Chomrong was the sacred sphere, hence no women were to pass through. In addition, our arrival marked the fifth year that the Nepali government had a country-wide ban on all expeditions, but also the first season for it to reopen to mountaineers. So, there we stood, on the doorstep of unfamiliar territory.

We asked Mr. Gopal to manage the situation and somehow gain permission to continue our travels through Chomrong. His reaction was one of confusion: "Why didn't you tell me about this earlier?" What? He had no idea about the restriction? In Japan we had been worried about it for months, wondering how to obtain a permit to access this particular village. We had already come to expect Mr. Gopal's expressive authority in dilemmas, to make things happen with the snap of his fingers, like the way he had hired forty-four porters in a single day, or how in a brief chat with a pilot, he had arranged to have his forgotten sunglasses returned to him (by airplane, no less). Surely, we assumed, he would achieve passage for us through the part of Nepal that forbade the entry of women. But for him to not even know about the problem that lay ahead – that was certain disaster.

With much discussion, we decided that Mr. Gopal and Miyazaki would travel ahead to diffuse the impact of 168 people, women included, descending on the village as one. "Mr. Gopal," said Miyazaki, "our mission today is to get there fast and early, please." She pleaded with her hiking partner and pushed him upright whenever he sat for a rest. His before-diet size required multiple breaks on the uphill, but Miyazaki would have none of it, and Mr. Gopal followed her with no complaint on that especially significant day.

When I first glimpsed the tiny village of twenty houses down the valley, I hesitated, fearful that I was looking upon a community of scavengers ready to attack. Aware that such fear would fail to get us anywhere, we approached Chomrong almost on tiptoe, as if to sneak by the entire issue at hand.

"*Namaste, namaste,*" the locals said, bidding us with their most respectful greeting. Having quickly assessed the situation, Mr. Gopal simply advised, "Nobody talks about it, so you don't start questioning, either." We followed his revered counsel and cheerfully returned the greeting to the villagers: "*Namaste, namaste*," and that was that. Later, when we mused at the ease of it all, we wondered, with some disappointment, if the locals recognized us as women.

The irony of that day came weeks after on May 25 when the mail runner from Base Camp en route to Pokhara had to arrange for porters to regroup and assist our team in the return from our climb. Plagued again by the timing of the British expedition, we were concerned that we would not be able to hire enough porters to help us descend. Imagine our shock when Base Camp was stirred to life with the sudden announcement on the evening of May 30: "Porters are here!" And who led the party of hired help? The people from Chomrong! Not only had they declined an offer to work for the British team, they clearly stated, "We're for the women's party." We were speechless and more than grateful for their assistance.

Their graciousness continued. On the hike out, the Chomrong porters urged us to hurry because they had scheduled a big party for us, one that was financed from their own pocket, with the very money we had just paid them for their services.

By the time a limping Mr. Gopal arrived in Chomrong that night, it had been dark for a while. Flames from the bonfire grew in height and swayed like dancers back and forth. The villagers gathered together and the party began. Unable to resist the music for long, Mr. Gopal danced and danced, sore knee forgotten. Soon enough he was singing his favourite Japanese *Soran-bushi*, his body moving in rhythm like a Hawaiian hula dancer. That was the impetus we needed – each of us stood up to join him. We tried to appear coordinated as we mimicked jitterbug-style moves, but our real strength shone when it came to eating the delicious meat and egg dishes served to us by our cordial hosts. The party came to a brief stop during a rain shower, but everyone stayed in position and minutes later the activities resumed until well past midnight.

The villagers placed wild flowers in our hair the next morning when it was time for us to say goodbye. History had occurred. A new wind had blown through this remote place in the Nepali Himalaya, changing a land that once forbade women to one that welcomed them. We left there in peace.

Loads Up!

March 29

In less than an hour we knew the approach route to Base Camp would be completely snow covered, and we had two days of hiking left to complete. The porters walked barefoot or in light sneakers, which meant it was impossible for them to continue. There was also no way we would let them sleep on snow without proper equipment. We had to think fast for a solution since we still needed their services. As it stood, they would have to return to Deurali to spend the night after having ferried loads to the snow line.

We knew money talked and decided to add an extra six rupees per day to the regular fifteen that the porters earned, to cover the expense of shoes. Since there was no place to purchase footwear anywhere nearby, the additional payment was more an acknowledgement of the danger and cold the group endured. An additional four rupees would be paid to each porter who carried a load all the way to Base Camp.

The next morning, I closely watched how many of our porter team would rather go home than push onwards. The ones who planned to leave stood as far from the loads of boxes as possible – forty-seven people in total. Footwear was not the determining factor after all: there were some with sneakers in the group that retreated, and there were barefoot porters among those who stayed. Hirano, the treasurer, paid out the wages to the porters as they left. She wore dark sunglasses and had a white bandana wrapped tightly around her head – like a pirate sharing her precious jewels. It was an effective guise because no one in line gave her any trouble.

Progress on the trail brought us to the unavoidable snow. Suddenly, everything changed. The colour green was entirely gone, replaced by a solid blanket of white. Only brush tips of bushes poked through the cold surface, giving a hint of the foliage below. I encountered a porter who had already dropped a load higher up and was retracing the route home. His bare feet were purple. "It's too cold," he said. "I won't go tomorrow." Our boxes had been dropped at the toe of the South Annapurna Glacier, at an approximate elevation of 3600 metres, 150 vertical metres below our forecasted Base Camp.

Advancement was slow. We had spent 9 days instead of 8 getting as far as we had, and there was still a day's walk to Base Camp. We had supplies in Deurali that needed to be ferried (which was ultimately completed by 6 team members and 10 Sherpas, each carrying 30-kilogram loads on their back), plus the abandoned boxes on the glacier. The British party, with Bonington as leader, was camped nearby at our established pseudo base camp, and was dealing with a similar problem. In the end, it came down to the help of the porters. Even though our initial group of 144 dwindled to 97, and then 22, most of whom were Tibetan, these amazing individuals pushed themselves to the limit, despite wintry conditions. When it was time to part ways, we thanked them with a sincere *arigato* and a hearty shake of the hands, hoping we would meet again.

At the pseudo base camp, we woke to the sound of clucking each morning, and the running joke became "The neighbour's food is calling." While some of us were tormented by the thought of the British party whittling away at their chicken population every day, others envied the thought of them dining on the freshest meat possible, but none of us could stand the daily wake-up calls.

To establish our bearings thus far, we retraced a short distance in the direction of Deurali and made our way in hip-deep snow down to the Modi Khola. There was a gorge carved out of layered black rock buttresses that eventually led to the West Glacier. Although this section was prone to rockfall, passing through it allowed us to view the summit of Annapurna III. Travelling a bit farther, across a pristine stream that flowed from Glacier Dome, we found a much safer spot with no risk of rockfall or avalanche. We guessed that it might have been Base Camp for the German expedition to Gangapurna in 1965; quite a few rusted empty cans remained strewn about. From that point, a ridge blocked the view of our summit goal, but Modi Peak and Glacier Dome shone bright. All things considered, we determined this to be our Base Camp, with clear drinking water from the glacier providing one of the best perks to our new home.

The next day's work was to establish the shortest route between the pseudo base camp and Base Camp to ensure quick transport of the remaining boxes. We fixed 120-metre ropes end to end to protect the descent from the pseudo base camp to the Modi Khola. For efficient transport, we split into two groups, one for each camp. At a mid-station between the two, loads were passed off from one group to the other, thus connecting the dots from the pseudo base camp to Base Camp. The process took almost two weeks, and while most of us settled into Base Camp, Mr. Gopal stayed at the pseudo base camp with Manita, where she endured non-stop nose bleeds. Miyazaki remained there, too, until the final boxes were moved.

Base Camp was at 3750 metres, almost the same elevation as the summit of Mount Fuji. Past climbing experience had shown we were all comfortable with that altitude, yet a few members began to suffer from nausea, headaches and menacing nose bleeds. The snow around the camp had turned isothermal and progress was again slowed. Tensions were also on the rise from the final stages of shutting down the pseudo base camp when we had decided to split into a third group that could begin fixing an ascent route to Camp 1. As team members poured their energy into advancement, some of them were already convinced of who would make the cut for the summit assault. Accusations and frustrations mounted, and I could sense the build-up of an "uh-oh, here we go" scenario. We pushed forward, and after four days we established Camp 1 (4350 metres) at the tip of the glacier that feeds the Modi Khola. Two days after that, we reached Camp 2 at 4800 metres. The summit stood more than 2700 metres above. There was much climbing to be done, yet we were still anchored to our pseudo base camp with an endless pile of supplies.

In a leap-frogging fashion, I moved back and forth between the established camps with the other climbers, constantly transferring equipment and marking the route. Although my job was physically tough, Miyazaki had the difficult task of determining the best rotation for the rest of the team. She worked late into the night, solving logistics and preparing the next day's plan, never flagging and always maintaining her healthy appetite and cheerful walks around camp. Her boots squeaked on the hard snow as she passed by and her signature black bag remained close at hand; she claimed it contained the team's "VIDs" (very important documents). Even as she performed her office-like duties, she also carried her share of 30-kilogram loads from the pseudo base camp, where snow conditions had deteriorated and travel was difficult. We felt some relief knowing that the British team was also challenged with ferrying loads from their makeshift base camp; the transport of boxes over rotting snow was everyone's nemesis.

April 14

The final boxes arrived at Base Camp, as did Miyazaki and Mr. Gopal – our dear Mr. Gopal, with his wide canvas army-style Kissling rucksack and ongoing good nature. "He fell big time when the rotten snow under his feet collapsed," said Miyazaki, excited to share her story and act out the dramatics. "He dislocated his shoulder. And you know what? He put it back in on his own, just grunting 'Yeah!'" We had already prepared a welcome song, to the tune of a popular Japanese ballad and accompanied by Urushibara's ukulele, and the story of the shoulder injury made it all the more humorous.

> Now! / Here we are at Base Camp
> Where? / Annapurna
> When? / Are we gonna stand on the top
> Why? / Because there is the mountain
> For Annapurna III / Our leader exists
> For Annapurna III / Our leader exists.

Two days later we officially celebrated our fully established Base Camp. Everyone – climbers, Sherpas and Mr. Gopal – was ready for a party. Afternoon showers ended by evening and a whitish mist hung in the air, giving the place an illusive atmosphere. A bonfire burned bright and the red of the flames highlighted people's faces, which were already tinged pink with drink and dance. We carried on, Sherpas and team members alike, relaxed and joyous, temporarily forgetting the seriousness of our mission in the Himalayas. The beat continued long into the night, and at some point, I remembered: *Here we are at Base Camp. Where? Annapurna ... Why? Because there is the mountain.*

The next morning was all business. Miyazaki and I met with Dr. O-no to discuss the health of the team with plans to start the more serious climbing the day afterwards. My anxiety grew as the conversation unfolded. There were three climbers under the doctor's watchful eye for high-altitude sickness – Hirano, Manita and Urushibara. When I crawled into my sleeping bag that night, I felt such desperation, as though I was clinging to God to get us through this. Never had religion played a role in my life, but at that moment I could not help but appeal to a higher entity. More than anything, I wanted the team to summit the mountain without peril, and return home. I had to erase from my mind the harrowing thought, "What if something happens?" And so, I prayed.

A Climber's Life

An added and often unspoken challenge in mountaineering is that of using the toilet. Of course, there is no avoiding it, yet when tucked in the cocooned warmth of a sleeping bag, climbers delay this task for as long as possible. Our team was no different. Every morning we would painstakingly sip a cup of milky tea, delivered by the Sherpas, to prolong the comfort of the tent and the pleasure of the hot drink. Meanwhile, our bodies were about to burst with the call of nature. The only disciplined soul in the group was Dr. O-no, who wasted no time stepping from the paradoxical comfort between wants and needs. Every day at 5 a.m. we heard her feet patter against the frozen snow as she scurried past the tents. Her routine quickly became a source of fun for us. "Oh, doctor, are you going out? How about a song before your business?" In our best pop-song voices, we serenaded her as she passed us by. "The path we take leads to the toilet / Why we persevere / The discomfort to the limit / Clenching our teeth / By all means." Secretly, we all wished we had her determination.

From radio talk on the airwaves, we deciphered that the other parties had already reached their respective Camp 3 and Camp 4, which meant they were on an ideal timeline for the summit, but we had barely established Camp 2 by April 11 and still had the crux of the ice wall ahead of us.

Following the same route as the 1965 German Gangapurna party, Hirakawa, Sato, Urushibara and three Sherpas spent three days climbing the most direct line up the right side of a main rock buttress, which would ultimately lead to the South Face; however, an impossibly huge crevasse mid-section brought them to a halt. Urushibara and Manita gave up, descended to Camp 2 and switched to the left side of the buttress (April 20), and a day later, thanks to their hard work, Manita and I were eventually able to climb even higher.

After threading through a series of small icefalls and seracs, we arrived on top of the first buttress, made up of rows of thick vertical ice walls with countless gaping crevasses in between them. Instinct told us to travel as quickly as possible through the potential danger, but our bodies felt heavy and sluggish and our feet moved forward with difficulty. Our only choice was to rely on fate and try to make it through the labyrinth unscathed.

To me, certainty equates to luck in the Himalayas. When one stands on a glacier that might collapse, the climber feels less sure than lucky if the ice remains intact. Amidst the East Glacier, I felt lucky, a fleeting sense of satisfaction at being there, standing on untouched land that had never before seen a human footprint. In order to keep a smile on my face and remain confident in such big terrain, I had to repeat the mantra, "It's OK," because I knew that in all its grandeur, the summit could easily escape us. In fact, it seemed like a constant trick – the higher I climbed, the farther away the summit appeared. I could never quite figure out the answer to that illusion.

At 5200 metres, we ran out of flags to mark the route. Although we turned back that day, we were set up for success to establish Camp 3, 100 vertical metres higher, on April 24. From there, it appeared we would not have to cross too many sketchy crevasses before reaching the base of the icefall crux that led to the col above. The views from Camp 3 were spectacular. To the west stood Modi Peak, South Peak, Annapurna Fang and the Annapurna I group; to the south was Machapuchare and Gabelhorn; and in between, to the southwest, flowed the Modi Khola. We were in the heart of the Himalayas and felt the elation of such an opportunity.

Unexpectedly, our joy was crushed with the news that Yamazaki, our Base Camp manager, had been struck with typhoid fever. It would take at least a week to help transport her to Pokhara. With our teammate's health first and foremost in our mind, we were instantly prepared to let the summit of Annapurna III slip away. Life and death issues outplay standing on a summit, without question. But our trusty Dr. O-no took matters into her own hands and assured us that Yamazaki's resilient nature would defy the severity of the illness and that she would recover, thus encouraging the team to continue the route upwards. Sure enough, with the doctor's around-the-clock care, Yamazaki recovered and rejoined us at Camp 1 on May 2, slightly more than two weeks after she fell ill.

Dear Junko,

I feel bad for causing you so much worry. But I'm getting better day by day, and my temperature this morning is finally down to 36.7°c, five days in. It was April 17, after you had gone to Camp 1, that I began to feel ill, then by that night I had a fever. By the 20th, I couldn't even stand on my feet. I had to use a container in the tent to go to the washroom, and that was the biggest task of the day.

Although it is still painful to sit up all day long, I feel it's much easier now since the fever at night is no more. As high as the fever was, it never let me sweat a drop, even in the daytime. I have never suffered like that before, and on the worst day, April 19th, I seriously thought it could be my last day alive.

I am as weak as having no vertebrae, like an octopus, and I have no muscle power at all now. But there is no choice other than starting to eat well and get better from here on in. Chloromycetin shots will continue for two to three weeks. I still positively plan to go up to Camp 1 sometime in the first days of May. No worries – I will behave and listen to Dr. O-no.

Don't let me forget to congratulate you for reaching Camp 3. We, the leftovers at Base Camp, wish you the best.

Sorry, I'm tired now; though I would love to write more, I have to call it a day.

Morie Yamazaki

April 27

It was my wedding anniversary, another cause for celebration. Manita pronounced the occasion with permission to indulge. "I allow you girls to open a can of peaches because it's Tabei-*san*'s marriage anniversary," she said from the depths of her sleeping bag, fighting the symptoms of altitude sickness. Well, well! I wasted no time in opening the biggest can in our supply and heartily dug in. We had a side dish of rations left over from the day's climb since we had turned back early at 5500 metres when Urushibara also showed signs of illness. Freshly brewed milk tea by Hirakawa had us relaxed and chatting throughout the afternoon. It had been a long time since we had lounged this way.

As it does in an environment where food is limited, conversation drifted to the delicacies we missed most. "What do you want to eat now?" someone asked. Tempura and sushi, warm *taro* potatoes marinated in soya sauce and sugar, *yakitori* (barbecued chicken shish kebabs), grilled fish with grated *daikon*, *gyoza* (Chinese dumplings), *ton-katsu* (fried pork wrapped in bread crumbs), strawberries, watermelon – the list of desired dishes was endless. "*Sake*," added Hirakawa, always the spirit of the party. "Drink *sake* with it." Indeed, we had room in our imagination for a glass or two of *sake*.

"Ladies, don't be disappointed. We're having freeze-dried rice and Knorr soup this evening. Actually, sesame and salt go well with rice; gives it a punch," said Hirakawa, casually bringing us back to reality. The truth was we had a food shortage. Prior to the trip, research of past expeditions taught us that climbers could only swallow liquid-like foods at high camps. Acting on that, we collected tons of items we thought would be easily consumable: canned peaches, condensed milk, powdered glucose, biscuits and wafers – a menu more suited to an infant's diet than that of a mountaineer. In short, we were starving. We craved rice and miso soup and begged for a load to be ferried up from Base Camp, but even that was not enough to appease our appetite. We were perpetually hungry, and the days seemed extra long as a result.

Nonetheless, we pushed onwards. The Sherpas returned to camp one day after fixing the route higher up the mountain. It was around 4:30 p.m. and dinner was ready for their arrival. A whiteout had settled outside our tents, and despite the gloomy setting, Girmi had a big smile on his face. "We found a very good spot for Camp 4. We can pitch tents tomorrow," he said. Whether his friendly smile denoted progress on the route or contentment that supper was made, I will never know, but I sure appreciated it.

April 29

Camp 4 was established at 5900 metres, which allowed us to begin focus on the route's crux, a steep ice wall that led to the col between Annapurna

III and Gangapurna. After a two-hour approach from camp, we encountered the 55° ice on the South Face of Gangapurna where we had to cut steps into the hard, blue surface, fixing rope as we climbed. We were as slow as ants struggling up the frozen face. Swinging an axe into the icy Himalayan wall had us begging for more muscle power. And the wall was not the only obstacle; the higher we climbed the more team members became sick from altitude. The remaining number of strong, healthy climbers began to diminish.

May 2

Fixing the route up the ice wall continued with Sato and Manita and Sherpas Pasang, Kitar and Girmi all tied to a 60-metre rope. From below, what appeared to be a giant crevasse at the bottom of those final pitches that led to the col was a bergschrund, where mountain meets glacier. To cross the bergschrund, the team placed an ice screw and climbed diagonally leftward, securing a 40-metre rope as they went. Task complete, they retreated towards camp, but on the descent, mid-traverse immediately below a series of seracs, Pasang slipped, triggering a domino effect. One by one, the five climbers were plucked from their stance and began to quickly slide down the slope. Fortunately, the fall stopped after 15 metres, but Girmi, who fell the farthest, bore the worst injury, making his right shoulder and arm non-functional. Manita suffered a large blow to her ribs. Pasang fell the least distance and had no injury but later explained that he had felt dizzy on the mountain face prior to falling, likely a result of one of us having administered too much pain medication for a headache he complained of the day before.

May 4

By 11 a.m. the usual crystal-clear sky at Camp 4 was layered with fog. Views beyond our immediate surroundings were hidden, which added doubt to the atmosphere. Despite orders from Miyazaki to return to camp no later than 2 p.m. from setting the route, we had no idea where Hirano, Pasang and Ang Mingma were by 4:00. Miyazaki and I went to look for them.

"It took us two hours to get to the bottom of the ice wall, then fixing the route started after that," Pasang said when we finally reached camp together three hours later. "The climber cannot move fast enough," he explained, using Hirano as the reason for their delay. In addition, Dr. O-no piped in that from the fall two days earlier, Manita likely had cracked ribs and Girmi had a broken shoulder. Both were to stay at Camp 1 and rest. This medical update made the fog that shrouded our camp feel even heavier. More so, Girmi had vented that his injury was Pasang's fault, that Pasang was never doing the right thing in fixing the route and that Girmi wanted him to stop. Without another word, a crevasse of our own began to open in the team.

As sirdar, Girmi's comment carried weight. His job was to assign the other Sherpas to their tasks, but in Pasang's case, Miyazaki had stepped in. Pasang, the strong one, seemed to have been tasked the job of ferrying loads more than anyone else. Even from our perspective, we thought it was too much. For a change of pace, Miyazaki asked Girmi to send Pasang up to fix the route as soon as Camp 4 was established. Then the accident occurred. Now with conflict and Girmi injured, and Girmi and Pasang having been the powerhouses and gutsy climbers of the Sherpa team, we were left to see what would develop.

Miyazaki, whose signature duty at Camp 4 had been to chase the miniature silhouettes of faraway climbers on the ice wall through her binoculars, was suddenly stricken with a severe headache at midnight. Her cries for help were a cause for instant reaction, given her otherwise perpetually calm and expressionless nature. I dug around in the first-aid box for the standard pain pills and passed her two. "Are these effective?" she said with skepticism, but within twenty minutes she was in a deep slumber. There I lay, wide awake in the darkness and cold of the Himalayan night, gently cursing her ability to sleep. "Thanks a lot, boss," I mumbled.

May 5

Another day of fixing the route, this time with Hirakawa, Pasang (again) and me on the rope. We had to brush away the 20 centimetres of snow that had fallen overnight before we could chip at the ice wall. We were showered with blue and white shards of ice as our work began. Each strike I made had me wish for more physical power; my lean arm drove a pick only so far into the ice. I needed brute strength, which was difficult to muster from my 5-foot frame.

Chips of ice continued to fly by us, as did small black rocks that rattled past. We were nowhere close to adding 100 metres to the route that day; it took us two hours to fix a 40-metre section, and each step we advanced was buried by slough avalanches. Our slow progress felt like torment. Thankfully, in the midst of it, Pasang caught up to me from the end of the line and kindly took over the lead.

By afternoon, the wind had gained in force and was gusting from below. With the added blowing snow, visibility was down to zero. My whole body was cold, a torturous state to be in, and my gloves were frozen solid, as though I had pulled them from a freezer. The highest we were able to climb in that weather was to 6300 metres, but I lacked the will to double-check the elevation on my altimeter. Hunger had peaked, too – I had not eaten since breakfast. By the time we rappelled to the bottom of the ice wall, on our way back to camp, my arms were tired and useless, and holding my ice axe took all my might.

It was a relief to arrive back at Camp 4, and our return was noted with a pack of *kibi-dango*, a sweet snack sent from Yamazaki with a message that said, "Take heart, ladies – high up there – for it's Children's Day." We broke into smiles in honour of this national Japanese holiday, an age-old celebration that recognizes and respects the younger generation every May 5.

Of all things, the very next day when I was meant to continue my fight with the blue ice wall, I developed a hemorrhoid from the extensive strain on my body. Doctor's orders had me tent-ridden, a point that I could not argue but irritated me to no end as I lay there, useless, dabbed with healing medication.

May 7

To save the two-hour approach from Camp 4 to the bottom of the menacing ice wall, a limiting start to a day's work, we established a secondary camp below the bergschrund and carried half our food and supplies to it.

> A father and a son who visited us from Chomrong had a dead deer they had hunted on the way. Mr. Gopal had been suffering with a bad throat and he didn't come out a step from his tent today; however, it wasn't the case that he was

uninterested in the fresh and tender venison that even a king of Nepal hardly had the chance to eat. So, for two hours he negotiated a price for the deer, sticking his head out a tiny bit from the tent, and finally succeeded in buying it for 12 rupees.

I hope he is re-energized by this, at least to some degree, since our Mr. Gopal-the-Joker has been less and less talkative these days; I guess life here for so long isn't in his favour. He had begun showing his wish to go down to Chomrong. "You want to go there, right?" I asked him.

"No delicious meals here, nor pretty women," he said. I see. Well, recently he had become quite depressed and self-confined in his tent most of the day, just like a frightened baby turtle.

– Yamazaki's diary, Base Camp

May 11

Manita had sufficiently healed, thanks to the extended care of Dr. O-no, and was able to climb to Camp 3. It was determined that Girmi's shoulder was not broken but badly contused, and it healed well with the use of ice packs, of which there was no shortage on the mountain. But the conflict between Pasang and Girmi continued. Their relationship was not openly nasty, yet Girmi's frustration with Pasang was felt in every word he spoke, especially since he had returned to Camp 4 and was giving orders to the Sherpas.

We were approaching mid-May, and my thoughts were concentrated on completing the ice wall. I felt nothing upon hearing about the successes of other parties; we had our own battle to wage. No sooner had I calculated the number of days still required to finish the job than Mr. Gopal informed us of the nearing monsoon. Pasang suggested that the Sherpas take over cutting the steps in the ice, thus speeding up the approach to the previous day's high point by not having to climb at our slower pace. Miyazaki and I considered the reality of the situation and gratefully accepted his offer. We had no other choice.

The entire route from Camp 4 at 6100 metres to the col at 6800 metres was fixed with 1000 metres of rope by May 14, two full weeks after we started up the ice wall.

Our attention was ready to shift to the summit assault team. The contest among members was on.

A Women's Battle

May 16

Everyone, except for Dr. O-no and Yamazaki at Base Camp, gathered in the Camp 4 mess tent. It was after 6 p.m. and supper was over. Miyazaki's words caught our nervous attention.

"Meeting starts now," she said. "Since the route to the col is fixed, I will announce the plans for the summit. With only a few days left to avoid the monsoon, I need climbers with great strength and speed. With that perspective, I chose the first assault members as Tabei, Hirakawa, Pasang and Girmi. The second is Sato, myself and Kitar. I'm not in favour of sending any more assault teams than these two parties – for now. My reason for this choice is that Hirano-*san* is too slow to keep up with everybody else, with her laboured breathing, so I don't think it's a good idea to dare let her go higher up. So far, Urushibara-*san* has suffered with altitude sickness every time we move up higher, which leads me to assume she'll most likely get sick at the 6800-metre col. Manita-*san* still has sore ribs from the accident and is showing some symptoms of altitude sickness, and so she isn't suitable to climb the long ice wall. Tabei and Hirakawa have been strong and in good shape from the start, which everybody here recognizes. And Sato and I have no reason to be denied further climbing at this moment."

So began the dispute.

> Manita: "Then this is the conclusion, not a meeting?"
> Miyazaki: "Please say your opinion, still, if you have one."
> Manita: "No sense if you've already decided."
> Miyazaki: "I would still like to hear it."
> Hirano: "Is our party really as cruel as this? I haven't come all the way up here only to ferry loads, having paid 1,000,000 yen! I would rather go down from here immediately then!"
> Miyazaki: "It's a common way to ferry loads in Himalayan expeditions. Did you think you could come to the Himalayas on your own?"

Hirano: "I shouldn't have stayed on this team in the first place. I should have quit when the others did." Then, turning to me, "Am I really that slow?"

"To be honest, I don't think you're that fast," I said, knowing my answer would further aggravate the situation.

Hirano: "I feel like a fool; I've never been so insulted before. Why can a person with a hemorrhoid go and somebody without one is held back? Himalayan climbing is supposed to take time for acclimatization with no need for speed, right? I shouldn't have come."

Miyazaki: "Urushibara-*san*, do you regret having come here?"

Urushibara: "No, I don't, because I was dying just to get to the Himalayas; however, now that I'm here, I'll miss going up higher. Though the final decision is what I had presumed, I would be happier if I could continue higher with my camera. I admit I get affected by altitude more than is desirable. But I thought I'd be all right if I took more time, if that was possible. I sorely regret missing my chance at the summit, but at the same time, I appreciate that I'm here now as a replacement member, after all. The conclusion of the party is the one I have to follow."

Hirakawa: "I'll take the summit as a serious responsibility, though I feel a bit nervous."

Sato: "Although I have been selected to be second, I know that attempt might still not happen due to poor weather."

Manita (resigned): "It's OK for me as I have my rib issue from the accident."

"I feel enormous responsibility," I concluded.

The weight of everyone's emotions bore down on me.

Silence. Then the falling snow, as it rustled down the side of the tent, became disproportionally loud. In the mixed soundtrack of weather and the settling of disagreement, Miyazaki continued. She directed each climber as to how they would best help prepare for the two summit assaults in the coming days. Miyazaki would climb to the final camp (Camp 5) with the first summit team; Sato would follow the day afterwards with a few Sherpas; and Urushibara and Hirano would climb to the Advanced Camp 4 (at the base of the ice wall) to film and photograph the ascents. Manita would stay at Camp 4 as the team correspondent. That was the plan. "Good night, then," said Miyazaki as she turned and left the tent, the matter closed to further discussion. A dire atmosphere filled the space where she had stood.

No sooner had I also left the meeting, on my way to sleep in the leaders' quarters, than angry yelling arose from the mess tent. "I'll tell everyone about this once I get back to Tokyo!" someone said, a statement supported by the back and forth of hushed voices that lingered long into the cold night air. I felt upset, too, and it took all my will to restrain myself from kicking something in annoyance. My mind reeled with frustration: "Was it really supposed to end up like this? Do it all on your own if you insist that much on not working as a team! You're missing the point of a group expedition." The emotions I had withheld in the meeting came to a boil as I walked to my tent. I was rapidly losing interest in reaching the summit myself, and was ready to tell people to do whatever they pleased.

Then I stopped myself. I was a candidate for the summit of Annapurna III based on my mountaineering skill and strength, and I was suddenly feeling more sure of myself, given the situation unfolding with the team. I even felt prepared to see how far I could push myself without using supplemental oxygen. What was the point of the night's meeting anyway? It seemed that Miyazaki and I were the ones who were fooled, given all that we, leader and assistant leader, had considered when making those critical decisions. Forget what others had in mind. "Know thyself," I thought, and clenched my teeth in sheer determination to continue.

Before slipping into my tent and warm sleeping bag, I stared straight ahead at Machapuchare, and facing the frigid beauty of the Himalayas, my angry heart began to soften.

Four hours prior to that group meeting, Miyazaki had consulted me in regard to possible summit teams. Her thoughts were conflicted. "A part of me resists considering Sato for a summit assault," she began, "seeing as how she's been complaining a lot since Calcutta. But it becomes too much of an emotional conclusion if I give in to that. This should never be decided by emotion. And I understand very well about Hirano's deep passion to grab the summit; however, it's impossible for now. Let's imagine Sato and Hirano as the second assault pair; they may not be able to make it to the top in a day with Hirano's pace, to which we also must add the fact that the route from the col to the summit is yet unknown to us. The math would dictate that Sato, who has potential, goes down without reaching the summit. Not good. So, I decided Sato and I for the second pair. This, I can explain, with a clear conscience, to everybody involved back in Japan. What do you think? Am I wrong? I hope not. All right?" Miyazaki repeated herself many times over in trying to come to terms with a final decision. I knew her ideas were well thought out.

I was about to ask why not send Hirano in a third assault, but I could tell this was an unlikely option when I looked into Miyazaki's grave eyes. Her initial plan was the appropriate one. In realizing this, I saw for the first time the absolute calmness and fairness that Miyazaki bestowed, despite the extremely difficult situation she was in as leader. I was immediately determined to do my best at whatever was asked of me for the success of the expedition. The more I knew of Miyazaki's agonizing decision making, the more upset I became with the fallout of the meeting. In truth, what other choice did she have? I had to admit, I could never be leader.

By that point in the expedition, fourteen months had passed since our joint commitment to the solitary goal of "doing anything" in the Himalayas. Countless tribulations had occurred since then, but there we were, on the eve of our ascent of Annapurna III. The time from when we made that commitment to this night felt simultaneously long and short. Now, everyone was left to embrace her own emotions that sprang from Miyazaki's plans for the summit. Pasang and Ang Mingma's tent remained lit up, too. Sleep was a distant hope.

> Now we heard the announcement. Anyway, I had never believed in "All of us for the Summit," which a few of the teammates advocated. But, though I admit the leader's choice a very reasonable one objectively, considering the condition of each of us and the weather, somehow, I still felt "That was it?" She asked us our opinions, probably trying to break off the distaste in the air. I almost felt like remarking, "Could you care a bit more for the members who are to stay at Camp 4?"

Anyway, I was mad at her for asking for our say. What was the use of asking for it when things were already decided? I trusted her to act in everyone's best interest, not in the interest of a chosen few, and wasn't the conviction of the final decision to come from the leader? Asking our opinion after that just sounded unprepared.

– Manita's diary

▲

I felt bad being picked for the first assault group since I knew and saw my senior Hirano-*san*'s dying passion for the summit. On the other hand, it's not an option to let her try as the first attacker because she's not in good shape at all. So, I had no other choice than to say yes to my leader. Of course, Hirano-*san* objected against the decision; it must be very hard for anybody not to be able to climb higher once up here. Having imagined it, I felt like curling up in to a ball and hiding somewhere. Voices of frustration and complaints throughout the night kept me from a good sleep. Come morning, I prepared for departing with my mouth shut. Am I to be the person thrown away by my teammates who are silently saying, "Do whatever you please," or to be cheered by the fact that I get to complete the task? Or am I the one who is too selfish to empathize with the ones who cannot go for the summit? Knowing well all those interpretations, I could hardly drag my heavy feet from Camp 4.

– Hirakawa's diary

Success

The shock of the summit announcements was over, yet the next morning dawned as gloomy as the night before. Visibility was poor. In quiet tents, we ate an instant breakfast the Sherpas had prepared for us. Hirano remained laying in her sleeping bag, to which nobody uttered a word. Reservedly, Hirakawa sorted equipment for the initial assault team to leave while Miyazaki and I packed away the leader tent. I was the first to speak.

"*Itte-kimasu*," I said, offering a Japanese goodbye. "Manita-*san*, please be the keeper of Camp 4."

"Yes, I will, but I feel like I'm holding a bomb," she said, referring to Hirano's volatility.

"I'm just worried that something life-threatening could happen." I had visions of Hirano leaving the camp alone. Manita understood my meaning and fell into silence.

The struggle was immediate as we left Camp 4 for the advanced camp at the base of the ice wall – trail breaking through knee-deep snow, our backs burdened with the weight of packs. It was nearly noon when we connected the camps, only to find the tents completely buried in snow. Incessant dust avalanches fell from the wall above, and it was obvious we would not reach the col that day. We would hunker down for the night at the wall's base instead. Girmi and Pasang made a round trip to Camp 4 to fetch an extra's day's food to support our decision.

May 18

Our tents were buried after a nightlong snowfall, and I woke to darkness when there should have been morning light. Disappointing weather again. My agitation was evident in the short breaths I expelled as I prepared to climb. The steps we had cut and the ropes we had fixed the day before were also covered in fresh snow. We had to dig our way up to the start of the route, aiming only for the col. I led the pitch with Hirakawa and Miyazaki tied into the rope behind me. The snow-filled steps up the steep wall were agonizing to navigate. Everything became an annoyance. I could hardly switch my carabiner from below an anchor point to above it to continue up the fixed line. Frozen knots connected frozen ropes that were barely malleable enough to trust, and once again I felt luck override certainty as we continued. Looking downslope through my stance, I could see Hirakawa's helmet inching upwards. Intermittently, I hung onto the mountainside while spindrift avalanches showered me from above.

Despite the depressed feeling I began the day with, my mind settled as we climbed. My breath became nourishing, and I felt like I could expand my entire chest full of oxygen. In truth, my breathing was laboured – I often had to rest for a moment, leaning my head on a minuscule shelf of ice while the continual rhythm of my lungs panted for air. I followed the only pattern of movement available to me: step, adjust carabiner, rest, repeat. I could sense – but tried to ignore – the pull of gravity from below.

Seven hours of this repetition delivered us to the col, marked by a surprisingly brown landscape on the far side of the ridge. We made it to our last camp before the summit.

As happy as we were to have surmounted the ice wall, we had other concerns to manage. Miyazaki was in poor shape. As soon as a tent was ready, she lay down without even removing her boots. The wind was merciless and the tents ballooned and swayed like mad, not helping Miyazaki feel any better. It was well past 5 p.m. by the time all the tents were pitched; too late to let the Sherpas return to the lower camp for the following day's repeat col ascent with Sato. Instead, they would descend early the next morning and then climb back up.

Hirakawa injected Miyazaki with anti-nausea medication. We tried to melt snow for water to sooth her distressed complaint of thirst, but given the elevation, the butane-fuelled stoves were diminished in their power output and the melting process took forever. Thankfully the medication kicked in and Miyazaki fell asleep. On the contrary, Hirakawa and I were starving, as usual, and had to satiate our bellies to some degree before we could attempt sleep. Admittedly, we ate Miyazaki's portion of dinner, too, and called it a night.

May 19

Weak rays of morning sun gently shone on Camp 5. I prayed for the weather to remain like that all day. The wind still blew, and to avoid its chill I stood on the leeside of the tent to tie on my crampons. Since the summit route was unknown to us, we added bivouac gear to the absolute necessities already packed. I mused that my load felt no heavier with the extra weight; perhaps I was just ready to get the job done.

To begin our final ascent, Girmi was in the lead position, myself second, then Hirakawa and Pasang. I left the camp with two concerns on my mind: Miyazaki's condition (which was improved from the night before, but not perfect), and that of Ang Mingma, the Sherpa who was meant to have descended from the col in the wee hours of morning to climb back up with Sato. He was also feeling symptoms of altitude sickness and was yet to leave Camp 5. Nonetheless, I had to let go of worries that I could no longer control and focus only on the summit ahead.

The route started on a broad, relatively low-angled slope without many crevasses. The creaking of crampons on snow somehow amused me. It distracted my mind from the constant, bitter wind that whirled around us and threatened to rip off anything exposed, my nose included.

From the ridge of the mountaintop, huge cornices hung to the south side and vertical buttresses of polished black rock stood jagged to the north, in the direction of the village of Manangbhot. A wide snowfield offered a reasonable spot for a break where Hirakawa and I put on down jackets, the first time we wore them other than at camp. Knee-deep snow met the ridgeline on the side of the ominous cornices, and the world around us seemed to grow foggy in eerie support of the dangerous landscape. I glanced back for a view of Gangapurna, and I could only recognize its vertical south face; the north side was fully hidden by a whiteout.

Our technique became even more precise as the ridge we climbed narrowed to knifepoint. There was no room for error – a step slightly too far right or left would mean a fast track to death for all of us. It would be impossible to arrest a person's fall in that situation. Particular attention was paid to each crampon placement. There has been no shortage of climbing accidents that resulted from a stumble on the two front points of the GRIVEL twelve-point design. I recalled easily the words that were drilled into me by the owner of a mountain equipment store in downtown Tokyo: "Be careful with your crampons when you see the head of the second person beneath you and when the slope starts to ease off."

"I've got a headache," said Pasang, an instant alert for us. The altimeter read just above 7000 metres. We sat on rugged rocks for a break, hoping this would be enough to ease Pasang's pain. A much-anticipated can of peaches was opened for a snack – but it was frozen solid, a cylindrical block of concrete. Our chance for replenishment was lost.

Pasang's headache progressed to severe. Unsure of the route and time commitment to reach the summit, we felt it unsafe to leave Pasang alone. We administered a single tablet of pain medication (not three, which he had taken before), and Girmi had a brief discussion with him. We had no idea what they spoke about, but soon afterwards we continued a slow ascent of the mountain, without incident.

It was past 1 p.m. and still we climbed. "Please let us get there," I wished to myself. "We'll be there if only we continue to put our feet forward, step by step." Then, through a brief opening in the fog, I saw two mounds in the distance, the left of which was the summit. "Continue on the snow-covered ridge, climb the rocky knoll and that will be it," I quickly surmised. We were so close.

Layers of fist-sized rocks were strewn right below the summit, as if tossed from the heavens above. With each weighted step, they collapsed with a startling rattle. But above the scree section was a stretch of solid snow, and at the end of that, the top of Annapurna III.

The snow on the summit was rock hard, deflecting my ice axe when I tried to dig in with its pick. Every movement was slowly executed. I placed my pack down and peeled off my over-mitts. The wind jabbed at my hands like needles. Carefully slipping flags from a plastic bag, we tied them off on our axe handles, the Nepali one by Girmi, the Japanese one by me and the team flag by Hirakawa. It was a clumsy task with bulky hands wrapped in gloves and a relentless wind pulling at the flags. I stamped my crampons on the small spot of summit snow that I could see through my sunglasses. "We're finally here. It's done." The temperature was recorded at −16°c, and the time was 2:45 p.m.

Visibility barely stretched 10 metres in front of us. Machapuchare and Annapurna II and IV were completely hidden. The only evident features were the sheer north side that dropped away from the summit of Annapurna III, and the summit itself. That was enough for us to maintain our bearings.

It never occurred to us to leave something on the mountain's peak to mark our ascent; instead we took numerous photographs. Standing beside Girmi, I watched Hirakawa switch from climber to photographer as she worked in the bright light. Her roll of film broke twice due to the cold temperature, and while she changed her camera over, I squatted for a moment and picked up a few stones. I collected these as souvenirs to take back from this place of greatness. I thought about how far we had come. As Hirakawa transformed our climb into pictures for others to see, I reflected on how we transformed the notion of wanting to climb in the Himalayas, any mountain in the Himalayas, into "Let's climb Annapurna III." And we had succeeded.

Tabei untied from the rope. It's the summit, no more climb-ing. Awkwardly, I looked down the north face. Unfortunately, I could only see the top of the icy cliffs below as it was too foggy. Relieved that my responsibility was finally over, I didn't feel happy yet; I wanted to go down sooner rather than later. Girmi the sirdar and Pasang were excited, bellowing "Success, success!" It must have been a different feeling for Girmi, who early on had strived so hard in making the route to then get injured and be frustrated until now. By the way, what about Pasang's headache? Better? Having finished our photo taking, we had nothing else to do, and quickly started going down within twenty-five minutes of reaching the summit. My lin-gering concern was for the descent. Looking forward to seeing our leader at Camp 5 kept me going. Oh, the summit is done.

– Hirakawa's diary

▲

The sunny sky in the early morning became cloudy after all, and the four attackers disappeared into it by 10 a.m. When Ang Mingma, who had been ill with a headache, went down to Camp 4 with Sherpa Sange, Kitar and I were left alone at Camp 5. So, I enjoyed chatting with him as I felt better today. Then I came back to my tent, laid myself down and stared at the ceiling. How long had passed I don't remember, but upon hearing people's voices, I shot out from my tent. Surprisingly, they were already near.

"Leader, we've been to the summit!" Tabei shouted. The three of us, closing the gap step by step, hugged each other when we had zero distance left in between.

"Great job! It's good, it's good!" Tabei, Hirakawa and I shared the joy, still entangled in each other's arms, stumbling on the snow, and Girmi held his arms wide spread around us. No tears were shed for this success; however, countless thoughts and memories of the last year and a half ran around inside my mind, supported by the feeling of "It's good, it's good."

After eating a repeated dish of instant stir-fried rice, Tabei and Hirakawa quickly fell asleep. Tired, of course. Have a good rest, you girls. I had no idea how the way up was to the summit. I could only imagine it from their sleeping faces.

– Leader Miyazaki's diary

It was past 6 p.m. by the time we returned to Camp 5. Miyazaki's condition was much improved from the previous day, and she whole-heartedly enjoyed our success on Annapurna III, especially the fact that it was accident-free. We learned of disappointing news for Sato. Her designated Sherpa, Ang Mingma, who was to accompany her from Advanced Camp 4 to Camp 5, was delayed in getting to her. His headache made him unable to descend from Camp 5 early in the morning as originally planned. By the time he arrived to meet her, it was too late for them to ascend the ice wall.

Miyazaki then had to rethink her summit strategy and decided that there would be a summit assault the next day with only Kitar. To make matters worse, the radio had been broken since we arrived back at Camp 5 after the summit bid, and no message had been sent down to Camp 4 with Ang Mingma and Sange to inform the rest of the team of the latest plan. I felt sick imagining how everyone was coping lower down on the mountain, not knowing of our success and managing Sato's expectation of climbing.

May 20

Miyazaki's health had deteriorated again. Despite much better weather than the day before, and the fact that Kitar was ready to climb, our leader made another announcement. "I'm not in good shape," she said, "and Sato, who is supposed to go up with me, is still at Camp 4. Our radio communication between camps has been non-existent for three days. Considering how Sato must feel right now, I prefer not to climb without her. I would have gone if the first assault had failed. The priority is that everyone returns home intact. Since the monsoon is just around the corner, we can expect unpredictable weather changes. There is no need for me to push today since we've already succeeded as a team. Call it a day. Period." Any chance for a second summit attempt was over. The time had come to head home.

Again, Miyazaki had made the right choice, and observing her swollen face as she spoke, I completely agreed that taking her down the mountain was top priority. So, we left Camp 5 behind, securing Miyazaki to the rope in between Hirakawa and me, with the two of us carrying as much of the gear as possible. Twice Miyazaki vomited on the descent, and it upset us to watch her suffer – in her condition, it must have been brutal to descend the ice wall. But we continued in the urgency to retreat to a lower elevation.

In the distance below, I began to focus on black dots milling around, and I soon realized they were my fellow team members. At that point, no one knew we had reached the summit, or that the second assault had been called off. Their agitation must have reached full intensity by that point, and I was nervous to confront them. What would I say? Radio transmissions had been impossible for three days. We had been isolated in our success, and in our defeat for a second summit. Now we expected the rest of the team to accept, without question, what we had known for days. The only buffer I could offer in hopes that they would understand was news that our leader was sick. Some teammates congratulated us with genuine enthusiasm; others, like Sato, strongly pushed for the original goal, but to no avail. There would be no reconsideration.

> May 20th, Sunny. Left Camp 4 at 7:00, skipping breakfast, to go up to Camp 5. I realized the climbing was over in the second I saw the figures of the other climbers coming down from the col nearby Advanced Camp 4. My wish to continue was rejected by Miyazaki, of course, and I was assigned to go with the Sherpas to clear Camp 5 the next day. There I spent the night hungry and cold, with no food or enough clothes. I bet it was the worst night of my whole life.
>
> – Sato's diary

From the next day onwards the weather turned nasty, and we had reached the bottom of our food barrels, which in retrospect, showed that the success of one group on the summit had pushed the limit of our supplies. The gloom that settled on the team was a result of more than just the change in weather. Shifts in allegiance among members ran rampant, and the success of the summit was no longer straightforward. A celebration was unlikely to take place.

I had mixed emotions, feeling guilty that I had reached the summit and confident that I could climb higher in the future without supplemental oxygen. I was worried about the well-being of my team members while imagining myself pushing harder next time. In other words, I had to remind myself that to each her own. I knew I would be back to the Himalayas, and for me, that was most important. Thus, our Annapurna was over.

Yamazaki, Hirakawa and I had plans to continue our travels to the European mountains via Pakistan and Iran, returning to Japan in November. Our sightseeing was shortened by two months due to the pending conflict between India and Pakistan. I still managed an adventurous trip when enough money and tickets, from my husband, arrived via a co-worker who had stopped in Kathmandu on her own travels. She timed her short visit with me to coincide with the end of the Annapurna expedition. This gift allowed me to travel to Europe and then return to Japan on the Trans-Siberian Railway from Moscow and across the Soviet Union. My husband's words of encouragement scrawled in a note handed to me by my friend were enough to further enhance my mountain dreams: "Have our house, have the debt. Moving in there in August. Aim for 8000er next."

I married the right man for me.

Aftermath

Part of our team's commitment to climbing Annapurna III was to publish a book under the aegis of the Ladies Climbing Club. When the book came to print, entitled *Annapurna: Women's Battle*, it caused trouble in climbers' circles. Complaints were made that the story was written in too direct of a manner, that the realities of the trip were too stark for the reader. At that time, mountaineering reports were transcribed in a poetic fashion, with flowery phrases like, "success from the unimpaired teamwork of all," or "caring for each other, to the point of success," "equivalent effort from all of us got us there." There was never any mention of the unkinder side of human behaviour. Our book stood out because it shared the feelings of team members when things failed to go in the direction they had envisioned. Much to the dismay of readers, we put our honest experiences on paper; we wrote about what people said and how they felt.

Over the years, I had heard many male-only expeditions tolerate unfriendly incidents, like someone having his teeth broken because he was hit by a teammate, a climber stamping his crampon-clad foot on another climber in rage, or loud verbal arguments between leader and team members dispatched over the radio. Yet, when the trip summaries were published, not a word of such stories was written. I find there is a vanity to that kind of presentation. It saddened me because a lot of male Japanese climbers, like Naomi Uemura, endured cultural doubt about their mountain endeavours and departed on expeditions as lone wolves. I felt that their stories were never fairly represented.

When I finally returned home from Annapurna III and reflected on the expedition, there were times I wanted to ignore the dynamics that unfolded amongst team members, to the point of not wanting to see certain people. Time was the healer, as it often is, and I chose to move forwards. I recognized that the variety of experiences I had on that expedition, positive and negative, were a treasure to behold and that without them, my later Himalayan climbing – Mount Everest, in particular – would never have transpired.

A dozen stories would be told if a dozen people were to experience the exact same event, just because each individual's interpretation of the experience would be different. In the case of Annapurna III, mine was simply one story of nine, which might or might not correlate with my teammates', but it was right to me.

As assistant leader on the Annapurna III team, I wanted to be seen as a good person, one who pleased both leader and team members, a trait that likely originated from my childhood. A social teaching that was deeply rooted in me when I was young was to be a good girl and do no wrong, so no one could accuse me of poor behaviour. This, in addition to the Japanese tendency to not be different from other people, made it difficult to stand by tough choices that were required on the mountain. It was unusual enough to be a female climber in that era of yesteryear, let alone to make a stand in front of your friends that would possibly upset them. Today, young people are encouraged to be unique, but in my day, we were strictly advised that being different was abnormal. Whether one belief is more correct than the other, I cannot comment, but what I do know (and it was the most crucial thing I learned from Annapurna) is that the old way failed me. Behaving as a social butterfly does not work in mountaineering – one must be clear with others; there is no time for mixed messages. Essentially, a person must be able to voice her opinion without worrying about criticism. To realize that for the first time at age thirty was eye-opening for me, and it changed my life thereafter. Once more, the mountains were my teacher.

At the time of our Annapurna climb, it was customary in Japanese mountaineering society for the successful liaison officers of an expedition to be invited to visit Japan afterwards. So it was with Mr. Gopal. Since he had lived short-term in Japan in the past, Mr. Gopal asked if his son could step in for him. We agreed, of course. The result was young Basanta, twelve years old, being admitted to Higashi-Nakano Secondary School in the district of Tokyo where Miyazaki lived before she was married. Basanta boarded with her, and she offered to finance the boy's entire stay. Miyazaki was also made guarantor of Basanta, a role that I also helped fulfill when a substitute was needed. Mr. Gopal's son practically became Japanese. He was a bright boy and such a hard worker that he was offered a scholarship from the Japanese Ministry of Education. In his post-secondary years, he returned to Nepal to study medicine at Kathmandu University, and then he revisited Japan to continue his studies at Hiroshima University. The young boy we took under our wing became a prominent brain surgeon in Nepal, a truly unforeseen additional success of the Japanese women's Annapurna climb.

Before Miyazaki passed away in April 2015, Basanta arrived on short notice to say goodbye, but he arrived too late. Miyazaki-*mama*, his honoured name for her, had died.

That fall, he also attended a fortieth-anniversary event for the Japanese Women's Everest Expedition in Kathmandu. His arrival there, straight from the airport on his return from a medical conference in Italy, kindly demonstrated his ongoing appreciation for the Japanese women's climbing effort.

Sadly, our well-respected Mr. Gopal died in a motorcycle accident in his fifties. His son certainly fills a gap there and helps the memory of our beloved joker live on.

Mount Everest Route Map, Japan Women's Everest Expedition, 1975
COURTESY OF TABEI KIKAKU/ LADIES CLIMBING CLUB

CHAPTER 4

Mount Everest

Sometimes, larger-than-life decisions are made in the strangest places. For me, Mount Everest was decided upon in a last-minute conversation with Miyazaki before catching the midnight train to Kawagoe. We had stayed late in the city to finish work on our Annapurna book. "Next one is Everest," she said, suddenly. I had to agree, as I had been considering the same objective since our trip to Nepal. My only stipulation was that she be the team leader. Happy that Miyazaki and I were in accord about a future expedition, I rode the train home that night curiously excited.

November 1970

A group from the Ladies Climbing Club were ready to consider which of the 8000-metre peaks should be our next goal. I had Everest in mind, largely due to having met Captain Kohli on my team's return trip from Annapurna III. Kohli was the expedition leader of India's successful ascents of Annapurna III and Everest. He welcomed us into his New Delhi home to show us a movie about his 1965 Everest expedition. Once I saw the route up to the summit from the South Col in the film, I felt for the first time that the mountain was climbable by women. In that moment, I was determined that Everest would be next. I kept the thought to myself until Miyazaki voiced her opinion that night at the train station.

I had to tread with care. Many of the Ladies Climbing Club members may have wanted to climb Everest, but I felt it prudent to discuss and compare it with other potential 8000-metre peaks to decide what was best for everyone. I wanted our goal to be one that our team chose to climb, not one that was dictated by me. Also, the club itself was on the verge of collapse and we needed it to regain strength before moving forward.

We had established the Ladies Climbing Club in 1969 as part of the requirement to climb in the Himalayas, when Annapurna III was first on our list. Strain on the club began before we even left for that expedition. Once on the mountain, certain decision making about the summit assault left some members of the team angry and upset. Disappointment ran deep as women had left their jobs and families for what they thought to be a sure thing: reaching the top of Annapurna III. The aftermath, in combination with the fact that most club members were in their twenties and thirties, caused the club to dissolve. Some members disbanded to return to jobs and earn a living, some for marriage and to have children. By the time we were seriously discussing the next 8000-metre peak, there were five of us left, and not all five were enthused about another large-scale expedition. If Everest was on the table, we had our work cut out for us.

First, money was an issue. "No more Himalayas," declared Yamazaki, tired of asking for expedition donations for something as basic as candles. As we compared the scale of Everest with Annapurna in actual size and monetary commitment, she simply said, "I'm out." We were sad to see her go, but we managed to re-establish a positive outlook and conclude that each member would bring to the next meeting her idea of the most suitable 8000-metre peak to climb.

I knew there existed a general difference between the power output of men and women. I learned this earlier when I climbed with the Ryoho Climbing Club. It was obvious that my speed in walking, running or hiking could not compare to a man's, and I had also observed a difference in strength between mine and a man's when hammering in pitons or executing explosive moves in technical climbing. It made sense to me that men and women competed separately in the Olympics, but in the mountaineering environment there is no separation. Mother Nature, for example, shows no mercy in the way of, "Oh, it's a women's party for Everest this year, all right, I will ease the degree of wind for them." We had to achieve our goals under the same conditions as men. In the early days of my mountaineering, it was considered impossible for women climbers to succeed at 8000 metres, where available oxygen is two-thirds less than normal, and speed and muscle power are in constant demand. While I found that way of thinking absurd, my drive was not to prove it wrong so much as it was to climb in a new place and experience the beauty and challenge of big mountains. Everest fit my ideals.

We met again to finally decide upon an appropriate all-women's climb. The peaks presented were Annapurna I (8091 metres), Manaslu (8156 metres) and Everest (8848 metres). Of course, Everest stood out for its status as the highest mountain in the world and a once-in-a-lifetime pursuit. It was also foremost in our minds since the Japanese Alpine Club's successful Everest expedition in 1970, the same year we summitted Annapurna III.

I originally became a member of the Japanese Alpine Club to facilitate my first trip to the Himalayas. It was in planning this second expedition that my true appreciation for the club developed. I cherished the stories and reports (especially those from the club's 1970 Everest expedition), books and Himalayan experiences that members were willing to share, and I would have been lost without them. It seemed all factors began to line up: Miyazaki's and my wish to climb Everest, the specific climbing route seen on film at Kohli's home, and the extent of mountain informa-tion available to us. The decision was unanimous – next would be Everest. Instead of a collection of random female climbers, the team would be one cohesive group that accepted Miyazaki as leader and me as assistant leader. I felt confident that with this format, we would succeed.

Masanobu was in support of Everest, but he suggested an additional step to the plan – for me to consider having a baby first. He disliked the idea of being without his own family while waiting alone for me to return from such a significant trip. Although I shared his desire to have a child, I was unsure that I could have a baby at the snap of my fingers. But I did. In March 1971, a few months after we had submitted our application to the Nepali government for the Japanese Women's Everest Expedition, I became pregnant. Not until fourteen weeks later did I realize it, though, when I was climbing one day and noticed that I felt heavier than usual.

Everest has long been highly sought after by climbers from all over the world. Although numbers on the mountain have increased since the 1970s, limits to how many expeditions can be there at once have always been in place. When we applied for our permit, permission for 1972 and 1973 expeditions had already been issued, and seven countries were in competition for 1974. The Nepali government offered us permission for 1974, but for another peak. We declined and decided to wait for Everest.

Meanwhile, we had a mountaineering team to build. Our approach was simple: visit climbing clubs with female members and ask them if they were interested in going to the Himalayas with us. On weekends, we extended our search to Ueno and Shinjuku train stations, both in downtown Tokyo, where people were lined up in droves, heading to various climbing and hiking areas across Japan. We chatted up the women climbers and spoke to them about Everest. A common response was: "Wow! Himalayas! I would love to go, even just to see Everest." Then, "But … I don't have that much skill, or time, or money…," and so on. I found it difficult to hear people crush their dreams with the word "but." My experience on Annapurna was that strong will, determination and the ability to problem solve in dire situations played a more critical role than physical ability when climbing in the Himalayas. We could help train a person to be a better climber, but we were unable to generate her willpower. An adamant desire to be part of Women on Everest was a critical factor in candidates being chosen for our team.

From a weather perspective, opportunities to climb the high mountains in Nepal are limited. Most expeditions base their timing on one of two eight-week periods in the year, April to May in the pre-monsoon spring, and October to November in the post-monsoon fall. Other than that, the months are dominated by monsoon season when jet streams of 100 to 150 kilometres per hour often rage at the top of Everest, offering no chance at all for a human to stand on its summit. But in May and October the wind is tamed to some degree, and the climbers ascend.

Records from previous trips showed that May 5 to 15 had consistently been the golden opportunity for crystal-clear days, so we made a long-term plan for a summit assault based on that time frame for 1975. We printed a specific calendar that addressed the four years leading up to that date and began to fill in the blanks. Members of the Ladies Climbing Club were divided into six groups, with each group responsible for researching climbing parties from one of six countries that had previously climbed Everest (1953, United Kingdom; 1956, Switzerland; 1960, China;

1963, United States; 1965 India; 1970, Japan). We needed facts: camp locations, climbing techniques and equipment used, number of team members, knowledge about the Sherpa people and where to hire them, and information on the roles and actions of each individual climber. Six months later, we were ready to present these details at subsequent club meetings.

In August 1972, we received official authorization from the Nepali government to climb Mount Everest. The news headline, "Permission Given for Japanese Women's Everest," spread and became the incentive we needed to attract more interest from other female climbers. The ten members we had stalled at prior to the go-ahead from authorities increased to as many as eighteen serious contenders. In the end, we were a team of fourteen women, plus a doctor, a number that was established far closer to the trip than in the early stages of planning.

With Everest 1975 tangible, we shifted gears and ramped up our focus on how to tackle the mountain. Attention to this complicated matter consumed us for most of the following year. In my combined role as expedition assistant leader and climbing leader, I had to determine the overall number of climbers needed for a team to reach the summit. That number would, in turn, help us establish the amount of resources, like food and equipment, required for the entire trip. I decided on fifteen members, including our expedition leader and a team of three for the final summit assault. From this, we created a blueprint of necessities for the last camp below the summit (Camp 6, at 8500 metres), in terms of supplementary oxygen, food, team and individual equipment, and number of Sherpas and porters. We traced and expanded these particulars every step of the way back down to Base Camp in order to precisely calculate the overall required amounts for every stage of the climb. The excessive number of meetings this entailed exhausted us.

Part of my personal long-term Everest plan came to fruition on February 18, 1972, when I gave birth to my daughter, Noriko. Although my intention was to continue to work, I left my editing position of ten years at the Physical Society of Japan due to new family logistics and commute times. We lived in a small home in Kawagoe, about an hour from Tokyo. Childcare was unavailable in our rural area, so I decided to stay home full time with my daughter. I supposed I had already learned what I could from a decade of employment and that it was unlikely I would progress much from that job anyway. I was concerned about our financial state as our income had been cut in half with me at home. This sparked the idea of instructing *koto*, which I still cherished. In my youth, I had to choose between the worlds of traditional Japanese art, forcing me to concentrate only on music, or mountain climbing. When Noriko was born, I decided to embrace both the harp and climbing as my pastimes. Optimistically, I let that new stage of my life unfold on its own in terms of music and climbing. Six months into motherhood, when permission for Everest 1975 was granted, I was confident that I would be ready for the expedition, and that my daughter (at three) would be fine, too.

JAPANESE WOMEN'S EVEREST EXPEDITION 1975 TEAM MEMBERS

Hisano, Eiko, 42	Leader
Tabei, Junko, 35	Assistant Leader and Climbing Leader
Manita, Michiko, 33	Management/Oxygen
Nasu, Fumie, 33	Public Relations / Equipment (Group)
Watanabe, Yuriko, 32	Public Relations / Treasurer
Naganuma, Masako, 27	Packaging and Transportation / Equipment (Radio)
Taneya, Yumi, 26	Equipment (Climbing Gear)
Kitamura, Setsuko, 26	Public Relations
Fujiwara, Sumiko, 26	Packaging and Transportation
Shioura, Reiko, 29	Equipment (Personal)
Arayama, Fumiko, 25	Equipment (Group)
Naka, Sachiko, 27	Equipment (Climbing Gear)
Mihara, Yoko, 34	Food Planning
Hirashima, Teruyo, 27	Food Planning
Sakaguchi, Dr. Masako, 29	Medical Doctor

Chaos

A thriving baby, a roster of teammates, approval to climb Everest – my road to the world's highest peak was concrete. Similarly, Miyazaki's life had evolved to new levels. She married in 1972, her surname changing to Hisano, and moved away to Nara, 600 kilometres from Tokyo. Although

I was concerned about the distance between us and the effect that would have on planning the expedition, her marriage became an inspiration among the single women of our club. If a thirty-nine-year-old mountain woman could find a husband, there was hope for them all. As for the distance, I figured the *Shinkansen* (bullet train) would help, as would the telephone, which had only just become prevalent with the general public. In addition, I foolishly thought, there was the abundance of free time I would have with my unemployment and being at home full time.

Unbeknownst to me, the crazy days had barely begun. I had to ask for club meetings to be held in the evenings and only when my husband was not working overtime, which was rare. Having finished bathing Noriko, preparing supper and readying the house for bedtime, I would rush out the door when I heard Masanobu's car pull up, hand him our daughter, tighten the grip on my bag of Everest documents tucked under my arm, and run to the train station for the hour-long commute to Tokyo.

As assistant leader, I was to attend all expedition meetings, including those about food preparation and equipment. I needed my husband's help to attend each meeting, and thankfully he was behind me every step of the way. He hated when I made the excuse of having a child at home or a family to care for in order to cut short or miss a meeting. He insisted that everybody should commit equally, regardless of their situation. Repeatedly, he sent me off with assurance: "Trust me, Noriko is fine. She adapts when you aren't with her." It was hard to let go of my role as mother after spending most days with my daughter. Sometimes it was hard to imagine her being fine without me. Yet, when I returned home, often on the last train of the night, and quietly opened the door, entering on tiptoe so as not to wake my sound-sensitive child, Noriko was peacefully asleep.

The tidiness of the house was another matter. I realized it was difficult for Masanobu to take care of such a young baby after his own full day of work. To ease his load, I prepared as much as possible for the evening routine before I left. But there were nights when I arrived home to the mess of dirty dishes, leftover food and used diapers dispersed all over the place, and my appreciation for his support would suddenly turn to anger. "What's this?" I would shout in my head, "Don't you have hands and feet?" I could feel the sweep of a mother's worry crush the last few thoughts I was still processing from the meeting about sponsorship or team members or supplies. Although I would never forfeit Everest, I felt pulled in the two directions of mountains and motherhood.

However, with time, I accepted that there was more to parenthood than tidying up. While a clean room might have been my priority, it was less so for my husband. I had to learn that even though I had diligently worked to make the evening run smoothly for my family in my absence, there was no ill intention on Masanobu's behalf in leaving a mess. He was tired, and he fell asleep with Noriko. No harm done. Slowly, I began to recognize that Masanobu's strength was his open mind and big heart. Still, on occasion, I had to acknowledge the feelings of frustration that managed to sneak in between us like the wind. To his credit, he continued to try, and as the demand for expedition meetings increased, and hence, my departures at night, so did Masanobu's attention to chores. Dishes were washed and rice was ready in the cooker for me to switch on for a late dinner. I welcomed this change in him and continued to appreciate his efforts in support of Everest, and I vowed to do my best with running the house whenever I was home.

As our partnership strengthened, Masanobu also become bolder in investments. With a real-estate plan in mind, he asked that I temporarily sign over to him my severance pay from work. I had originally intended for this source of income to be a part of my Everest fund, but I agreed based on his words, "You will go to Everest no matter what." He then secured a bank loan and bought a strip of land near the Minami Ski Hill in Niigata in the northwest part of the main island of Japan. Much later, we would sell that land to purchase a lodge in Numajiri, near the Bandai mountains. At the time of the expedition, though, he confidently followed through with his investment idea, despite our employment revenue having been reduced when Noriko was born, and the expense of train travel to meetings and phone bills to cover my high volume of communication. Our pile of debt grew as my preparation for Everest progressed – I literally had two mountains to climb.

I was not the only one who struggled with the overwhelming demands of life that revolved around Everest. When Hisano (nee Miyazaki) visited Tokyo, which she did for important expedition meetings, I received a few phone calls from her husband in the middle of the night, and he was as frantic as I felt. The same chaos that had seeped into my home was shared with everyone on the team. The number of phone calls I had to manage, for example, was too much. I would begin laundry first thing in the morning and barely finish hanging it to dry by late afternoon due to incessant phone conversations. In the evening, the situation would escalate: the food I cooked prior to leaving for a meeting would often burn because I was stuck on the phone; in turn, this would create an added mess to clean up, with Masanobu caught in the middle. Even my mother, who had come to visit from my distant hometown of Miharu, left sooner than planned in order to find solace from the onslaught of calls. Eventually, the phone found its place at the back entrance of the house with cushions to cover its unnerving ring so as to not wake up Noriko. In the chilly winter nights when I was engaged in a long conversation, Masanobu would come to me and place a blanket or down jacket over my shoulders as I dissected the world of big-mountain climbing from a chair. After a year of this, when Noriko was two and half, she said, "Mom, isn't Everest hard work?"

It hit me how much my family supported my Everest dream when one time I watched my husband walk towards the house. He carried a shopping bag in his arm that overflowed with longs stalks of green onions, and our daughter on his back tucked in a *nenneko*, a traditional puffy winter jacket designed to hold a baby. At other times, he would wrap Noriko in a blanket and drive in circles on local roads until she fell asleep. He would do this to accommodate Everest meetings in our home while keeping our child peaceful.

Masanobu helped keep the chaos at bay, and I was lucky to have found a husband like him.

Frustration

Generally, the team met every other weekend from Saturday to Sunday. Members would travel far distances overnight by train on a Friday with sleeping bags at the ready. Finding locations for these weekend meetings was not easy, as we tried to incorporate some level of physical training into the agenda. We often invited climbers who had experience on 8000-metre peaks to share their stories. We would cook and sample foods that could work well as part of a high-altitude menu, and we woke at 4 a.m. on Sundays for a run, workout and basketball game. By 9 a.m. meetings would resume with presentations and discussions of trip details. Frustrations, however, quickly mounted amongst the younger new members of the Ladies Climbing Club. They shared a common feeling of doubt based on the disproportionate amount of time spent discussing equipment, supplemental oxygen and food supplies rather than with actual climbing.

Unfortunately, annoyances began to run deep. Some women were skilled at taking notes or organizing files of information while others were not, and this bothered people. We talked about these administrative tasks countless times to no avail, and conversations on the way home after these weekends escalated. I began to feel hollow inside and was asking myself why we were so disconnected as a team. I questioned if it was because Everest was not their dream after all. I suddenly felt irritated at that possible truth. I was also hurt by accusations that were directed right at Hisano and me, harsh words that were spoken without thought. Comments like, "Looking at past grand-scale expeditions, the leaders and assistant leaders usually worked with all their might for the team, almost abandoning all other responsibilities for the couple of years prior to the actual trip. The leaders in this team are too lazy, and that's why we lack sponsorship."

It made my heart sink.

I understood the importance of socializing with potential sponsors, of having a couple of drinks with them to share stories of our endeavour. An evening like that was critical to receiving funding for the expedition, and to decline an appearance could be detrimental to the team. Yet I was also stretched to my limit by attending the mandatory club meetings. When I excused myself from a sponsors meeting, having received an invitation at short notice, I was met with unsympathetic support. "In other climbing parties, progression of a trip was dependent on the assistant leader's positive attitude. Perhaps we need an assistant leader who doesn't have children." This argument was presented to me several times, and it caused turmoil in my mind. When Noriko was born, I had decided not to use daycare because I wanted to raise her myself, at least until I left for Everest. I knew more effort was required for a married woman with a family to pursue an expedition of this grandeur. I worked relentlessly to establish a solid home life for my daughter while remaining 100 per cent committed to the team. I had to ask, would a single person devote every aspect of their life to this expedition? If yes, then I would not only give up my position as assistant leader, I would step down from the team.

When I shared my concerns with Hisano, she wasted no time in fixing the situation. She immediately travelled six hours from Nara to Tokyo and spent two days speaking with team members. In an unusually intense tone for Hisano, she clearly spelled out her wishes: "With few exceptions, everybody has family and a job, so it would be natural to say it isn't feasible to concentrate all of one's attention only on Everest. And the members who live farther away take more time and pay higher costs than the ones who live in Tokyo just to attend the meetings. If this is a big problem, the members who complain about these conditions are welcome to make a new climbing party, choose a new leader and go their own way."

Hisano's intervention kick-started me as well. I should not have been the one to complain about travel, living in relatively nearby Kawagoe. In addition, my family had made sacrifices to support me thus far; I was unwilling to waste their contributions to my goal. More so, what about my own passion for climbing Everest? I could not let that die. If other members failed to trust Hisano and me as leaders, then I would dismiss them – they were welcome to run their own expedition.

I remained strong-willed about Everest, but tears of doubt fell down my cheeks at night. In those moments, I would turn to my little girl and hold her sleepy warm hands and exclaim in my heart, "Mom will fight! Get going, Junko!"

In February 1974, one year before departure to the Himalayas, we held a winter training camp at Gaki-dake. On a snowy day, we broke trail in knee-deep powder the entire way from the train station to the mountain's summit. There, I finally witnessed what the team had to offer: thirteen women setting a solid pace uphill with no complaints. A renewed strength bubbled up and filled my entire body, convincing me that, yes, we would achieve our goal on Everest. I often drew from the feeling of that day to get us to the summit.

However, no sooner would I feel confident in our team than another argument would develop. A repeated subject for discussion at our on-going meetings was how to save money and resources. For instance, based on a person drinking 300 millilitres at a time, and to save fuel from heating more than the allotted amount, we aimed to use cups sized at that exact measurement. As minor as these details seemed, we had to scrutinize them from all angles because once on the mountain, every facet of planning would count. Still, these conversations remained triggers for dispute. "We wouldn't have to talk like this if we had good sponsors," was the common rebuttal. The constant conflict of deciding whether or not to seek sponsorship was a major cause of headache.

We were torn between the desire to remain financially independent as an expedition and having the advantage of monetary support to cover expenses. We neither preferred external pressure to perform successfully on the mountain, nor, as Miyazaki stated, someone else footing the bill for us to have fun in the mountains. Yet, the outlay was simply too high. Multiple times I recalculated how much it would cost for fifteen women to climb Mount Everest. The answer was always the same: 60,000,000 yen, which equated to 4,000,000 yen per person, a small fortune. Granted, this included everything from air tickets to Duralumin ladders for the icefalls to the 300-millilitre cups we needed, but in Japan, it was equivalent to the cost of having a house built. None of us could afford such a price. It was clear we needed financial assistance.

We approached major Japanese corporations for donations, but the country was in recession from the 1973 oil crisis, and available funds were limited. It was a period of rampant rumours about jumps in gasoline prices and toilet paper disappearing from store shelves; people lived in fear of running out of basic supplies. Women stood in endless lines at grocery stores to ensure that they could provide food for their families. Not many businesses were in favour of an all-female team on Everest. It was considered unrealistic, unproductive and most of all, detrimental to our families. "Raise your children and keep your family tight rather than do something like this," potential sponsors said. I quickly realized that past success on Annapurna III was not enough to draw from in terms of being respected as an international mountaineer. I was disappointed in the disdain my teammates and I experienced as we reached out for support for our trip.

Finally, a phone call from a correspondent at the national newspaper *The Yomiuri Shimbun* finally suggested we were making headway. Having heard of our women's Everest team, the paper's journalists were interested in an interview. Shortly after, two reporters attended one of our weekend sessions at Okutama. They could not have appeared any more different from each other. Yoshinobu Emoto easily looked the part of a mountaineer and had been a member of a mountaineering club in university. He was fit and agile. Setsuko Kitamura, a young woman fresh from university, appeared to have no previous relationship with the mountains whatsoever, and she looked like a big-city fashion model. We were quick to judge her as an unlikely candidate for a reporter on a mountaineering expedition such as ours, and we were adamant in thinking she was more suited as a soap opera star than a climber, at least until I received a call from her three days after we met.

"I'm Kitamura who visited your club the other day," she said. "I know I'm asking abruptly, but please take me in as a member for Everest." At our meeting, she was relieved to see that none of the team members looked like superwoman with bulging muscles but instead were ordinary ladies with normal jobs like office workers, housewives and school teachers. She was so impressed by how all of us were throwing our passion into this non-profitable idea of climbing Everest that she begged to be a part of it. She explained that with her past work experience in mountain rescue in the Northern Alps of Japan, she, in fact, loved the mountains as much as I did. "Please, take me in," she said.

I, the seeker of strong will in people, could not deny Kitamura. I recalled her fashionable presence that seemed unsuited for the mountains but was intrigued by her determination. Unable to say no on the phone, I invited her to my home to discuss the possibility. After spending time with her, chatting in my living room while we played with my daughter at our side, my intuition buzzed: "This woman is a strong one. She would be useful to the team."

Shortly afterwards, we received the significant break we needed. *The Yomiuri Shimbun*, in conjunction with its branch of Nippon Television Network Corporation, was willing to sponsor us. "We're impressed by your indefatigable will, despite desperately scarce resources and funding, and that's the very reason we'd like to support you." Well, how about that?

The power of the media was not to be underestimated, a lesson that was evident with our Everest expedition. Immediately after the news of our sponsorship spread, the corporations that were reluctant to support us in the first place began to make donations. The Ministry of Heritage and Education offered use of its name as a sponsor, which provided a tone of authority to the expedition. A local transportation company organized space for us to store our expedition equipment and packaged supplies. We were shocked by how in place everything felt as support for the climb grew.

The number of women who had first joined the team dwindled due to a few people's disappointment with the burden of the unexpected desk work. It was obvious they were only interested in the expedition for the Everest name and were unable to commit to all aspects of trip preparation. No problem, we let them go. In the end, we were a team of fourteen women plus a female doctor, who joined in 1974. With this consolidated party of women, any lingering doubts about our dream dissipated, and our meetings became highly active and realistic.

The list of the Japanese Women's Everest Expedition official team members was announced in October 1974, four months before we departed for Nepal. Following that, the remaining task was to actually pull together the equipment and supplies we needed according to our previous two years of trip research. Simply put, the crazy days were on the rise.

Pack and Go

I knew The Japanese Mount Everest Expedition 1970 was in a different league than our trip in terms of scale (thirty-five team members versus our fifteen) and budget (their 100,000,000 yen to our original estimate of 60,000,000), but I soon realized that any big-mountain expedition cost a significant amount of money, regardless of party size. To offset our expenses in any way possible, we drew from numerous resources that were already part of our regular life. We saw no need for tables and chairs; we planned to use boxes from loads being carried up and down the mountain. We based most meals on the ingredients of miso and soy sauce, which we all had plenty of at home. One of our proudest innovations was transforming car covers, which are windproof, into the outer layer of gloves. Our creative thinking reduced trip expenses to 43,000,000 yen.

Still, half of our load consisted of the six tons of food we brought from Japan. We made all efforts to reduce weight, one gram at a time; we stripped every item of its wrapping, we dried and powdered heavier condiments (the necessary miso and soya sauce), and we transferred items into light-weight plastic containers. Even the cardboard centres (at two grams each) of toilet paper rolls were discarded, and the paper alone was carried in plastic bags that also doubled as cushioning in our packs.

By October our supplies were ready for a final inventory. We camped for a week at the Yamato Transportation warehouse to sort everything into very precise 30-kilogram packages. When our job was complete, we celebrated with a soak in a nearby *sento* (public bath). We must have been a sight, a group of giddy women with months of preparation behind us and Everest in our future. From onlookers, it was assumed we were part of a prevailing youth program that supported movement from the countryside to Tokyo for employment. We laughed when asked if we were in the city for work. "Yes, something like that," we replied, bursting into more laughter once we stepped away from the front desk. As I smiled at the scene around me, I was flooded with a feeling of anticipation – the next time I would open those boxes that we had so carefully organized would be in Nepal.

Supplies were shipped from Yokohama to Calcutta, India, where they would pass through customs and then be transported overland to Nepal. I volunteered to oversee this process, along with fellow climber Yumi Taneya. The two of us left Japan in December 1974, one month ahead of the rest of the team, in order to keep track of the countless and valuable boxes that were key to our expedition.

In Japan, families have a special celebration, called 753, for their child's third, fifth and seventh years of life. Prior to my departure in December, my husband and I chose to commemorate Noriko's first 753, on November 15, 1974. Noriko was not quite three at the time, but with the "just in case" mindset I had in leaving for Everest, I felt the need to honour my daughter's age. For all I knew, it could have been my last chance to do so. This was how I began to compartmentalize thoughts when a big climb was on the forefront – what if...? Every day, I considered what would happen if I failed to return from Everest. As I walked by kindergartens and elementary schools, I wondered if I would be present for Noriko's first-day ceremony for school. I began to record conversations between us, Noriko and me, and her favourite songs and stories that we shared at bedtime. I did all I could to show my daughter that I loved her.

I would be gone from home for at least five months. Masanobu and Noriko were to live with my sister Fuchi's family while I was away. The act of moving Noriko's belongings – clothes, dresser, tricycle, dolls – to her aunt's house added to the hectic final weeks of preparation, and I caught myself a few times wondering how much simpler it would be for a single woman with no children to organize herself for a trip of this magnitude. Then Masanobu stepped in: "Don't worry about us. Trust me to provide a good life here in Japan. Focus only on yourself and your team; complete your mission from your heart without regret." His words allowed me to move forward.

Family support extended beyond my husband. Fuchi's seventy-eight-year-old mother-in-law, who also lived with my sister, said, "We'll look after Nori-*chan*. Go to Everest, don't be worried." Like the thaw of snow in springtime, her assurance warmed my heart. I needed this kind of encouragement to reassure me that everything would be all right. Fuchi was exceptionally helpful. Although we shared different interests and activities, and she was not a mountain person, she supported my endeavours and welcomed Masanobu and Noriko. It must have been difficult for her to see me leave my little girl behind, yet she did everything she could to make it the best for Noriko, even with three sons to care for. Funny enough, after Everest, I heard Noriko say, "Hey, Mom, is *meshi* ready yet?" *Meshi* (meal) is a word used only by men. Clearly, she had been well looked after by her older boy cousins in my absence.

Finally, my departure date arrived. On December 22, 1974, I bid farewell to the closest people in my life. Despite my repeated practice with Noriko of me saying, "Hey, Noriko, I'm going now," and her reply of "Go ahead, Mom," when the actual day came, she cried and screamed on the spot.

"Don't leave, Mom," she pleaded, clinging to me. When I pulled away, I dared not look back as I walked to the gate, my daughter's cry trailing behind. Her tiny voice filled my head for days after I left Japan.

CHAPTER 5

To the Top of the World

After long months of preparation, arrival in India felt abrupt. The country's humid tropical air hit us with gusto and the mixed smell of rotten fish and human sweat drowned our nasal passages. Our T-shirts were soaked in minutes and dragged at our skin, discomfort setting in like a monsoon. Welcome to Calcutta.

Taneya and I were the first members of the expedition team to leave Japan. We had slightly more than a month to organize everything before the main party would meet us farther afield in Nepal. As two Japanese women alone at night in Calcutta, we were on full alert, not to be mistaken as vulnerable tourists. As we stepped from the airport with our valuables hung around our necks and hands clutched to the handles of our bags in thief-proof fashion, we were ready for the onslaught of locals. "Taxi, taxi," the drivers solicited, and we prepared ourselves for any potential scams. Some taxi drivers liked to trick foreigners with excessive fares. I remembered this from my previous visit and understood that part of reaching Everest was surviving the city's mayhem.

Bribery seemed second nature in India. Even public servants used it as a starting point in conversation, looking to receive anything from a pen to tobacco. Upon arrival, we answered the constant pleas by saying "we have none" and passing the locals by with a pleasant smile. As climbers, we refused to succumb to bribery, and in later years, I still never gave in to it while negotiating costs to climb mountains in China. I have heard people whisper behind my back that as women, we were second rate because of our inflexibility with bribes. To me, it was a matter of principle. In the event of an emergency, however, I would concede and exchange a bottle of whisky for a seat onboard a plane or helicopter.

I had visited Calcutta on the way to Annapurna III, and my familiarity with the embassy and required documentation for expedition travel helped us efficiently complete the necessary jobs this time around. An unexpected bonus was that the employees from the transportation company that we hired for Annapurna remembered us. For Everest, they miraculously arranged four trucks to transport our 11 tons of equipment to Nepal – all organized on schedule and before the Christmas holidays, with no bribery required. On January 1, New Year's Day, 1975, we waved goodbye to the convoy packed full of our boxes and covered in tarps, heading towards Himalayan soil. Taneya and I then flew to Kathmandu, reserved a room in a small hotel, ate a quick meal and collapsed into bed. Relief and exhaustion flooded in – the expedition was truly under way.

We had a taste of home in Kathmandu as our team's communication headquarters was based at the house of Takashi Miyahara, a Japanese man who lived there and ran his own tourism business in Nepal. Amongst a mound of envelopes that had already arrived for us was a letter from my husband. He told me that Noriko's tears quickly ceased at the airport after I had stepped on the plane and that she had settled into life with my sister's family, playful as usual. She even referred to my sister as Mom. "No worries at all," he wrote. As I read those words, the lump of emotion that had been stuck in my throat since the moment I left Haneda Airport in Tokyo finally dissolved. My daughter was in good hands and happy, and my mind could be at rest. I was suddenly able to fully focus on the task of Everest. Another rush of relief washed over me.

Miyahara's home office was on the main street in Kathmandu, which allowed us easy access to everywhere in the city. The backyard was large, providing us with enough space to store our load of supplies. Miyahara also had a guesthouse in the back, equipped with a kitchen and room for a dozen guests. Taneya and I shared accommodation with the other ten lodgers, but our host assured us we would have the entire house to ourselves when the rest of the team arrived.

The weeks to come were occupied with intense groundwork, two of the main tasks being to obtain 4 tons of local food and fuel, and to prepare tobacco and local currency to pay porters and Sherpas. We also had

to unload all the boxes that arrived from Japan via Calcutta and sort
and repack the countless items necessary for Base Camp, an exercise
in craziness. And there was still the most important duty to address:
the selection of Sherpas. A liaison officer was assigned to our team by
the Nepali government, but the sirdar and other Sherpas could be requested in advance by the expedition party. Selection would be based on
a Sherpa's experience with previous Japanese teams, physical strength,
personality and ability to speak English. Sirdars and Sherpas with good
reputations in the climbing world were quickly booked up, which made
hiring them fast enough one of the most critical undertakings for a successful expedition.

We strongly requested Lhakpa Tenzing as sirdar, since he had been on
several previous Everest expeditions and had summitted the mountain.
Instead, he was assigned the position of liaison officer despite not being
a government official. Apparently, there was a shortage of officials to
draw from that year due to events revolving around the coronation of
Nepal's King Birendra. We were satisfied with Lhakpa Tenzing as liaison
officer; his appointment showed that he was trusted by the government.
He appointed to the role of sirdar his brother-in-law, twenty-seven-year-
old Ang Tsering. At first, I was skeptical. He was far too young for such
a job, especially on Everest. Aside from a muscular build, his big smile
and innocent-looking face gave him the appearance of a happy-go-lucky
boy. The commands of the sirdar were to have absolute authority over the
Sherpa team; the group would have to respond to him without question.
I could hardly imagine this youthful lad delivering that kind of control.
In addition, there would be many Sherpas older than him, and his style
would have to be one of dignity. Furthermore, this was to be Ang Tsering's first experience as sirdar. The more I thought about it, the more my
doubts grew.

Nevertheless, with Lhakpa Tenzing as liaison officer and Ang Tsering
having to answer to him, we surmised it would all work out. Immediately, Ang Tsering produced excellent work and responded to our many
requests long before we even began the climb. He assigned a team of
Sherpas with no fuss, mostly choosing from his own relatives and Sherpa
clan, some of whom were from Kathmandu and others from Namche,
his home village.

The work day started early in Kathmandu. Bazaars opened at 5 a.m. while the city was still shrouded in a milky morning mist. Taneya and I usually woke at 4:30 to be ready to shop in the wee hours. It was difficult to buy items in large quantities due to short supply, so we would load ourselves up with 5 to 10 kilograms of goods, and then return the next day for more. In particular, fuel was an issue to obtain. There was a limited volume imported from India to Nepal, and the government controlled by permit how much, if any, was purchased. Thankfully, we were issued the necessary permit due to the nature of our expedition, but still, the regulated amount of fuel one could buy per day had us line up at the distribution station with an 18-litre container time and time again.

The total weight of trip supplies quickly increased as a result of our vigorous shopping in Kathmandu. The original 11 tons we had shipped from Japan became 15 tons in Nepal, which seemed ridiculous, but compared to previous Everest parties, it ranked as minimal. The 1973 Italian team was said to have had 80 tons of supplies, including individual tents for each climber and a carpet-laden floor for the team leader's tent. They enjoyed full-course meals on the mountain, allotted by a budget of roughly 300,000,000 yen – a lot of money at the time. The 1970 Japanese party spent one third that amount. And compared to those numbers, ours was a super-saving expedition at less than half the cost. The Sherpas, however, were leery of our minimalist approach. "That's it?" they repeatedly asked with a hint of worry in their voices.

It struck me in Kathmandu how important it would be to remain true to myself on this expedition. I had to make decisions based on the goal of the trip regardless of how some members might interpret a given situation. For example, one night, Taneya told me that a teammate had suggested to her that she decline travelling to India with me as part of the initial party to leave Japan. She argued that the extra work would exhaust Taneya before the climb even began. Conserving pre-trip energy had never occurred to me. Then I remembered when Manita said, "I envy you." She was referring to the fact that I would be paid for my duties in Kathmandu while being able to save my own money. Those two perspectives – a person saving energy for the climb and me saving money while working for the team – surprised me. I realized that the rest of the trip would be like this, that everyone would have different ideas and views on how and why things were done. I was determined from then on to not whine or worry over trivial matters. Instead, for Everest, I would focus on empowering my *tanden*, my gut strength.

"*Memsahib*, trouble!" Breathless, a Sherpa knocked on my door one morning. There was an unusual restlessness in the backyard. Wearing only a T-shirt as pajamas, I ran outside to see some of our boxes gone, torn away from the ropes that bound everything together. I immediately knew that a brand-new tent, among other items, had been stolen. My heart dropped – every piece of equipment had been bought with our hard-earned money and represented the amount of sweat we had put into our accomplishments so far.

It had only been the day before that we had removed the solid wooden frames from around the boxes in order to add to our recent purchases from Kathmandu. My guess was that whoever robbed us had patiently waited until the crates were dismantled, at which I felt nothing but anger. I was mostly mad at myself, though, for not having heard any disturbance in the night while sleeping close by the crime scene.

Shocked and upset, I asked the four Sherpas we had already hired in Kathmandu to take turns standing guard over our supplies each night until we left for Everest. With little choice, we bought a tent that was used by the 1973 Italian party. This reduced our capacity to one mess tent at Base Camp that would house as many as twenty-three of us at a time.

On January 30, the main party of our team arrived in Kathmandu, along with our assigned journalists. Exploding with excitement, Taneya and I welcomed them at the airport. While the two of us were dressed in dusty jeans and native Nepali wool shawls, running around in well-worn sneakers, our teammates stepped off the plane wearing the most fashionable attire. Pantalon suits, long skirts and fancy hats, one-piece dresses covered with floral designs – straight from the boutiques of Tokyo. In a flourish, the Japanese Women's Everest Expedition brought a big-city atmosphere directly to the tarmac. Travelling abroad was an extremely rare event, so my friends embraced the chance to go all out for the occasion. When the fragrance of their perfume struck me, I jokingly extended my hand from under my shawl and mumbled, "Madam, *paisa*?" suggesting a meagre donation of less than a rupee.

The guesthouse became lively once the entire team arrived. As the first women's expedition to Everest, we were invited to several parties held by government officials. As a result, when we left Kathmandu, we felt enriched and well-supported by the Nepali people. Our departure went in stages. The Sherpas and Nasu and Naganuma flew ahead to Lukla. Hirashima and Fujiwara remained in Kathmandu to safeguard the remaining boxes of gear until the last of thirteen flights was under way. Meanwhile, the main party of climbers left Kathmandu on February 9 by minibus for the 80-kilometre drive that preceded our hike, with camping along the way, to Lukla. This served as the first stage of altitude acclimatization. Day after day we climbed passes as high as 3500 metres and then descended to valley bottoms, passing through villages and pitching our tents on the outskirts wherever there was drinking water. As we put distance behind us, the fluctuations in elevation became more tolerable, and after twelve days, we reached Lukla. Poor Mihara had caught a cold, and a stubborn cough led her to be carried on a porter's back for part of the way.

Leader Gone

The team of journalists flew straight from Japan to Kathmandu to Lukla, and on February 21, the entire expedition was gathered together for the first time. There were twenty-two of us, fourteen women climbers, a female doctor and seven journalists. We celebrated with an official ceremony to greet one another and matched each Sherpa with the team member in his charge. This was common practice to help formalize the team and establish a general safety net, although Sherpas were not expected to remain solely with their partners at all times.

The airport in Lukla was unique. It was built on a slightly upward slope barely scraped out of the mountainside. The planes used the uphill to slow them down when they landed. To take off, they relied on the gravitational pull of the downslope to pick up speed and soar above the sudden space of the valley below. Our boxes were left piled high at the edge of this wild landing strip, alongside a deserted Pilatus Porter airplane (a model known for its short take-off and landing capabilities) that had experienced an unsuccessful arrival long ago. Although under a beautiful blue sky, the barrenness of the scene was apparent to me. We were amidst unforgiving terrain.

The work of nearly six hundred porters was needed to carry the 15 tons of equipment to Base Camp, plus a number of reliable yaks. Lukla itself was a village of very few houses, and thus we were apprehensive about finding the number of porters required. Yet, word of the women's team had spread from our Sherpas, who had arrived in advance, and an influx of helpers presented itself, some from villages as far away as a two- to three-day walk.

A porter's job was not only pursued to earn money but also for the rare chance to interact with other cultures, and our women-only Everest expedition added even more diversity to the cause. Despite there being no telephones or organized communication channels from one village to the next, it was unbelievable that news of our trip, and request for assistance, had spread lightning fast and with stunning accuracy – all by word of mouth. I was witness to the same phenomenon on the Annapurna III expedition, and I was no less impressed on Everest. Theirs was a system of communication that could not be beat.

Managing the caravan of people that unfolded was an art unto itself. On the first day, our liaison officer, Lhakpa Tenzing, wrote down the name of each porter and the exact number of boxes we had to transport. The porters who hung around the easier-looking loads were quickly redirected to more suitable boxes by the responsible Sherpas, and number cards were hung around their necks to match them to their specific boxes. Every box weighed approximately 30 kilograms, but some were thought to be easier than others to carry because of their size or shape. When asked for their names, the same list repeated itself: Ang, Kami, Phurba, Tenzing, Kitar, Dorje or Lhakpa. When asked how old they were, most replied, "*About* 20" – there was no official registration of births in the small villages of Nepal, so no one knew their age. Since not many of the porters knew how to write, we jotted down their names and had them place a stamped thumbprint alongside it. This way, when payday came, we could match the worker to the correct name (thumbprint) and to the loads they had carried. I could only imagine a long meandering snake of a lineup when that time came.

We had already prepared the money for the porters in Kathmandu, and the number of bills and coins was so immense that it filled two Duralumin boxes. Of course, we had to hire porters – the most trust-worthy – to carry the special contents. To further ensure security, we marked the boxes with the large *kanji* character (金), meaning money, so only we knew what was inside.

About 10 per cent of the porters were women, dubbed *Sherpani*, and they often carried their babies' baskets on blankets atop the 30-kilogram boxes assigned to them. Regardless of weight, they nonchalantly hiked with support bands that connected the boxes to their foreheads. I saw some of the women knit hats while hiking in this manner. They chatted or sang in groups of five or six, quite enjoying the work. This, in combin-ation with watching children run barefoot through villages as we passed by, made me wonder about my daughter in Japan. "How was Noriko?" I asked myself with tender heartstrings, but the reality in front of me snapped me out of that sensitive place.

The procession of our group began at 9 a.m. with the first porter bound for Base Camp, and shortly after noon, the final porters were on their way. By the time the rest of us were walking, a kilometre of distance had stretched between us and the tons of gear being carried in.

Sixteen days after we left Kathmandu, and just before arriving at Namche Bazaar, we saw Mount Everest for the first time. There was no sweeter sound than the porters announcing the mountain to us in Nepali: "*Memsahib*, Sagarmatha; *Memsahib*, Sagarmatha." Their excitement was as genuine as ours. Far in the distance stood a black rock face, sticking high up into the dark blue sky, with a white, triangular, snow-covered peak, casting filaments of persistent cloud.

"That's it," I thought, "*the* Everest."

It was easy to acknowledge the peak in front of us as the highest place on Earth, yet because we were so far away, I lacked the feeling of being face to face with the mountain we were meant to summit. We stood there for some time, absorbing the enormity of our objective. Meanwhile, I silently prayed, "Please, let us climb it."

Namche sat in the steep bowl of a mountain slope at approximately 3800 metres in elevation, similar to that of Mount Fuji. At that altitude, the houses were cool enough inside that one would wear a warm sweater at night. We pitched our tents on top of a hill that overlooked the village, while most of the porters dispersed to their nearby homes. Since they are born and raised at those elevations, it is no wonder how strong and energy efficient the Sherpa people are on the high mountainsides.

On Saturday, in the early morning, the market was set up along the village streets. Vegetables, rice, sugar – whatever we needed was available for purchase. We almost cleaned out the vendor who sold logs, which we bought in anticipation of staking our way through the Khumbu Icefall. We left Namche for Tengboche but stopped part way at the aptly named Hotel Everest View, owned by our gracious host from Kathmandu, Mr. Miyahara. It was impressive that such a quality hotel could be built and operated at an elevation of 3962 metres. Thankfully, the management staff of the hotel was also our communication check-in for the climb. How many hotels offer that service? Once communication was established, we continued on our way. The date was February 27. Our hike descended to the Kali Gandaki River and then up again through forested terrain until we arrived at the monastery in Tengboche. A large grass field surrounded the grounds for animals to graze, and nearby was an elementary school that Sir Edmund Hillary helped build, along with three tea houses that encircled the area.

The village was blanketed in fresh snow as we arrived, and on sunny days, staggered layers of white peaks filled the horizon. Thamserku, Kangtega and Ama Dablam were in the immediate forefront; Lhotse, Nuptse and the southwest face of Everest stood in the distance. Still far away, Everest was immense – an outstanding monstrous massif of giant rock.

It was a four-day hike from Tengboche to Base Camp, but the change in elevation from 3900 to 5350 metres between the two was the precise range where people suffered from altitude sickness, particularly on such an uphill route. To acclimatize, we planned to stay in Tengboche for two weeks and organize training climbs from there. We paid the porters to take the time off and go home. We would see them again in a fortnight.

As predicted when we first labelled the boxes with the Chinese symbol for money, payday was chaotic. As before, we had the porters make thumbprints by their names in the record book, indicating receipt of their dues. The red muddy paint from the ink pad splashed all around as though to emphasis the day's excitement. Those Sherpas who were able to count money kindly helped those who could not. With cash stuffed in their shirt pockets, some porters scurried home while others went directly to the bars in Tengboche.

Unexpected incidents had more impact the farther away we were from home. We had travelled a long distance by the time we reached Tengboche, and acclimatization was well under way. The trip was unfolding as planned. So it was a great surprise when a scene presented itself on an overnight training session to the Ama Dablam Base Camp. Six of us and Ang Tsering were slowly making our ascent. We were busy chatting with Sherpas along the way and enjoying the landscape while enduring the difficult approach. Ang Tsering spoke of his climbing experiences on Dhaulagiri IV with a party from Japan's Gunma Prefecture and a French team on Everest. As elevation increased and we tired, we could barely nod in support of his stories. The weather was beautiful and one of us dared to say, "Looks like we can summit Ama Dablam tomorrow."

Then a Sherpa yelled, "Somebody is running up here!" None of us could see anyone at all, but Sherpas have keen eyes and I knew better than to doubt him. He could already discern who it was before we could even place the figure on the trail. "It's Karma; he's running. Something must have happened."

When Karma arrived to where we stood, he handed me a letter from the journalists, the tone of it curt and unforgiving. "Leader Hisano has gone back to Japan today. We hope this is not some kind of joke. What do you take us for? We are here to work as journalists, not to play around. Needs to be explained as soon as possible."

I felt sick, like the wind had been knocked out of me. Without hesitation, I left the group, leaving someone else in charge, and returned to Tengboche. On the way, the breathtaking scenery failed to come into view as I ran downhill then up the final slope to the village, barely keeping pace with Karma.

The seven journalists were sitting, having tea at the round table in a nice, sunny spot at our camp. Iwashita, the chief director of Nippon Television, wasted no time in thrusting the letter at me that Hisano had left behind. I immediately recognized her handwriting. I stormed to my tent to read it, not even taking my boots off.

Dear Tabei-*san*, and all the members and journalists,
I have decided to go back to Japan. Though it's for a short visit,
I feel awful. All I can do now is ask for you to be OK with it. I
plan to come back to Tengboche so that I can leave for Base
Camp together with you. Please take care. Hisano, March 1
at Kathmandu.

When I reappeared from my tent, the journalists threw their questions
at me.

"Didn't you know this beforehand?"

"Explain the reason."

"What will you do if the leader doesn't come back?"

"How can I report this mess to my office in Japan?"

"Will you welcome her back and treat her as leader if she returns?"

I had no answers. I was utterly shell-shocked by Hisano's behaviour. I
could not believe it. The longer I stood there, speechless, the more irritated everyone became with me, and slowly, every ounce of my energy
drained away until I felt entirely empty.

At the time, I had no idea why Hisano had left, though hints from
members whispering back and forth about her conduct reminded me
of a phone call she had made in Kathmandu. That call must have been
the turning point for her; words must have been spoken that made her
abruptly depart. Nonetheless, Hisano's actions were out of my hands, and
something suddenly tweaked in me when I reached my limit of assault
from the journalists. Recharged, I stood up to the team and declared that
Hisano would return during our stay in Tengboche, and if by chance she
did not, then I would take over. End of discussion.

As confident as I was in front of everyone, once alone, I was flooded by
tears of frustration and misery.

I sympathized with Hisano, as it must have been difficult for her to
have written that letter, but I was convinced that no matter what the
situation, I would never have walked out on our team. To me, without total commitment, especially from a leader, Everest could not be
climbed. There was no turning back, risks and all. My thoughts began to
churn; I knew sleep would not come easily that night as concern shifted
from whether or not the team would accept Hisano when she returned

to the question of *would* she return. The answer was revealed ten days later.

The sound of a Cessna aircraft filled the sky above Tengboche. "She's back! Our leader is back!" was the cry that promptly dissolved the lump in my chest. Was it fear that had been lodged there for the past week? Anger? Either way, relief made its way in, and I could breathe again.

The members of the team, along with Iwashita and Emoto (representing the journalists), sat down with Hisano to hear her story. Mostly what we received was a heartfelt apology as she chose not to disclose why she had left. She knew we were annoyed and simply asked for forgiveness. Everyone was willing to move forward with the promise that such a thing would never happen again. The issue blew over, and discussion turned to more imminent issues related to the climb. Another hurdle was behind us.

To Base Camp

At the end of our two weeks in Tengboche, we split the team into two parties. The second party would stay an extra night at each stop along the way from Pheriche to Base Camp while the first party stayed only one night. This approach would allow for a more gradual and continued acclimatization but was considered a variation from previous men's expeditions. Our team's main concern was to arrive at Base Camp healthy and fully adapted to the higher altitudes. We knew the value of morale and how quickly one's spirits could decline when unwell, and with only fourteen climbers, we could ill afford to have anyone suffer from altitude sickness. Still, as hard as we tried to avoid symptoms, a few of the members complained of headaches at 3900 metres, and only Nasu, Watanabe, Kitamura and I could move around with no difficulty when we arrived at Base Camp on March 16. We appreciated that everyone would acclimatize in time, but it took some longer than others.

At 5000 metres in elevation, the mountain terrain of the Himalayas is dominated by moraines, which are loose rocky remnants of moving glaciers. On our approach, Base Camp was soon upon us when the landscape changed from moraine to blue-white ice. Then, Nuptse's knife-sharp ridge stood above us, and frozen icefalls, like huge building blocks piled atop one another, filled the view. Once again, in the distance, Everest showed itself, the black, rocky West Ridge marking the horizon. The summit remained hidden behind the up-close angle of the blocky icefalls, giving Pumori the chance to loom above in all its beauty. Had we been any higher in elevation, we would have seen Cho Oyu stand even taller. At Base Camp, we were pinpoints, tiny dots, on the world's greatest real-life topographical map. There we stood, amongst giants, humans in these vast waves of glacial ice. The essence of the scene took my breath away.

Essentially, we moved into Base Camp, making the place inhabitable for our group of seventy. We were a mix of women climbers, Sherpas and journalists calling the location home. We established camp on the glacier far above where past parties had pitched their tents, deterred by the amount of scattered garbage that had been left behind, a sight that surprised us. We knew then that we would strive to leave less of an impact on the mountain. For our team, toilets for men and women were set up. Then the ground ice was levelled and covered with flat rocks to create platforms for the many tents our horde required. Boxes of food and equipment were piled up in disarray, ultimately needing to be placed in order, depending on which of the higher camps they were destined for, and stored in our warehouse of sorts, which was walled in by stacks of rocks. Deemed straightforward tasks at sea level, these jobs demanded a great deal of time and effort at Base Camp. I could barely carry a 30-kilogram box more than a few steps before needing rest, my throat instantly parched. We were already paying our dues in the thin mountain air.

When it came time to bid the porters farewell, our sentimental side kicked in. We had trekked many days with this group and felt part of a cohesive team. "Come back to help us when we return," we said. "Thanks for carrying our loads. Go straight home; don't lose your money." We could barely sum up what they meant to us as we shook their hands, and in jumbled Nepali, English and Japanese, said goodbye. Once on their way, they hurried down the path, leaving the rest of Everest for us to navigate. The yaks and yak handlers departed as well, and the snow began to fall.

I stood there for a moment, watching the porters disappear from view, reflecting on what it had taken so far to reach Base Camp. The events that would occur from then on were anyone's guess. The number of days on the mountain, success on the summit, people's ability to rise to the occasion – it was all a mystery at that point, but I was ready for the story to progress. Then, sure as I was that the demands of the climb would be incessant, shouts began to pour in from behind me: "Tabei-*san*, where should we store all these boxes?" "Tabei-*san*, someone says the camera box is missing." "Tabei-*san*, how many tents for the team?" I turned towards the camp, finally face to face with our Everest.

By nightfall of the first day at Base Camp, we were exhausted. After a simple supper, we collapsed into various tents, me with five teammates – Manita, Watanabe, Nasu, Naganuma and Kitamura. One after the other, we squeezed in like sardines, slipping into our sleeping bags, alternating head and feet so we could all fit across the tent floor. Once settled, I lay wide awake. My mind whizzed with general excitement at my whereabouts, plus the logistics and plans that ran through my head for the coming days. Then Kitamura began to cough, and as though a dam had been released, so did the others, one by one. Sleep hovered around most of us that first night, but maybe we needed to get the worry of a wakeful night out of our system.

We were unaccustomed to mornings at Base Camp. Instead of the sound of chirping birds, as in the various villages on our approach, silence in the wee hours was encroached upon by the roar of distant avalanches and rockfall. A sea of orange-coloured tents brightened as hints of sunshine gently reached us at 6 a.m. By 8:00, complete daylight poured over the camp and the surrounding ice seracs twinkled in its illumination. Ribbons of smoke rose from the site of the Sherpas' routine prayer rituals. So, began our days in the wilderness of Everest.

By the time the entire team was at Base Camp, the second party having arrived on March 18, our home felt properly established. On the Khumbu Glacier, Nepali and Japanese flags swayed from logs that were used as poles and secured by a base of stacked rocks. We gathered around the flags for an official prayer to grant us safe climbing. Several of the Sherpas had trained as lamas, or teachers, and were able to lead us in the proper chants for the occasion. The ritual was quite beautiful. A prayer book was placed on a rock, and beside the book was a plate filled with mounds of *tsampa* (like buckwheat flour), butter and rice. Pleasant scents from a variety of smoked tree barks wafted in the air around the flags. A string of *tarcho* (prayer flags) were hung from the logs of the two national flags and tied out to the sides of the main poles. It reminded me how we hung flags at school athletic meets in Japan, and I smiled at the memory.

In front of the makeshift altar stood the Sherpas, then the kitchen staff and high-elevation porters. Next were the climbers, and behind us, the journalists. Everyone listened with quiet minds, humbled by the experience. The mantra "*Om mani padme hum*" was chanted into the thin air. My fellow Japanese team members and I joined in, and we threw the *tsampa* powder over one another's shoulders after the prayer was complete. We added a toss of rice in the direction of the summit of Everest, wishing for a safe ascent. I also threw the rice grains towards the Khumbu Icefall, adding my own silent prayer: "Please let us maintain the same number of people on the way up and on the way down. And may success on the summit also be granted."

After a few more days of acclimatization, Hirashima, Arayama, Fujiwara and Naka descended to Pheriche, unable to shake the signs of altitude sickness. As soon as they descended to a lower elevation, their symptoms would subside. But, by way of past example, we were not a team to put one problem to rest without another coming to light. One of the Sherpas who had accompanied the four sick team members to Pheriche had a fight with a Sherpa from another party and sustained an injury. A message had been sent to Base Camp requesting our team doctor go to Pheriche and check on him. The general reaction was one of frustration: "It's not a good time to fight. We need to establish Camp 1."

On it went with daily dramas. I not only had to complete necessary administrative tasks, like writing to the Ladies Climbing Club headquarters and each of the sponsors in Japan to announce our safe arrival at Base Camp, and share in the demands of climbing, I also often acted as team mediator. There was no shortage of problems to solve. Demands poured in like a waterfall: "Tabei-*san*, the pair of crampons we gave to the Sherpas was the wrong size." "Tabei-*san*, the journalists need to know who will go to the icefall tomorrow." "Tabei-*san*, a French trekker asked to stay in one of the team tents overnight." "Tabei-*san*, is *gyoza* all right for supper this evening?" The repetitiveness was tiresome, almost funny, but necessary. Solving each dilemma at Base Camp, as was done

in Japan and Kathmandu and Tengboche, contributed to headway on
the mountain.

CHAPTER 6

The Route

The scale of expedition dilemmas varied from minor to serious, and one day, right after Taneya and a few Sherpas had scouted the Khumbu Icefall for the first time, Nasu raised a concern that needed attention. "Isn't it a bit off our goal to do the scouting with Sherpas? Shouldn't we do it all by ourselves since we are a women's party?"

Until then, I had given little, if any, thought to this point. We had planned to use Sherpas from the get-go. A women-only ascent, without Sherpa assistance, was never discussed in our four years of trip preparation, and suddenly, the idea was being raised for the first time at Base Camp. I tried to swallow my surprise. Hisano, who must have been equally caught off guard, replied, "I hadn't thought about this before; does anyone have an opinion to share?"

Nasu continued, "We should make our own route, because we're a women's party, and if we can't reach the summit and have to turn back halfway up, then so be it." A few people offered a slight nod in agreement, but mainly we were silent.

I asked Taneya what she thought since she was the first to scout the icefall earlier that day. In a barely audible voice, she replied, "I think it's hard to fix the route all by ourselves."

Had we judged Nasu's input and stated that her idea was wrong and that a women-only approach without the help of Sherpas was not an option, she would have lost face amongst her team. It would have been unfair to disregard her input. "All right then, let's go out by ourselves, alone, tomorrow and see how it goes," I said, and the meeting was adjourned.

I spoke with Ang Tsering afterwards, summarizing the discussion, and he nodded in support. With respectful understanding, he said, "We don't want to waste even a day, so we'll take up the things needed for going through the icefall, like ladders and ropes, by ourselves, the Sherpas, and try not to disturb the ladies' activities."

The next day's events yielded a different result than what Nasu had hoped. Even with lesser weight to carry, the women team members were stressed to keep up to the Sherpas burdened with heavy loads. For one, our smaller muscular stature limited our performance in comparison to theirs. As well, the Sherpas' capabilities at high altitude provided them with an advantage we could not compete with; we needed their assistance. Gradually, the goal of tackling the route setting unassisted was forgotten and became that of an innocent dream.

The Khumbu Icefall is a notorious feature on Everest. It continues from the elevation of Base Camp (5350 metres) to Camp 1 (6050 metres), blocking the summit from view. Safe passage through the icefall was considered the key to success on the mountain, and here, input from the Sherpas was invaluable. Drawing from previous experience with other expeditions, they could quickly surmise conditions and offer advice. "This part was good last year, but it's not good this time. Let's explore more to the right side," they said, their opinion worth its weight in gold.

We had hired ten high-elevation porters, and they transported ladders and logs to bridge the crevasses in the icefall. They hiked behind all of us, carrying the heavy equipment on their backs. It was a dangerous maze. Countless deep crevasses existed in unpredictable locations throughout the rugged icefall and, at any time, posed the threat of possible collapse. The gaping cracks were pitch black to the very bottom, making the measure of their depths impossible. If a person were to fall into one, they would likely perish. We found ourselves chanting "*Om mani padme hum*" along with the Sherpas as we crossed the monstrous chasms.

In a feat that was more construction than mountaineering, we positioned the logs across the "crevasses of no return," as we came to call them. This was a job much easier said than done. It was physically difficult but also technically challenging – a little to the left, a little to the right, a shallower angle, more upright – as these wooden structures were hard to steer.

The ladders were easier, and thankfully we had two of them. They were custom-made out of Duralumin and cost 150,000 yen each, an expense we were happy not to have scrimped on. A ladder stretched 15 metres, which allowed us to cross the largest of open crevasses, even the ones we considered impossible at first glance. Crossing the ladders with crampons on was a challenge; it required guts. When tied into the rope for safety, the weight of it gave a backward tug, and I felt like I was being pulled into the gaping space below. With every step, the ladder flexed with no warning, and my gloves, smeared with snow, slipped on the metal as I longed for a secure grip. Fixed ropes that were relied on in the morning dangled powerlessly into the abyss by evening due to the collapse of ice at the crevasses' edges. The process of trusting our set-up was unbearably tense, yet we repeated it over and over and over, one crevasse at a time, up and down and up and down the Khumbu Icefall. It was a treacherous gateway to Everest that had to be surpassed.

Meanwhile, we were threatened by building-sized chunks of ice that could collapse, triggering a domino effect and crushing everything in the immediate area, including us. Enough accidents had happened to previous parties that we wished to minimize the number of times we had to pass through the icefall. Ironically, however, the Khumbu Icefall's elevation fell within the precise zone that was critical for our acclimation at high altitudes. We were required to repeatedly go in and out of this zone to ensure our body's physical adaptation and thereby reduce struggle higher on the mountain. It was a stressful predicament to send members back and forth into the dangerous icefall, but it was necessary to acclimatize and to continue building the route. I cringed every time part of the team was headed there.

All precautions were made to reduce the risk of ice collapse. To avoid warmer temperatures, the party in charge of building the route on a given day woke at 2 a.m. and departed camp within the hour. We had a system. A party consisted of two climbers and six or seven Sherpas. Two parties a day would work at higher elevations, constructing the route from Base Camp to Camp 1. Ideally, each climber would only work that stretch once in the rotation, but by way of numbers and the effects of altitude sickness, the stronger climbers ended up working there more often. Slowly, they began to tire and needed a day off. In an effort to ease the load for my teammates, I assigned myself the higher-elevation work seven times. Later, I learned that my efforts were considered by some as a scheme to better acclimatize myself for a selfish chance at the summit. I wish I had *that* calculating of a mind for my first-ever attempt on Everest.

The Sherpas managed the crossings differently than the climbers. In the chest pockets of their parkas, they always carried the rice that had been given to them at a prayer ceremony in the Tengboche Monastery. At the dangerous sections, they threw the rice high up into the air while chanting the now-familiar words "*Om mani padme hum.*" Many of their colleagues had lost their lives in the Khumbu Icefall. In 1970 alone, six Sherpas were killed there on Yuichiro Miura's ski expedition. The icefall was a daunting place for everyone.

Beyond the Khumbu Icefall, the Western Cwm Glacier expanded indefinitely, like an ocean, and there on its horizon stood Everest's Southwest Face, radiating an enormous sense of power. The Lhotse Face loomed in the distance like a colossal headwall, and to the southeast was a panoramic view of the knifepoint ridge between Lhotse and Nuptse. Runnels laden with snow fell from the ridgetops, beautiful pleats of symmetry in the landscape. The sheer beauty of our surroundings had us instinctively saying a unified "wow." Our joy was well-earned; we had safely navigated the Khumbu Icefall, and there was Everest. Our plan would progress like clockwork.

April 3

Nasu, Watanabe and four Sherpas established Camp 1 higher up on the glacier. It took us fourteen days to reach that site from when construction of the route began from Base Camp. We had another 2800 metres to climb to reach the summit, determining Camps 2, 3 and 4 on the way. Camps 5 and 6 would be reserved for the summit-assault teams and their required support. At maximum, each person was able to carry 15 to 20 kilograms as we climbed. To bring the necessary two tons of provisions to Camp 2 required mindboggling calculations that seemed to push the summit farther away. Everything came down to numbers.

The route from Camp 1 to Camp 2 was a gradual uphill on the easier topography of the Western Cwm Glacier. The terrain was less technical, the crevasses easier to skirt, and the climbers more adapted to the elevation. Camp 2, also called Advanced Base Camp, was to be the main base for the climbers, so its location needed to be precise. We were aiming for a small glacial mound that sat between the West Ridge of Everest and the Lhotse–Nuptse ridge; it was a spot considered safe from avalanches due its geographical location, and most expedition parties chose to stay there.

As I arrived at Camp 2, one of the several Sherpas I was with said, "Last year the Spanish party camped here," as he dropped his pack. "Let's make our camp here, too." Slightly taken aback by the cardboard and other remnants left behind by previous parties, and unsure what other garbage would be exposed when the snow began to thaw, I suggested we pitch the tents a bit farther uphill from the initial recommendation. We trudged another 15 metres to select a site, unaware of the future impact of that decision.

April 8

Camp 2 was established, and the focus shifted to Sherpas and climbers ferrying loads nonstop up from Camp 1 while simultaneously fixing the route to Camp 3. It was an enduring game of leap frog, and the gruelling efforts began to take their toll. Manita announced on the radio that the trip to Camp 2 in one day then onto Camp 3 the next was too much. She was concerned about lack of acclimatization. "I may die going up another 500 metres in that short of a time period," she said. "The Sherpas are tired, too. Camp 3 is not going to be set up exactly as you had planned."

I waited for the Lhakpa Tenzing's version of the story at the end of the day and was able to respond to Manita with confidence. "The Sherpas are not tired yet. We couldn't reach Camp 3 yesterday because the climbers were tired. We'll ferry up only those things necessary to establish Camp 3 tomorrow," I said.

The inevitable friction between me and some of my teammates was on the rise. I was aware of our limited time on the mountain and the waning strength of the climbers, so my attitude was for us to quickly move forth and establish camps as fast as we could. I was disheartened to hear comments that suggested a possible us- (or me-) versus-them relationship. I thought we were comrades who shared the same goal. I persevered through those heated moments, and sure enough, the young climbers (those below thirty) began to feel the positive effects of acclimatization.

April 13

Camp 3 was established by Manita, Naganuma and four Sherpas.

Meanwhile, Kitamura, the super-model of the team and the person we (wrongly) judged to be most unlikely a mountaineer, was naturally drawn to the role of manager for Camp 1. I recalled her comments at her first official interview with the team a couple of years earlier. "I would be totally happy to stay at Base Camp," she had said. I was amazed to see how far she had climbed. She embraced all aspects of camp management and was in great shape and well-acclimatized.

At high altitude on a sunny day, the blue sky took on a blackish sheen speckled with white dots – which, at first, we failed to recognize as stars. The reflection of the sunlight on the snow surface was extremely intense, much like walking on a heated fry pan. When conditions changed, we would experience the exact opposite: a blizzard of snow that had us braced against tent poles from the inside to keep our shelters upright.

Sunburn was a constant problem. The sunscreen lotion we had was insufficient, and we all developed blistered burns. Even our mouths burned, from having them wide open to laboriously breathe as we climbed. It was painful to eat with such swollen, damaged lips. Left to our own devices, we invented sun-protection masks from medical gauze that covered the lower face and allowed us to breathe. It was totally effective, but when several of us gathered as a group with our masks on, we looked more suited to have guns in our hands than ice axes.

Various other side effects from altitude kicked in as well. Some climbers lost their appetite and their faces began to show their newly acquired slimness, whereas others, like me, maintained our exact weight for the entire trip. Several women's menstrual cycles shifted – some did not menstruate at all, others had to endure two weeks of menstruation, and others still struggled with such pain that they could barely move – all symptoms that subsided once off the mountain but experiences we had to manage on Everest nonetheless.

A women-only expedition certainly made the discussion of such issues easy and supportive, but we still had differences to sort through. In the small space of a tent, for instance, it quickly became obvious who was organized at sorting their personal gear and who was not. Kitamura,

Shioura and Fujiwara were the queens of searching for lost things – one sock at the entranceway and another under a sleeping pad – and so it went, continuous moments of lost and found for every one of their outings. It was impossible to help them keep track.

The picky eaters were another matter altogether. If a person disliked a certain dish, say, stinky cheese, then she applied her dislike to the other people who ate it. Slowly, food choices began to determine who hung out with whom, and a comical social structure developed.

Thus, life at altitude and in close quarters took shape. Privacy was non-existent; alone time came when, heads down, we ferried loads from camp to camp, one step after the other, slowly making our way up the mountain. The only other precious private time a person had was in the toilet, and for me, particularly on a clear night with a sky full of twinkling stars, that was my chance to really absorb where I was, on Everest. Stars danced like diamonds in the beam of my headlamp as I walked along the midnight pathway to and fro, and I often wondered how my family was doing in Japan under the same lively sky.

We secured the route between Camp 3 and Camp 4, running 700 metres of static climbing rope through carabiners that were clipped to pitons hammered into the icy slopes. It was tough work as the air thinned, carrying heavy loads and pounding metal into frozen fixtures. By then, we were reduced to four climbers (Watanabe, Nasu, Manita and me) who could perform at the higher elevation of 7600 metres at Camp 4. Our climbing ability at altitude was peaking at the critical time of the expedition, and for that I was grateful. Disappointingly, though, I heard rumours that the journalists were betting on us like horses, stating the odds of who would make it to the summit or not. I was sorry to have let such talk reach the climbers who were on the battlefront, striving hard day after day to fix the route and ferry loads in impossible conditions. Our efforts were no joking matter.

We were constantly reminded of the limited budget we had for our expedition. We lacked appropriate equipment for every aspect of the route, especially the number of ice screws and snow anchors we had brought. In normal mountaineering practice, climbers would anchor themselves to the slope with an ice screw for every 20 to 30 metres of displayed rope, 40 metres at the most. With minimal gear, we self-anchored every 80 metres. In terms of safety, that was a ridiculous length of runout rope; a fall would be injurious, to say the least. On top of that, we could only afford two jumars, and we had offered these to the Sherpas because they carried heavier loads. Meanwhile, we climbed with a carabiner on our harnesses, through which we ran the fixed rope, and the grip of our fist was the only stopping mechanism in the system. This was totally dangerous, and I still advise people: "Never do that, please!"

The process of kicking the toe of the crampon into the frozen uphill slope, one foot at a time, while attempting to grab the rope with a free hand, was monotonous, made worse by the rope's extensive stretch that threw us off kilter with every reach. Focused balance was required to maintain unity with the heavy loads on our backs. Had we the pleasure of using jumars, our method of ascent would have been entirely different. We could have rested hands and feet while relying solely on the bite of the jumar into the rope to hold us stationary. Instead, we had no respite. Our calves burned and our hands gave way to the bitter cold and intense work of hanging on for dear life. We maintained this painful effort from 7100 metres to the South Col at 8000 metres. At times, I questioned why I was there. I had visions of my family and friends tucked into a *kotatsu*, warming their toes, and I longed for the taste of the mandarin oranges they would likely be sharing over relaxed conversation. Clearly, I was in another world. I missed my home.

On the steepest terrain, we fixed the route with rope ladders. One person climbed ahead using two ice axes and without the weight of a pack, fixing anchor points to the slope as they progressed upward. The rope was tied at the climber's waist on the harness, then threaded through each anchor point for security; the next climber below was tied into the bottom end of the rope, which was pulled taut once the lead climber was at the top of a pitch. This allowed climbers to be on a safe belay as they moved upwards. Ladders and other equipment were continually brought higher and fixed to the route. On some days, we could only progress 300 metres while working at +7000 metres in elevation – even standing still at that altitude was cause for exhaustion. After a full day of fixing the route, we were simply too tired to move an inch, greatly in need of a rest.

We were at the crux of the climb in terms of maintaining good health.

One after the other, teammates began to succumb to altitude; first, Naka, our star youngster, and then Naganuma, who suffered from a relapse of severe pain from a long-ago broken leg. But we endured, and on April 27, ten days into our struggle with the Lhotse Face, Watanabe and I finally arrived at Camp 4.

It took us almost nine hours to achieve the 700-metre elevation gain from Camp 3 to Camp 4. We climbed without oxygen, which we saved for sleeping, and our packs were notably heavy. The result was two self-induced oxygen-deprived hypothermic climbers who were almost driven insane from nearly frozen hands and feet. The severity of that day, both in terms of cold temperatures and hardship, remained imprinted in my mind's eye for decades to come.

We cut a small flat surface into the steep and hard ice slope with barely enough room to pitch four small tents, one for four Sherpas, one for Watanabe and me, and the other two for the journalists and their Sherpas. Chopping into the frozen mountainside while on belay seemed to take forever. The winds picked up to double that of the lower elevations, and the simple job of going to the toilet became a scary adventure.

"*Pugyo*," I said (Nepali for "enough") to Hisano on the radio that night. "There is no other day that I desperately wished we had brought more jumars as badly as today. I'm exhausted enough to almost declare that I quit mountaineering. Let's have the next Ladies Climbing Club expedition at a beach, not in the mountains."

"I second that!" Kitamura said from Camp 1. "Hawaii would be great. We'll take lots of jumars then! In the meantime, best wishes for the Kawagoe Housewives Association." Watanabe and I laughed – there we were, two married women from Kawagoe, both of us mothers, on Everest. We felt rejuvenated once again.

I felt pleased when I looked down the sheer ice slope that draped from our tent entranceway to the distant bean-sized silhouettes of the Sherpas who continued to ferry loads on the Western Cwm Glacier. "How fantastic that we have come this long way," I thought. Right in front of me was Pumori, the Himalayan pleats of Everest's West Ridge, and Nuptse – all of them bathed in an incredible evening light that made a person's dignity shine bright. It was a picture beyond words.

Watanabe and I had climbed to nearly 7800 metres, and we were close to the Yellow Band. The Geneva Spur would be next, and then the South Col. The Yellow Band is the signature stripe of limestone rock, formed millions of years ago when Mount Everest was below sea level, that cuts across the upper third of the mountain's face. It is a hazardous feature that threatens the climber, whose crampons are likely to skid out on the steep rocky surface. Numerous old ropes lay hung from worn anchors, left by previous parties and tempting us to use them. The amount of energy required to fix our own ropes was excruciating, but the thought of clipping into partially eroded lines that had been long exposed to Everest's harsh climate made us think twice. We added to the milieu of tat and fixed our own ropes on the limestone band.

Watanabe and I had taken turns with Nasu and Manita, each pair ferrying loads from one high camp to another and flip-flopping who stayed where. After Watanabe and I had spent three nights at Camp 4, Nasu and Manita were on their way to join us there. On the morning of the day they arrived, the Sherpas had fixed ropes to Camp 5 (7986 metres) at the South Col, a worthy accomplishment. It was regrettable that Nasu and Manita missed the chance to reach that higher elevation with the Sherpas. In the name of success, though, the route had been built, enabling our climb to progress to its final stage.

I also regretted that only the older team members (Nasu, Manita, Watanabe and I) had reached as high as Camp 4. I really wanted the younger stars – Shioura, Naka, Taneya and Arayama – to surpass the Lhotse Face. But once again, I had to accept certain disappointments, as did others, as part of the greater team effort. It was difficult because I wanted everyone to experience Everest as they had dreamed it.

Then logistics changed. On May 2 Arayama relayed a tense message from Camp 3. "Naka fell ill while climbing the lower part of Lhotse Face. We should take her down as soon as possible." On Everest, the time frame of "as soon as possible" means hours later. Not until the next day could we implement a team to accompany Naka down to Camp 2. Watanabe, Mihara, Shioura, Taneya and I shuttled loads from Camp 2 to Camp 3. Shioura and Taneya were to stay at Camp 3 and then progress to Camp 4 on May 4. Watanabe, Mihara and I would descend with Naka. Instead, on our way up, we crossed paths with Naka below Camp 3, escorted by Arayama and Sherpas. It was obvious she was suffering from altitude sickness – unable to put on crampons by herself, for example – but she remained able to walk. After a quick assessment of the situation, I decided that Naka should stay at Camp 2 for the night then continue down to Base Camp the following day. The plan for May 4 read like a hit list as I dictated it over the radio for the rest of the team. This was how I kept logistics direct and organized.

> May 4
> Naka, Tabei: descend to Base Camp
> Shioura, Taneya: Camp 3 to Camp 4
> Watanabe, Mihara, Nasu, Manita: Camp 2 to Camp 3
>   (ferrying up two oxygen bottles each)
> Arayama: stay at Camp 2
>   (take care of Naka for night of May 3)
>
> Tents—rooming
> 4-person tent: Naka, Arayama
> 6-person tent: Watanabe, Mihara, Nasu, Manita and Tabei

In an unusual turn of events, as many as seven climbers stayed at Camp 2 the night of May 3. I slept next to Watanabe, who was camped right at the tent entranceway, and beside Mihara, who lay in the middle of five climbers. Three of us were headfirst towards the icefall side of the camp, while Manita and Nasu slept with their heads pointed at the Lhotse Face. An earlier mistake in ferrying loads meant we were short one sleeping bag. Together, Watanabe and I stuffed ourselves into a single bag – room for legs only – with down jackets zipped around us for upper-body warmth. We settled in for sleep, unaware that plans were about to change again.

CHAPTER 7

Finalists

May 4, 12:30 a.m. (recap)

First, silence. Then a whole-body vibration, a deafening noise and – WHAM – impact. Avalanche! Before I knew it, I was tumbling fast. Then, stillness, and an unrelenting pressure that pinned me down so I could hardly breathe. I felt suffocated. I desperately sought escape as I reached for my knife.

"Everybody OK?" I yelled at the top of my voice, startled by its loudness. There was no response. I realized that someone was on top of me. It was Miharu, her hair smothering my face.

The night of disbelief unfolded from there, an entire camp wiped out by tons of snow and ice. The saving grace, summarized best by one of the Sherpas, was that "Nobody is die."

Nearly a week had passed since the avalanche, and timing to reach the summit had become imperative. We had to get a move on. From a recovery point of view, we were steady enough. It was the other calculations that were the threat: the amount of available food and bottled oxygen dictated that not many of us could stay at high elevations for much longer; and the weather forecast reported that India's monsoon would begin around May 20. Supplies were not the only thing being depleted. The human body is driven to deterioration and exhaustion purely by existing at 6400 metres – slowly, we were wasting away. In all of this, each of us felt the urgency of the final assault on Everest. Whom that would involve was yet to be determined.

May 10

An evening meeting was held to announce the finalists for the summit team. Hisano, with the weight of the world on her shoulders, led the discussion in a slightly tense voice. She admitted to how upset she had been when first informed of the avalanche, and then how her hopes for continuing the expedition plummeted when she saw in person the scale of the disaster. As team members began to recover, and word from the doctor assured her that the injured Sherpa would be fine, the summit assault returned into view. Hisano was convinced a miracle had kept the team alive, and she felt ready to shift that positivity towards the goal and joy of climbing again. "Having considered Tabei's unwavering request to continue," she said, "the team is being given one last chance to succeed."

It was with a deep respect for each team member that Hisano presented her conclusion. Watanabe and I would make the final push to the summit of Everest with Ang Tsering. We would have added support from the Sherpas since, unfortunately, there were not enough resources to fuel the remainder of the team to the South Col.

When a summit team is chosen, it is vital for everyone to remain united in their support, but often it can be the cause for an expedition party to disband. Thinking back to Annapurna III and the upsetting arguments that ensued when the summit team was selected had me in mixed emotions on Everest. I cautiously waited for the group's reaction, but no sooner had I comprehended the announcement myself than a barrage of hands appeared for a heartfelt congratulatory shake. As I vigorously accepted each one, my broken glasses slid farther down my nose. They had been snapped in half by the avalanche and were now held together by tape; an inconvenience, but not enough to hamper the moment. I would summit Everest, and our team was unified in the effort.

I was surprised to feel unburdened by Hisano's decision. I thought that if I heard my name as part of the summit team then responsibility and obligation would descend on me like a heavy blanket. Instead, I was wrapped in a certain kind of relief emitted from the rest of the team. We had already spent more than fifty days at more than 5000 metres; living in such a stark environment had begun to wear on us – we had been pushed to the far edge of tiredness. The unspoken thought that we shared was that if someone, anyone, could reach the summit, then please let them so we can go home. It was nice to feel the genuine support from everyone.

That night, as a fresh start was needed, we scrubbed each other's backs with 5-centimetre-square cotton sheets soaked in rubbing alcohol. It had been more than two months since any of us had soaked in a hot bath and the itchiness of dry, sweat-smeared skin was a serious annoyance, even taking into account our noble pursuits. The mere luxury of feeling clean had us revelling in our Japanese ways. Watanabe spoke of bathing in *onsen* water, and how beautiful the early summer greens would be in Japan. Hiking in Kamikochi was on her list of things to do when she returned home. A flurry of responses followed: "We must eat sushi first, and eel and *ramen* served with traditional thin noodles, and *gyoza, chaw-an-mushi, hiya-yakko, hatsu-katsuo* and *sashimi*." As we cleansed our tired selves, the conversation lingered on food, from barbequed *sanma* with shredded *daikon* to cream puffs and chocolate parfait. It was as though the topic itself would fuel us. Hirashima, in charge of food for the ex-pedition, added: "Tabei-*san*, we've packed a can of the best tasty ham for your last camp before the summit attack – eat it up. No leftovers allowed." I was grateful for her dedication and thoughtfulness, and it highlighted the group spirit. Our enthusiasm had gained momentum based on the shared feeling that the climb would soon be over. Freshly washed, our bodies felt rejuvenated as well.

May 11

We woke to a sunny, cloudless day, perfect for the team to jump into action and ferry loads to Camp 3. Kitamura, who at first declared that Base Camp was more than enough for her, had eventually become the manager at Camp 1, and then she progressed to ferrying loads between Camp 1 and Camp 2 based on her quick adaption to altitude. We pushed her farther and were happy to see her climb as far as Camp 3, almost 7000 metres in elevation. Hisano did the same. While the expedition leader usually oversees the team from Base Camp, Hisano's choice to climb to Camp 3 meant that everyone, except for Dr. Sakaguchi, made it to that high of an elevation. This alone emphasized the unique strength and adaptability of our team, which to us was an accomplishment in itself.

We were never considered a group of elite mountaineers in the Japanese climbing community. We were a team of women who shared the dream of climbing Mount Everest; a team that readied itself for such an opportunity despite the obstacles met along the way. The success of all climbers reaching Camp 3 was enough to keep me up that night with pride and excitement.

The low-angled glacial slope between Camp 2 and Camp 3 dramatically changed at the looming buttress of the Lhotse Face where the steep, polished ice seemed an endless obstruction. We had already succeeded on one of the three notable, difficult sections on Everest, the Khumbu Icefall. Next was the Lhotse Face, which would lead to the South Col at almost 8000 metres, and then the knife-point ridge that connects the 8700-metre South Peak to the true summit. The intimidating features ahead made it feel like the mountain could still refuse us the summit, yet my attitude remained steadfast: Go for it!

May 12

We woke to a cloudy early morning, knowing there would be snow later in the day. With two preparation days already complete on the Lhotse Face, and fixed lines established above Camp 3, we were ready to resume the route. Watanabe and I tied into a shared rope and climbed toward the Lhotse Face once more. We left the camaraderie of Camp 3 for the earnestness of the summit, the entire team waving goodbye behind us.

The steepness of terrain was intense right from the start. Step after step, we kicked the two front points of our crampons into the glacial ice, like metal teeth biting their way up the frozen slope. With mitted hands, we clipped the slings from our harnesses to the fixed rope, each of us relying on a single carabiner that was the only attachment point between us and the mountainside. We were immediately aware of the 20-kilogram packs on our backs, each one containing a 7-kilogram bottle of oxygen. This was of little concern on an earlier scouting mission, but now the weight was a noticeable addition. Climbing with no jumars and the added strain of altitude had us breathing hard within minutes. Our pace slowed – step, stop, deeply inhale, repeat. The sheer angle of the route made it impossible to plant a foot flat on the ground;

my weight was fully supported by the forefront of my crampons. My calves screamed in pain, and my knees and thighs were as heavy as lead. Hardly any distance had passed between us and Camp 3, yet my body already felt consumed by the demand of the route. The summit was approximately 1850 vertical metres away.

The glittering glacial ice continued to stretch endlessly in front of me. As hoped, by the time I reached the rope ladder that the Sherpas had fixed on a steeper section of the face, I had settled into my usual climbing style. The remnants of aches and pains from the avalanche had dispersed, and I felt strong again, until I stepped onto the ladder. The rope structure stretched like a rubber band as I placed my entire weight on each flexible rung. Patience and accuracy were required with every foot placement as I positioned the space between the points of my crampons onto the narrow horizontal strands, twenty-eight steps in total. My balance was repeatedly tested, and fatigue set in. Slowly, Watanabe and I staggered upwards.

The weight of the packs and the lack of supplemental oxygen also began to take their toll. The sun had started to slip behind Everest's neighbouring peaks, the temperature dropped and our hands turned numb. We were still on the ladder. Camp 4 stood directly above the pitch we were on, taunting us to climb faster.

I was almost at the point of collapse when the Sherpas came into view, busy expanding Camp 4. The site was no bigger than the footprint of a tent, a no-frills flat spot cut into the steepness of the slope. A few steps higher up, a similar platform had been built. Watanabe and I shared a tent with the two cameramen, Ajisaka and Nakamura, on the lower level while the Sherpas were stationed above. There was a toilet a few metres away at the end of a narrow path, and we had to remain on belay to use it. In such close quarters, there was no room for modesty.

By the time we greeted each other with Japanese pleasantries, evening was on the cusp. Our hellos were interrupted by Ang Tsering's urgent voice: "*Memsahib, memsahib!* Tabei-*san*, I have to talk to you." He guided me to the second tent. Three Sherpas lay flat out in their sleeping bags, looking grave. My initial thought was if the Sherpas were suffering at 7600 metres, how did we stand a chance? "We have to get them down due to altitude sickness," Ang Tsering said. The severity of the situation hit fast with his next words: "That means we cannot shuttle enough loads for three people to make the summit assault."

The sound of falling snow on the tent grew louder as I tried to digest our options. Conditions had turned to whiteout and daylight was fading; there was zero visibility for the Sherpas' proposed descent. They would have to wait until morning. Their departure would mean that 90 kilograms of supplies could not be shuttled farther up the mountain in our effort to reach the summit. The weather was worsening with the monsoon pushing ever closer to the region, and I felt a sense of now or never if we were to succeed on Everest.

I tried to calculate what we could accomplish with three fewer Sherpas. Could the rest of us ferry enough resources to establish Camp 5 and 6, and support one cameraman at Camp 6 while three of us continued to the summit? No. It was impossible.

Ang Tsering suggested we reduce the number of climbers required to reach Camp 6. Although I had not thought of that, it made sense, and I radioed Hisano to explain the scenario. After some consideration, she responded. No matter how many times she reviewed the numbers, the result was negative – we lacked the support for three of us to reach the summit. "You'll have to decide," Hisano said, "Tabei-*san* and Watanabe-*san*, who is going up."

Instinctively, I felt that since I was assistant team leader, my job was to provide backup to Watanabe. I would support her to the South Col, and then she would make the push for the summit. I had learned my lesson on Annapurna III that when a person is in a leadership role, she is better off not to choose the summit for herself in a case like this. "Let Watanabe-*san* climb," I said.

Watanabe grabbed the radio transmitter from my hand. "No. Tabei-*san* should continue climbing. I'll go down with the sick Sherpas."

Hisano was silent.

"Watanabe is in good condition today. I can support her to the South Col," I said.

"Leader Tabei-*san* has better experience at high altitudes. I'm totally inexperienced from this altitude on. Reaching the summit is much more certain with Tabei-*san* climbing higher."

Hisano was indecisive. "Give me more time. I'll call you back tomorrow morning," she said and turned off the radio. For a moment, it felt like time stood still, but the camera kept rolling as Nakamura shot footage of our expressions during the radio call, finishing with our looks of uncertainty.

The evening storm picked up speed. The intensity of the falling snow erased any hint of our surroundings; we could have been anywhere. Tied to the fixed rope, Watanabe and I made our way to the toilet, the sky pure in its darkness with only icy flakes whirling in the beams of our headlamps to provide perspective.

I peeked inside the Sherpas' tent on my way back. It was obvious how sick the three of them were, pale-faced and complaining of severe headaches. Morning could not come soon enough. I reported to Ang Tsering about the radio call with Hisano. His response was adamant: "The camera guys should go down." An obvious answer from a climbing perspective, but not an easy decision given that media sponsorship funded the expedition.

Tucked away in our tent, and seeking a distraction from the heavy mood of the camp, Watanabe and I sat wrapped in our sleeping bags to begin the ritual of wiping off the thick layer of sunblock from our faces. We focused on remaining calm, clearing our minds as we cleansed our skin. Late at night, with heads side by side, we each fell asleep inhaling one litre of oxygen per hour from a shared bottle through a two-pronged nasal tube. I tried to relax to the hiss of the oxygen flow and the gentle sliding of snow from the tent roof. No thinking, no emotion, only sleep was needed.

May 13

The radio call from Hisano finally crackled in the morning air. Her voice was low and obviously strained. No doubt she had not slept much the night before. "After considering all potential scenarios, I've decided to have Tabei-*san* continue the climb. Watanabe-*san*, nothing could be harder for you than this, but please come down with the sick Sherpas." Hisano was choked up after the announcement and unable to speak. She had such respect for every climber on the team that to pull one of us from the impending summit, to disappoint us, weighed heavily on her. Sadly, some members of the team misinterpreted Hisano's intentions with this decision, and after the expedition unkind accusations were made against her.

But, with no hesitation, my partner replied to our leader, "This is Watanabe. I got it. I'll go down to Camp 2 with the sick Sherpas." She was resolute and clear-minded as she turned to me "Yes, this is the right thing to do. We're better off with Tabei-*san* climbing. *Ganbatte!* Show your good fight on it."

The dice were thrown, the curtain was up, and the game was on.

May 14

Snow fell through the night and at 7 a.m. it was still falling. As I stirred from the tent, visibility remained poor. Regardless of weather, the three Sherpas were ready to descend. They refused my offer of hot tea, claiming it was a waste to consume goods that they had worked so hard to carry this far. Two more Sherpas, who had always been in great shape on the expedition, were also suffering from severe headaches. We had no choice but to bid them farewell as they also left with Watanabe.

Before she stepped away, I shook hands with Watanabe. "Take heart," she said. "But don't take it too hard." She pulled out an *omamori*, a good luck charm, from her pocket and with a bright smile placed it in my hand. I could barely express my thanks as I hid the treasure deep in my jacket. The warmth of her gesture seeped into my heart like healing water. From that day onward, Watanabe's smile remained ingrained in my mind.

For efficiency and safety, the order in which our friends would down climb the Lhotse Face had been decided before they left. Watanabe clipped her carabiner into the fixed rope and began her descent. She looked back at us only once and waved her hand, and then continued to lead the Sherpas on their way. Her silhouette quickly disappeared into the heavy falling snow, and I was the lone climber of the Japanese women's team en route to the summit.

The poor weather had Ang Tsering and I declare a day off. I radioed Hisano with an update of the team on its way to Camp 2 and us remaining at Camp 4 for another night. Concern flowed both ways across the transmission, me asking Hisano to take care of Watanabe and the Sherpas, and her assuring me they would be welcomed with a full heart and that I was to also take care. Her reassurance enabled me to focus on the task ahead.

Limitations of living at 7600 metres in elevation kicked in. Ang Tsering gave up trying to ignite a temperamental kerosene stove to boil water for soup. Logistics dictated that we only use kerosene stoves at Camp 4, reserving the butane gas for higher up. An unlit stove meant we were forced to eat lunch from the stash of already prepared food, diminishing supplies we would rather not touch. For every action there was a reaction that further hampered specified plans.

Returning to the tent with food in hand, I found Ajisaka hugging a plastic bag full of snow stuffed between his jacket and sweater. "What are you doing? You'll get hypothermia!" I said.

"I'm making water by melting snow this way," he said. I was impressed by his effort to help us, and my disposition softened. I recalled how upset I was with the journalists after the avalanche at Camp 2. They obviously never meant any harm.

The unfortunate part about forgoing soup for lunch to save butane gas was that our thirst became insufferable. As we waited for the weather to clear and the day to pass, our discomfort became excruciating, but with the weather delay, we had to save our fuel.

The snow continued to fall into the night and the potential for an avalanche hung over the camp. There, perched on the middle of the Lhotse Face, we had no control over our surroundings. We had only luck to rely on to make it through the night. I had Watanabe's *omamori* and knew I could call myself alive if I woke up in the morning. I burrowed deeper into my sleeping bag, feeling the lonesomeness of my tent with no female teammates around.

CHAPTER 8

South Col

May 14

After two days of continuous storm, a vast blue sky finally spread over the mountainous world of white. Across the valley, Pumori and Lingtren were heavy with new snow and shone in the distance. Shortly after the Sherpas and cameramen Nakamura and Ajisaka left Camp 4 for the South Col, Ang Tsering and I packed up to follow behind. As I tied off the strings to the doorway of the tent, before I really stepped into the unknown of Everest, I prayed that I would safely return to this spot. Roped together, we began to climb.

The weight of my pack with an oxygen bottle and personal equipment felt so heavy that it drew all the energy from my body. The allotted two litres per hour of oxygen supply was not enough for me and again I struggled with every step of the climb, not to mention the knee-deep snow. When we hit the steep ice slope, my breath became even more laboured and the speed of my beating heart increased, as did the height of our view.

Eventually, we reached the Yellow Band, its exposed layer of rock from several thousand million years ago depicting the fact that Everest was once covered by ocean. Next was the Geneva Spur, the rock buttress that leads to the South Col. Ajisaka turned around then, and as he passed me on his descent, he offered the cheer: "Have a good fight!"

We had hardly crossed over the Geneva Spur and my legs felt like stiff sticks. Ang Tsering had followed me the entire way with almost no space between us, showing no sign of difficulty. Considering that he had only one litre per hour of oxygen at his disposal, his constant strength irked me.

My mood continued to worsen. The morning's bright clear sky had turned grey without us even noticing, and it began to flurry. Even the tiniest of snowflakes falling around my face frustrated me to no end. Into the lacklustre weather, I began the traverse in slow motion – hike, rest, resume, over and over again.

A while after we had passed the Geneva Spur, the angle of the slope eased off and boulders came into view with a still-distant but wide space in front of us. Two tents that the Sherpas had pitched also became visible and my spirits lifted. "Tabei-*san*, South Col," said Ang Tsering. We had arrived at Camp 5.

I knew of the South Col being referred to as the place that smells of death. I thought this to be a rather unusual reference as all I could picture when I arrived was how its spaciousness could accommodate a baseball field, a volleyball court and a tennis court all together. I wondered if that reference simply meant that at 8000 metres elevation, the threat of death was enough to keep most humans away.

More than sixty oxygen bottles and various tent poles were strewn around the camp, left from previous expeditions. In the monochrome of rock and snow, the yellow of the abandoned bottles was the only vivid colour. It broke up our moonscape-like existence and, somehow, I felt relief more than anything that other climbers had been there beforehand. It was encouraging. Where one might see garbage, in this case, I saw hopefulness.

"Tabei-*san*, the other side is Tibet. We can see Makalu very well," said Nakamura. He had already finished shooting some footage of the area, and so he walked with me, his heavy camera equipment slung on his shoulder. His balaclava was outlined with frost and icicles hung from its mouthpiece. From where we stood, facing east, the South Col stretched up to Everest north–northwest and south to Lhotse, the fourth highest mountain in the world. Beyond the col stood Makalu.

The South Col was like a giant wind tunnel. Pitching a tent was almost impossible and required a group effort for fear of equipment being blown away. When Ang Tsering and I were still roped together, any slack in the line between us was lifted upwards in an arc that hung in the air by the constant force of the wind. Six Sherpas and I managed to help set up two tents, one of which I would share with Nakamura and Ang Tsering.

An attempted radio transmission to Hisano at Camp 2 failed with nothing but static over the airwaves. As a result, I left the refuge of the tent and walked in earnest to find a spot with better reception. The work it took to establish our camp had exhausted me – carrying rocks to secure the tents to the ground was one thing; doing so with no supplemental oxygen was quite another. Life on the mountain usually entailed collapsing in the tent and not moving from there once prone, but in this case, the importance of the radio call was critical. It was our only thread to the others below at Advanced Base Camp. Finally, after walking around for some time, I made contact. "Given good weather tomorrow, we'll leave the South Col for setting up Camp 6 at about 8500 metres, and will attempt to get to the summit next day. Everybody here at Camp 5 is fine," I said.

After a brief discussion with Hisano, reporter Emoto jumped in. "Tabei-*san*, Tabei-*san*," he said. "It's not in our favour to have our news scooped by any other climbing team nearby since the South Col sits in a good location for radio waves going through. I ask you not to mention your own name but to call everybody with a code number, yourself as Number One, Ang Tsering as Number Two and Nakamura as Number Three. OK?" Even though I agreed to his suggestion, I had no idea why we needed such covert action in our summit bid.

By the time I finished the radio call, I felt the last of my body heat drain out of me. My nose, ears and hands were almost numb, and I rushed into the tent to warm up. Then I was hit with thirst, a hellish thirst that burned my throat and made me throw back several cups of black tea as though I were on autopilot. The sweetness of the hot drink seeped into the dried-up tissues throughout my body. I felt somewhat revived. That night, I would share with Nakamura an oxygen bottle tuned to an added half litre of oxygen per hour for a better sleep.

May 15

At 3 a.m. I woke with a start when the oxygen flow suddenly stopped. Once awake, it was nearly impossible to fall asleep again, as the cold invaded my body as soon as I was alert. I must have dosed off enough to pass the time until 6 a.m., when I could no longer defer morning. For a moment's reprieve from the bulky oxygen mask, I took it off and was surprised by the layer of slimy frost that lined the inside. Hence, the lack of flow that woke me up in the first place.

The wind gusts that had beaten against the tent all night had finally subsided. My face met sunlight as I popped my head out the door, and in looking around I realized that we were camped at a higher elevation than the summit of Pumori to the west–northwest from us. The day to reach Camp 6, the final camp before the summit, had arrived. I begged the weather to stay steady for two more days.

We were a group of eleven broken into three teams: eight Sherpas, one cameraman (Nakamura), and Ang Tsering and me. Each team checked and re-checked all the life-line equipment we would need to ascend: a tent package for Camp 6, cooking equipment, fuel, food, rope and enough oxygen bottles for Ang Tsering and me to make the return trip to and from the summit. It occurred to me that we would also have to account for necessary supplies for Nakamura, who would return to the South Col after filming our arrival at Camp 6. I processed this thought but was unable to tend to it with any speed – my actions were slowed by the high elevation. At 7906 metres, even tying a boot lace took forever due to lack of mental clarity and the additional clumsiness of thick over-mitts.

"Can we leave the ham? It's too heavy," Ang Tsering said as he put aside the tinned meal Hirashima had specifically prepared for us for the last camp. Resigned to losing the ham, I insisted that we should not leave any drink powder behind. With diligence and sacrifice, we were able to reduce the food weight by half.

Above the South Col, even the Sherpas used supplemental oxygen. Their gaits were strong, and I heard their crampons scratch into the ice and rock more solidly than usual. I watched as four of them in a row carried all the Camp 6 necessities across the terrain, with Nakamura and his Sherpas following behind. Meanwhile, I placed boulders around the tent to secure it from the powerful gusts that threatened to flatten Camp 5. It was my best effort at ensuring a place to return to when the job higher up was complete. Again, tying off the entranceway to the tent, I made a wish to come back to this spot with no accident. "When I am to be here next," I thought, "the result of Everest will be with us, too, success or not." I had two big days ahead of me.

At 8:30 a.m. I left for Camp 6 roped to Ang Tsering, just like the day before. We were the third of our three parties starting out minutes apart.

Prior to climbing Everest, photographs I had seen of the South Col showed it to be fairly barren with prominent black boulders exposed to forceful winds. But the day I walked away from there, summit bound, the scene was one of pure white, a blanket of fresh snow. Only slivers of ground around our tents showed the colour of the earth. It displayed a stark beauty all its own.

We climbed the slope that directly connected to the summit, and at 8020 metres, the angle steepened and we were on more of a ridge, bare rock to one side, windblown snow on the other. The angle was so steep that when I looked up to see where Camp 6 would be situated, I almost fell over backwards. Otherwise, I was in good shape. My gait felt light and I was not burdened by the weight of my pack, probably due to the 3 litres per hour of supplemental oxygen (compared the one litre per hour I was restricted to the day before, which I did not appreciate very much).

My pace was solid, and thanks to the oxygen and my strong partner, Ang Tsering and I passed Nakamura, and even caught up to the lead Sherpas. This was a good sign. At 8300 metres the slope angle eased a bit and the wind lessened, suggesting a break. Our tents at the South Col were far below, and we were high enough in elevation that soon we would surpass the summit of Lhotse.

Slowly smoking his tobacco, Ang Tsering pointed out the surrounding area. "Those are Cho Oyu and Gyachung Kang; Tengboche is somewhere there, and Gaurishankar is that one," he said. He looked as relaxed as if resting at a tea house on a moderate pass somewhere other than Everest. His gentle demeanour showed no sign of anxiousness, which in turn helped me to relax.

I began my first radio call in code, as requested yesterday. "This is Number One. Camp 2, can you hear us?"

I laughed at the response from Emoto: "This is Camp 2, where are you Tabei-*san*?" Did he not instruct us to avoid surnames on the radio for fear of giving away our status on the route? I still had no idea why that was important, which made me laugh even more at his use of my name. So much for incognito.

We continued on our way, up a gully flanked by rocky outcrops. Each step was tentative in order not to bang our oxygen bottles against the sidewalls. Another snowy steep slope led to a flat area the size of a *tatami* mat where the lead Sherpas had already dropped their packs, signifying Camp 6 – the final stop before the summit.

It was shortly after noon hour and snow flurries had begun again. The peak of Everest was hidden, but its presence was forthright. Our location at 8500 metres was almost equal to that of Lhotse's summit to the south.

The Sherpas had chopped out enough space for a two- to three-person tent. Sixty-centimetre bars were hammered into the snow through the corner loops to secure our home for the night. For added peace of mind against the wind, we crisscrossed 8-millimetre rope over the top of the tent and secured it to the frozen ground. I was familiar with the potential danger since one of the Sherpas had shared with me the story of a tent being blown away in similar conditions.

An almost fully buried blue tent left by a Spanish team was still visible. The team failed to reach the summit due to high winds despite their success at making Camp 6. Also left behind, although possibly by another team, were eleven bottles of still-usable oxygen, jam and soup mix. The regulators for the oxygen were incompatible with ours, so we also would have abandoned them if it were not for the work of our Sherpas. They carried the bottles down from the mountain since such equipment is considered precious, thus lucrative, to them.

I shook hands with the Sherpas, so grateful that they had climbed this far. My appreciation of their day's contribution was immeasurable. They had relentlessly ferried loads, set up camp and collected snow to melt for water before it was eventually time for them to return to Camp 5, all in the effort to get Ang Tsering and me to the summit of Everest. Soon, it would just be the two of us.

Gyaltsen spoke first: "Don't go up if it's too gusty tomorrow." My heart warmed from his gentle voice, such an unlikely match to his large size. "Give us a shout on the radio, whatever happens. We'll be waiting for you guys at the South Col. Take great care."

"We'll come up to get you the day after tomorrow, no matter what.

Never be too daring. Make sure you return," said Reenjee and Lama-*san*, both vigorously shaking hands with me. I poured my thanks out to each of them: Lhakpa Tsering, Ang Phurba, Anima, Phurba Tenzing and Ang Mingma. Thus, I bid our Sherpas farewell as they climbed down the steep slope from Camp 6 in lightly falling snow.

Nakamura, who had carried heavy TV cameras up this far and was filming Ang Tsering and me busying ourselves at the last camp, also prepared to go down. "Wait a second," I said, thrusting at him a cup of leftover black tea, still slightly warm from the Thermos in my pack.

"No, thank you. I'll rehydrate when I get down. Even a drop is too precious here to share," he said. It would take nearly two hours to reach the South Col so I forced him to enjoy the drink. Shoulders buried in gear, he was off. "Be careful and hang in there," he said to me.

Then Ang Tsering and I were alone.

The daily routine of entering the tent began. We cleaned snow from our packs and stored them inside, sat at the entranceway facing outdoors and removed crampons, tapped overboots together to shake off more snow, secured crampons to the outer tent straps so they stayed put, then peeled boots off and retreated indoors. Straightaway, I felt cozier.

We unpacked the food, stored the oxygen bottles away from where we would light up the butane stove and readied ourselves to cook. Due to the high elevation, the stove barely cooperated, but we managed to melt some snow. We drank milk tea, coffee, hot chocolate, green tea and hot lemon juice, one after the other until each of us had consumed six cups worth, but felt no difference. Rehydrating was nearly impossible, and my lips were dry before the next batch of snow began to melt.

Ang Tsering stopped me short of trying to grill frozen cheese directly over the flame. "It's not good to burn food in the sacred fire," he said. Although I craved the taste of warm melted cheese, I would never do anything to upset him, for the faith of the Sherpas is one to uphold.

We finished our supper by 5 p.m.

"What was on the menu for dinner tonight?" Advanced Base Camp asked the same question every evening.

"All right, here I present the menu for the last official dinner at the final camp on Mount Everest. To start, we had dried spinach soup to which we added dried green onion and carrot and miso flavour for perfection;

followed by the main dish, which was freeze-dried instant rice with *nori* mix sprinkled. Delicious!" We laughed as we spoke in a dignified manner, like waiters at the finest of restaurants. Our high-quality radios made it sound like our teammates at Camp 2 were in a neighbouring tent, and I found that encouraging. By then, our thirst returned with a vengeance, and the simple conversation tired us out. Having had no supplemental oxygen for the duration of mealtime and the radio call, I felt light-headed and I already longed for the 1 litre per hour that was allotted for quiet time in the tent. Meanwhile, Ang Tsering had a look of contentment on his face as he puffed on a cigarette.

Despite our best efforts, the tent lay victim to the winds of Everest. The gusts were strong enough to nearly lift us off the ground, even with the oxygen bottles in position to weigh down the corners. Ang Tsering checked each bottle one by one, worried that their rolling around from the wind would reduce their set pressure, a disaster that would kill us on the summit. Deciding to check the pressure on the bottles or not was in itself a dilemma, because by simply opening the valve to test it, we would lose oxygen and decrease the available amounts for the next day. Thankfully, the pressure in each bottle remained at the necessary level for the summit assault.

Ang Tsering and I spoke in a mixed language of Nepali, English and Japanese. Flavourful as it was, we had no difficulty communicating with one another. When I had to go to the toilet, he secured me to a rope from inside the tent. When I was about to change my socks to a dry pair, he took out a thicker pair of his own and suggested I use them. "These are better," he said, "French made." Not only were we climbing partners, we were friends.

On the pre-summit evening, I thought to myself, "Whatever we smile at or cry for, tomorrow will be the day we get the result, the result of 1,400 days of preparation." Unfortunately, I was unable to feel the excitement of my own words since my main concern was the potential change in the weather. Ang Tsering was equally as worried, and he continually stuck his head out the tent for an update. Thankfully, the light snow from earlier in the day had ceased and it was a strikingly clear night full of stars. The black silhouettes of Lhotse, Nuptse and Pumori were sharp against the stellar sky, the beauty of which made our nerves and the wind tolerable.

Dressed in down jackets and tucked into sleeping bags, the extinguished stove between us and a few more cups of tea gone by, and with oxygen set at a flow rate of half a litre per hour, we were ready for lights out by 9 p.m. Outside, gusts of wind as loud as subway trains roared us into a fitful sleep.

CHAPTER 9

The Summit

May 16

After two hours, I was awake, trying to convince myself that lying stationary was enough to provide the body rest. I checked my watch: 11:30 p.m. I closed my eyes but sleep evaded me. I checked my watch again: 1:20 a.m., 3:00, 3:50. I listened to the outdoors – silence. No wind. I woke Ang Tsering. Still embedded in my sleeping bag, I raised the front flap of the tent to a sea of stars that twinkled in the serene air high above the hovering 8000-metre peaks. It was almost eerily quiet as the mountains stared back at me. I knew the weather was good for a climb to the summit.

Slowly, I crawled from the warmth of my cocoon and began to pack things away. Every movement was sluggish. I had to rest after pulling up a sock. My brain was sending the message to hurry but my body found it impossible to cooperate. My actions were that of a slow-motion film. Sloth-like, I fired up the stove to melt the frozen chunk of concrete that had been hot water the night before. The thawing process allowed me enough time to put on my over-pants, leather climbing boots and nylon overboots, which had holes in them, mementoes from Annapurna III. When we eventually earned the morning's first mouthful of milk tea, the heat spread through me like life itself. "*Mitho*," said my companion. Tasty.

We had two more cups of coffee each and filled our Thermoses with black tea and our pockets with candies, and were out the tent at 5:50 a.m. It was dawn and neither wind nor a wisp of cloud was evident. In front of me lay the route to the summit, a long white ridge that we would follow. Every other peak – Makalu, Lhotse, Pumori – was vibrant in its presence. The scenery was one of crystal clearness, like the air we breathed.

I put on my crampons while staring at those beautiful mountains in full morning light. I thought of how unlike this day was to the Japanese harp concerts of my youth where I could calm myself with the assurance that no matter how poorly I performed, it would not kill me. Everest was different; performance was everything, the line between life and death. Nonetheless, to my own surprise, I felt at ease.

My pack was ready with two cameras, an 8-millimetre movie camera (the journalists asked us to bring two as a backup but we decided against it), one radio, a spare pair of gloves, food, drink and emergency kits. The two oxygen bottles I also carried, plus the regulator and mask I wore on my face, forced the straps of the pack to dig into my shoulders and accentuate the weight of the 20 kilograms on my back. Ang Tsering saw the problem and grabbed the movie camera, Thermoses and emergency kits, and buried them in his pack.

No sooner had we left camp than we were breaking trail in knee-deep snow, which, unbelievably, became waist deep. Essentially, we ploughed our way through in a whole-body tackle of the conditions. Five metres of climbing made my heart want to leap from my mouth; my mask was covered in snow from leaning into the steep slope. My breathing was so arduous that it erased the sound of the supplemental oxygen flow, which was usually a loud hiss in my head. In a persistent action of first padding down the snow with knees and then stamping feet, Ang Tsering and I alternated breaking trail.

Two hours of desperate work led to a ridge of steep rock and snow. Although very rugged and unstable, it was not technically difficult. We continued to climb, tied into the rope with 20 metres between us and alternating leads. Our only chance for rest was when we belayed one another. I suffered less than expected, likely a tribute to the supplemental oxygen, and mainly felt the weight of my pack and a screaming pain in my ankles from the steepness of the pitch.

"South Peak!" bellowed Ang Tsering, his face mask removed so he could speak. Although not the true summit of Everest, the South Peak marked significant progress. We arrived there at 9:40 a.m. Almost four hours had passed since we left Camp 6. We stomped out a spot in the snow, dropped our packs, and for the first time since dawn, sat down.

"We have just arrived at South Peak," we reported to Camp 2.

"You'll be at the summit in about an hour then? The radio will remain on. Have a good one," Hisano said, her voice cheerful.

"I don't think we can get to the summit in an hour due to the tremendous amount of snow. Please estimate two to three hours," I said. Then I took a moment to pour tea into a cup, soak three biscuits in the lukewarm liquid and eat them with a handful of chocolates.

I glanced in the direction that Ang Tsering pointed towards. "That's the summit," he said. From where we sat on the first peak, our route descended a sharp upside-down V-shaped ridge that abruptly dropped from our perch. After a bit, it trended upwards into a rocky gully with the crack pitch called Hillary's Chimney (now, the Hillary Step), and then onto the final snowy ridge above.

Even though I had read from the records of prior Everest climbers that the terrain between the South Peak and the summit was difficult and dangerous, I had not read a description of the sheer drop and knife-point ridge that we encountered. I immediately begrudged the lack of detail in previously written Everest reports but knew I had to accept the route in front of us. Simultaneously, I realized this was the section that Lhakpa Tenzing, our sirdar-turned-liaison-officer, had warned us about earlier.

We exchanged our used oxygen bottles (leaving them at the South Peak) for full ones, and began the final push to the summit at 10:10 a.m.

Carefully, I made my first downward step onto the two-pitched knife-point ridge, one side of which descended east into Tibet, and the other west into Nepal. The exposure was dizzying. My movement mimicked a sideways crawl, with my trunk on the Nepal side of the ridge and my arms swung over to Tibet. I kicked into the slope with the toe of my crampons and placed my weight on the platform of my boot, knowing that each time I relied entirely on a foot placement was the very moment I risked my life. Would the next kick be faultless? A minuscule sense of balance came from grabbing at the sharp ridgeline positioned at chest height in front me. It was all I could do to hold on. There was no option to use my ice axe for stability. It was more a matter of precisely shifting my body weight inch by inch in the direction of the summit.

Leaning over the ridgeline for a glimpse down the Tibetan side caused my body, chest to toes, to hang freely towards Nepal. I could see the slope run at least 3000 metres nonstop into the country below. Dropping my head and peeking at the Nepali side between my legs, I saw our bean-sized tents at Camp 2. Nonchalantly, clouds like cotton candy floated below me, as if I was looking out from an airplane.

It was surreal to be at such a high altitude, knowing there was no room for mistakes. Neither one of us could have stopped the other if we had slipped. A fall would mean death. My hair stood on end beneath my helmet, my scalp shook, and goose bumps crawled up my back. I felt on the verge of madness from the extreme tension of the situation. Yet we were able to continue.

Forty metres along the ridge was a spot where I could finally place my feet side by side instead of supporting myself on one foot at a time. Next was the freshly snow-covered rock gully that marked Hillary's Chimney. I cleaned the new snow away with my ice axe and over-mitts and readied myself to climb. The initial overhang required me to wedge my entire right leg into the crack as I reached both arms outwards and up diagonally to my left. With nothing but air between my backside and Camp 2, I managed to climb the chimney. How would we descend this on the return trip? As soon as that thought popped into my mind, I was driven to anxiety, knowing that 90 per cent of climbing accidents in the Himalayas occur on the descent.

Thirty-seven climbers before us had successfully summitted Mount Everest and safely descended. For now, my job was to climb. Later I would concern myself with the descent. As we continued, another 7 metres of the shallow crack deposited us on an upward ridge of solid snow.

Although the labour-intensive trail breaking in deep snow ended with Hillary's Chimney, the slope remained steep. It was critical to not be drawn too far to the right of the ridge where huge cornices crested on the Tibetan side. The blue sky was almost touchable, and I was baffled by how many times I thought we were at the summit, only to be mistaken. Repeatedly, the highest point of Everest seemed to grow taller as I pressed forward. I could barely lift my legs any more. The utmost I could raise my feet from the snow was the nail-length of my crampons' teeth. Basically, I dragged my body up the mountain.

I thought of the previous climbers who had succeeded on this face of Everest, among them the five Japanese mountaineers Teruo Matsuura, Naomi Uemura, Katsutoshi Hirabayashi, Hisashi Ishiguro and Yasuo Kato, all of whom I admired. As my mind travelled, my body fatigued. Again and again I had to rest, leaning onto my ice axe with my forehead slumped on top. Every step was agony, but I persuaded myself to continue; soon there would be a final uphill step. The view of the Tibetan landscape grew increasingly larger as I climbed. Then, Ang Tsering, who was a few paces ahead of me, stopped. The rope between us no longer pulled at my waist.

"Tabei-*san, tyojo dayo,*" he said in Japanese. "It's the summit."

I lifted my feet up one by one, slowly wrapping the rope in a rough coil as I walked. Then, I took my last step to the summit of Mount Everest. It had been six and half hours since we had left camp earlier that day. I felt pure joy as my thoughts registered: "Here is the summit. I don't have to climb anymore."

My crampons bit into the snow as I firmly stood beside Ang Tsering. He stretched out his big mitt and we shook hands. His sunglasses shone with the reflection of the sun, highlighting our success. The time was 12:30 p.m. on May 16, 1975.

The summit of Everest was narrow with snow thrusting up from both sides of the mountain to form its pinnacle. In ankle-deep snow, which was unpredictably soft, we stomped down a flat spot about .05 metres wide by 1.5 metres long. We secured ourselves by anchoring the ice axes through loops of the rope and driving them deep into the snow. The mild-featured mountains of Tibet spread vastly to the north, and the gentle curves of Rongbuk Glacier were easily identified. In contrast, the rugged slopes, rock and ice of Nepal filled the view to the south.

Since we had no room to offload our gear, I asked Ang Tsering to grab the radio from my pack. I embraced our success for a moment longer, not quite ready to share the news. Then I made contact with Advanced Base Camp. "ABC, ABC, we arrived at the summit at 12:30. Both of us are in good shape," I said.

We were met with the cheerful singing of the Sherpas, and our teammates and Ang Tsering laughed out loud listening to them. "*Otsukaresama deshita!*" they said in Japanese. Good job!

"The black and white contrast of the Tibetan mountains that we can see from here is of outstanding beauty. Please say a big thanks to all the Sherpas and team members," I said, trying to give justice to the view from the top of the world.

We readied the movie camera and began to film as I continued to speak on the radio. Spanning from the Nepali side of Everest to Tibet, there was Lhotse in front of us; Makalu, big and beautiful, to its left; and then in the distance, Kanchenjunga and the graceful Jannu. Layered beyond the sharp ridgeline of Lhotse and Nuptse were Thamserku and Kangtega; to their right stood Gaurishankar, Cho Oyu and Gyachung Kang, and below them was the brown basin of Namche Bazaar, home of the Sherpa people. Silvery clouds floated around the summits of the giant peaks, emphasizing the dramatic difference between Nepal's rugged Himalayas and the endless, mildly sloped mountains of Tibet. One could imagine the smell of the Tibetan soil it was so prevalent in the rolling landscape, while the precipitous environment of the Nepali side remained breathtaking.

When I looked through the camera lens to take a photograph of Ang Tsering and saw him standing there with flags from two nations in his hand, the reality of the Everest summit touched my heart for the first time. I was warmed by our success. There was no higher place in the world than where we stood, and the sensation was tremendous.

Time was short. In the background of Ang Tsering's stance, a misty cloud rose around the peak of Makalu and made me feel unsettled. We quickly snapped photographs of each other, me asking Ang Tsering to take several to ensure an in-focus shot. Fifty minutes passed in a second. Ang Tsering spoke again on the radio with the Sherpas, his voice song-like with excitement. I experimented with removing my oxygen mask for a while and was pleasantly surprised that I could do so without any immediate problem. Then came the time to descend. We had to return to the South Peak before our oxygen supply ran out. A moment of fear set in: could we climb down without trouble? I yearned to be in a spot where I could stand on both feet, in safety and without feeling anxiety. Fear aside, the clarity of knowing there was only one direction to go – down – offered me relief.

To mark our victory and embed the moment in our minds, we left a green Thermos on the summit along with the Nepali and Japanese flags thrust into the snowpack. Fifteen metres down from the top, I asked Ang Tsering to pick up souvenir stones for all my teammates. As I looked back at the summit once more, our flags proudly flapped in the wind, connecting earth and sky, and bidding us farewell.

We began our descent at 1:30 p.m., and it became obvious that going down would require far more nerve than climbing up. Humans were not made for this. Climbing, yes; descending, no. As I tucked my chin to see the security of each foot placement, the oxygen mask stopped short like a barrier. It nudged out of place, and cold air leaked in and fogged up my sunglasses, which immediately froze. Trying to clear the frost with my over-mitts made things worse. Ultimately, I pulled off my glasses for comfort and clearer vision, but Ang Tsering berated me, "Though it feels OK now, you'll be snow-blind by tomorrow if you continue without sunglasses."

"Heck, I know that! But I don't care," I thought. I was fixated on ending the relentless step after step of the descent. I was dying to stand on flat terrain. At the same time, my mind tried to gain control: "Stay calm, one slip could end your life. Bear with this tension; it's now or never." My fear was a safety net, and if kept in check by my inner voice, it enabled me to continue. The visible tracks from our ascent also provided encouragement. The much-anticipated knife-edge ridge that fed from the South Peak was easier to traverse on the way back, and that felt good. In almost the same amount of time it took us to reach the summit from the South Peak, we had returned there. The main hardship was over.

The oxygen bottles we had switched to at the South Peak on the ascent were almost empty upon our return so we dug them into the snow to leave behind. To our surprise, we found a couple of old bottles of an ancient type, and my heart raced with exhilaration, imagining them to be the ones left behind by Everest's first climbers, Sir Edmund Hillary and Tenzing Norgay. In admiration, we buried our empty bottles beside the old ones before switching to our other bottles for the remainder of the descent.

The cloud – more like fog – around Makalu was a growing concern. It forced us to continue, heads down, radio silent. When we arrived at the section where we had broken trail through deeper snow earlier that day, we knew we were close to Camp 6, and we eventually arrived at 4:30 p.m. Tired, we clambered into the tent with crampons still on, pulled off the oxygen masks and quickly fired up the stove. Hot coffee was in order, then a tin of pineapple, which was frozen solid – we had to thaw it directly over the flame. An exquisite after-summit meal!

Nervous about the weather and confident we had enough energy in reserve, Ang Tsering and I decided to descend as far as the South Col that evening. We reported our plan to Advanced Base Camp and asked them to inform the Sherpas so they would be ready for us later that night. It was 5:20 p.m. when we left Camp 6, and even though we had only stayed there one night on our way up the mountain, I felt regret leaving the pitched tent behind. Later in my life, I would act on that regret.

The monotony of descending resumed. One saving grace was that my pack, despite the added weight of restocked personal equipment from Camp 6, was manageable. Unsure why, I felt no further distress from the extra load. As we worked our way down the route, darkness gradually filled the sky. The summits of Makalu and Cho Oyu were tinged a reddish brown from the reflection of the sunset, the last bit of colour bringing closure to the day.

Black dots moving on the ice below came into view. Ang Tsering shouted to Lhak-pa (Lama-*san*), his older brother, and Reenjee (Reen-*chan*). They were there to welcome us. Ang Tsering and I turned to each other and acknowledged our appreciation for such a gesture, then Ang Tsering quickly sped up and the rope between us became as taut as a cable. "No rush, no rush, make one firm step after the other," I told myself in order to stay in control of my footing. I had to remain careful on the descent of the steep rock and ice. This was no place to be complacent, but Ang Tsering was on a mission. My only choice was to follow.

Two lights swirled in the not-too-far distance, voices percolated into earshot, and then the two parties – us and them – became one. Lama-*san* and Reen-*chan* leapt at me and heartily shook my hands then patted my shoulder over and over, saying, "Good job, good job!" They were oblivious to the steepness of the slope on which I still stood, not entirely stable.

The 8000-metre peaks that were wrapped in twilight hours before were now transformed into a deep purple. The drape of night had gently settled upon them. Ang Tsering spoke incessantly in Nepali, surrounded by the magnificent mountains he called home. All the while, the summits maintained their whitish glow in the night sky. I sat heavily in the snow, immobile, and listened to his words, which danced around me.

In 1975 I had no idea that the equipment we left behind on Everest would be considered garbage in the future, partly because we were following suit of all the expeditions prior to ours. Discarded items like oxygen bottles and tents were not considered a wrong-doing, and I never gave it much thought. We had made what we presumed was a reasonable effort in asking the Sherpas to remove everything from Camp 5 and lower, leaving only fixed ropes on the mountain. Nevertheless, when I walked away from the tent at Camp 6, I felt an unidentified tug at my conscience.

In 1975 I was the thirty-eighth person to summit Mount Everest, twenty-two years after Sir Edmund Hillary made the first ascent. By May 1993, thirty-eight climbers reached the peak in a single day, part of the increasing rate of climbers that would ensure Everest was scattered with garbage in no time.

Interest led me to became passionate about the health of mountain environments. In 2000, I completed a master's course in social culture with my focus on the garbage problem in the Himalayas. I also acted as chairperson (until 2014) of the Japanese branch of the Himalayan Adventure Trust, an organization that was formed by Sir Hillary and stands under the umbrella of a larger international mountain ecology association whose motto is "Carry down everything you carry up."

Along with my commitment to the role of chairperson came regret for leaving the empty oxygen bottles at the South Peak and the tent at Camp 6. I cannot change those occurrences, but I am the first to admit they make my voice stronger in encouraging as many people as possible to keep mountains clean.

CHAPTER 10

Endgame

May 17

Our tent shook in the vicious morning wind, and we knew all would have been lost if this was the day meant for the summit. We had succeeded in our goal on Everest, so weather was no longer a deterrent. In one sense, we could relax.

Since the summit radio call on May 16, we had been unable to make further contact with Camp 2. We could receive their calls, plus ones from Base Camp, but they were unable to pick up our signal. We had tried to transmit every half hour until 9 p.m. the night before with no luck. Anticipating their worry, we thought it best to quickly descend in order for the team at Camp 2 to spot us when we reached the Geneva Spur. We left Camp 5 with the three Sherpas who had stayed overnight at the South Col. There were no usable oxygen bottles left, and in climbing down I required multiple rests. I wondered at my tiredness.

We arrived at Camp 4 by noon, just in time for the midday radio call between Base Camp and Camp 2. Hastily, I turned on the radio and made contact. I could feel their enormous sense of relief wash over the airwaves as I spoke. Hisano had been unable to sleep a wink the night before out of concern for our safety. Although we tried, I felt sorry that I could not have eased her mind any earlier. I knew the amount of strain she would have felt wondering how her team was faring higher up on the mountain. What I failed to realize at the time was that some team members considered Hisano's concern for me and Ang Tsering to be too much and at the expense of the other climbers. The result was a widening division, like a deep crevasse, between leader and teammates, and the anguish it caused was immeasurable.

The tents that had remained at Camp 4 from our ascent were packed and dispersed among Ang Tsering and the three Sherpas who were with us, making their loads extremely heavy. Ang Tsering and I continued to totter down the slope, staggering on the Lhotse Face, thoroughly relying on our carabiners and the fixed ropes to guide us to safety below. Thank goodness for the Sherpa who met us at Camp 3 to help lighten our load by taking the packs and slinging them over his shoulder. Even then, my footing remained ridiculously tangled and my body unintentionally swayed on the long descent.

Countless times, even that strong sirdar Ang Tsering said, "Let's take a break." I hated to stand up after we sat, but we needed the longer breaks every fifteen minutes, with lots of short rests in between. And that was how we progressed down the mountain. Finally, Camp 2 was visible, and the shapes of our team members gradually took form, scurrying about, busy in anticipation of our arrival.

By that point in the expedition, I had no energy left for personal care. Sixty-two days in the Himalayas and I was not worried about how I looked. Appearance meant nothing as I reeled along, happy to be within sight of Camp 2. But the camp stretched away from us, like a mirage in a white desert of snow, at an unreachable distance. Then, at long last, I heard the words that ensured I could finally rest: "*Omedeto!*" Welcome back! Great job!

We made it. We had climbed to the top of Everest and back down again. We had survived the mighty ordeal of mountaineering at high elevations and safely returned to Camp 2, the very spot that could have changed our fortune a couple of weeks earlier on the night of the avalanche. Totally spent, Ang Tsering and I collapsed like rubber dolls, unable to stand upright for another minute.

We handed out the little stones that we had collected from near the summit, a gift to each of our teammates. We drank black tea and embraced the camaraderie of our friends, though only for a short while. Fatigue overcame me and I retreated to my tent, where Hisano had spread out my sleeping bag. Too tired to speak another word, I lay on my back and fell asleep.

May 18

I woke up numerous times in the night to reassure myself that I was, in fact, at Camp 2.

Comforted, I would sleep again until the next startled jolt of concern about my location. I was having difficulty determining my whereabouts and realizing that the task of climbing to the top of Everest was complete.

First thing the next morning, Hisano said, "You should come down to Base Camp with me right away."

I hesitated. "But I have to dismantle Camp 2."

"It's all right. You're too tired to do that," she said.

Part of my responsibility as assistant leader was to disassemble the camp, and it pained me to leave the job for Shioura, Taneya and Arayama. Supportively, they understood and encouraged me to descend. "It's OK," they said. "It's best for you to go down." The level of exhaustion I felt allowed me to be easily persuaded, and I prepared for the long-awaited return to Base Camp.

Roped up to one another, Hisano, Watanabe and I began to retrace the familiar route to Camp 1. Sentimental thoughts matched my steps, and I found myself saying goodbye to the landscape, even to the monstrous crevasses that somehow looked lovely to me. I felt a pang of emotion knowing that I would probably never see this place again in my lifetime. I looked back at the distant Lhotse Face and it shone like a polished prized possession. Stage by stage, we had pieced the mountain together and climbed to its magnificent summit. Tired, I continued my descent as though in a reverent dream.

Reality shifted when we arrived at the Duralumin ladder just below Camp 1. It hung there miserably broken, dangling in space, as though to remind us of the constant focus required by climbers. Hisano was first to descend the ruin, on belay by one of the Sherpas. When she was out of view, I realized I had one too many ice axes in my hand. "Oh, this is Hisano-*san*'s ice axe," I mumbled to myself, but my comment was met with frustration by Watanabe.

"You'd be rebuffed by everybody if you mention Hisano's name, or openly call her our leader these days," she said.

"What? How come?" I was confused by the direction of the conversation.

"Because, Tabei-*san*, she had only you and what was happening at the higher camps on her mind, nothing else."

The signal for my turn on the ladder was yelled from below, and with no reply to Watanabe, I stepped forth, one cautious rung at a time. My mind was a flurry. Something must have gone wrong between Hisano and the rest of the team. I had sensed a difference at camp the previous night but was unable to identify the cause. Now, after hearing Watanabe's unthinkable words, it was clear that built-up tensions needed to be addressed. Everest was a team effort, and I had no intention of losing what we had conquered to such dramatics.

We were back at the Khumbu Icefall. The upper section was like giant ocean waves frozen in time, while the lower part was visibly melting, and the sound of spouting water filled the air around me. How long had I been gone? It was late winter – mid-March – when I first reached Base Camp on our ascent, and now the thaw of springtime was everywhere. I walked through a stream of meltwater, tapping my crampons in the splashes of seasonal warmth. Our liaison officer, Lhakpa Tenzing, and Nasu and Manita added to the scenery by hiking partway up from Base Camp to greet us, a pot of hot black tea in hand.

"*Hontoni omedeto*, Tabei-*san*," said Lhakpa, his face overcome with joy and his hand tightly shaking mine as he offered a heartfelt congratulation. Next, I recognized Mihara approaching us, and then Hirashima and Dr. Sakaguchi.

"Sorry I talked back to you," I said to the doctor, asking forgiveness for ignoring her orders to retreat from Camp 2 after the avalanche. That, too, seemed ages ago, but was hopefully put to rest.

A few steps before we reached Base Camp, a front tooth on my crampons snapped off. I was impressed by the timing of it, so close to the end, as I walked the final distance in front of me. Once at Base Camp, all the Sherpas, the cook, the kitchen boys and the rest of the party welcomed us back. I heard Ang Tsering repeatedly say in Nepali, "*Dherai dherai thakai*" (very very tired), and I had to agree.

One factor I wanted to ensure upon arrival back to Base Camp was a doctor's checkup. I was curious as to how my body had held up to the higher elevations and its progress in recovery. Also, as premature as it may have seemed, I wanted a positive medical reference for future expeditions. The appointment failed to take place, however; and whether that was due to the general commotion at camp or my previously blatant disregard of doctor's orders at Camp 2, I was unsure.

After a hot bowl of *ramen*, and having handed out the remainder of the summit stones to our teammates, I desired nothing more than rest. I laid myself down in Hisano's small tent to sleep, but my mind fitfully wandered about. I should have felt safe, secure and tired there at Base Camp, yet sleep evaded me again. I was filled with a mixture of thoughts left to absorb.

May 19

I had hoped my fatigue would be gone after the first night back at Base Camp. Instead, the opposite was true – I was unable to lift myself out of the tent in the morning. I was painfully heavy with exhaustion, to the point of forgoing use of the toilet. Even to rise enough to catch sight of the oncoming climbers took all my might. As I watched their silhouettes – Shioura, Taneya, Arayama and several Sherpas – navigate the icefall, my only wish was for them to arrive at Base Camp as quickly as possible, then everything would be over. After seeing them descend, I burrowed back into my bag to rest.

An intense argument had been brewing amongst the Camp 1 team before they made it to Base Camp. I could hear their raised voices from afar. "Why wasn't any rope brought up to us when we had asked for it? We badly needed it! You don't care about us, the ones who stayed up there!" The confrontation highlighted Watanabe's earlier comments about team disruption, but, in all fairness, the Sherpas who could have taken ropes up to the icefall were occupied with ferrying loads between camps. They certainly were not sitting idle.

My attitude was that everyone had arrived at Base Camp unharmed, and by May 18, our entire team was in one place. No one had to climb through the daunting icefall anymore. We were done. Safe. *Finito*. For me, any residues of concern melted away. Everest was complete.

Hisano called a meeting in the mess tent for every climber to attend, except me. I could barely stand and remained sunken in my sleeping bag like a heavy sack. Akamatsu suggested I breathe with supplemental oxygen, and even though I would usually deem the gas too precious to use at a lower altitude, I placed the mask on my face and turned the flow dial to 0.5 litres per hour. The comfortable hiss of the oxygen as it seeped from the bottle lulled me to sleep.

I awoke again, this time to the sounds of boots stomping on the snow and a conversation I was likely not meant to hear. "Well, for whatever reason, Tabei is the one to be blamed most." The words stung as they hit me from the neighbouring doctor's tent. Why me, and what was I being blamed for? In a desperate state of tiredness, I had no energy, physically or mentally, to react, and again I succumbed to the hiss of the oxygen bottle. The team members, with all their opinions and criticisms, would have to sort themselves out. All I could manage was sleep.

Each time I woke, my thoughts would quickly see past everyone's blaming and whispering and recognize that the climb was over. All of us, every single climber and Sherpa, made it down the mountain. Period. I recalled how much I prayed, on the hike in, that the same number of people would be present on our way home. We succeeded. There lies the satisfaction of our expedition.

After four hours of supplemental oxygen, I stepped outside the tent and was immediately struck by the brightness of the day. I had assumed that the weather had turned when the light dimmed earlier, when in fact, it was the weakened state of my eyes. Despite poor vision, my body was alive enough to venture to the toilet, a feat I had been unable to accomplish hours earlier even by way of crawling.

Slightly revitalized and making my way around camp, I sensed the unsettled atmosphere that resulted from Hisano's meeting. The cause of frustration for the party arose from me not being able to communicate by radio from the South Col. Knowing that missed calls could indicate an accident, Hisano was so worried that she was unable to be calmed until she was confident we were safe.

In the eyes of the team members who were with Hisano at Camp 2, their leader only cared about the climbers on the upper part of the mountain, and not the rest of the team. They felt that it was an embarrassment and unacceptable for a leader to remain that agitated and nervous simply from lack of communication with a party at the South Col. How was it inappropriate to be concerned about a scenario of that magnitude? What would they have done as leader?

Hisano remained completely silent for the next two days. Her lone-liness and sorrow was understandable, but I desperately wished for her to speak up before her silence worked an opposite effect on everyone's well-being. In response to the tension between team members, the layout of tents had been completely rearranged, and a plume of cigarette smoke rose from the camp. Since none of the women on our team smoked, the fact that some had turned to cigarettes proved to me just how strained the situation had become.

By the day we were ready to dismantle Base Camp, our team was in-delibly divided in two. One group worked hard to clean things up, and the other stood by in observation, nonchalantly flipping through maga-zines, sunglasses on and cigarettes in hand. The workers paid attention to detail so as not to disgrace the reputation of an all-women's party: toilets were buried under stones; burnable garbage was set alight; emptied cans were collected and thrown into the deepest of crevasses, even though we were concerned that those tins might resurface one day.

I was ready to leave after I watched the logs that were used as poles for the kitchen tarp burn to nonexistence. Hisano and I turned to leave Base Camp behind, waving farewell to Hirashima, Kitamura and Mihara, the three who stayed to finish the last of the kitchen cleanup. Their faces were smeared with black from the ashy smoke, highlighting the filthy nature of the job.

The gap between leader and climbers grew and followed us down the trail. In its wake, it dragged all other frustrations from the trip, trivial or otherwise. Accusations were made about who was chosen to climb to higher camps and to the summit. As climbing leader, I was ridiculed, too. "Tabei didn't bother passing on any more instructions to the others once she was selected for the summit assault," said one teammate. Another declared that it was Annapurna all over again. I realized that frustrations originally directed at Hisano had shifted to complaints against me.

Some climbers stayed clear of the negative backtalk, murmuring under their breath that enough was enough. Unfortunately, this passive re-sponse did nothing to erase the bad taste in the air that hung like a wet blanket on our route to Lukla.

It would have been impossible to fully satisfy all fifteen members of the expedition, regardless of who was leader. When two or more people are involved in any situation, let alone the number we had and the setting we were in, compromises must be made. Curiously, though, even when annoyance, fatigue and disheartened emotion exist, the physical pain of it heals and is forgotten with time.

Standing on the summit of Everest lasted a moment in time, a moment that resulted from the joint effort of all the women on our team. We came to the expedition with greatly varied backgrounds and strove together for nearly four years to reach the mountain. It was our combined determination that made the summit moment a significant one.

There lies the most precious thing about our trip: teamwork and commitment to the goal. Yes, the summit was an unforgettable experience for me, one that crystallized as a memory for life. But the reason for our success went deeper than standing on the summit – it was the result of will and endurance. I believe that a person's will is innate – it comes from a fired-up passion that begins in the bottom of the heart, and takes over from there – and I equate will to power. That power was what steered the 1975 Japanese all-women's team to Everest in the first place, and more so, to the summit.

The news of our success travelled fast. A speech by King Birendra of Nepal was aired on the radio and a message from Nepal's queen was also delivered. Telegrams arrived in Kathmandu from Japanese Prime Minister Mr. Miki and former Heritage and Education Minister Mr. Nagai, as did many other congratulatory well-wishes from numerous other countries. It was during these celebrations that I heard for the first time that the United Nations had designated 1975 as International Women's Year.

Ang Tsering, team leader Hisano and I were awarded the Order of the Gorkha Dakshina Bahu – one of the highest honours in Nepal – directly by King Birendra himself, and we paraded through the city of Kathmandu, riding in a convertible car decorated with flowers. Before us, Sir Edmund Hillary was the last foreigner to receive the award, twenty-two years earlier. After the festivities, and having said goodbye to the Sherpas and the others who had assisted us on the expedition, we travelled to India, where we were met by more than a hundred reporters awaiting interviews. Prime Minister Indira Gandhi was also slated to meet with us. Overwhelmed by our reception, I remained unconvinced that we had done anything worth this scale of treatment.

June 8

Almost six months after I had left Japan for Everest, Hisano, Watanabe and I landed back in Tokyo. Ang Tsering accompanied us as an invitee of *The Yomiuri Shimbun* and Nippon Television. Reporters and cameramen crowded around us, blocking our way as we descended the steps of the airplane. We still could not believe the reaction to our climb. What was all the fuss about?

After I passed through customs, I finally saw my daughter. She wore a new long dress and had a yellow ribbon in her hair. My mother clasped her hand and led her towards me. Noriko's lips were tightly pursed; she was unsure of how to proceed. "Noriko, it's your mom," I said. It had been half a year since I had seen my only child. Her growth in that time filled me with joy. I hugged her in my arms, so grateful for our reunion. The moment was rushed as a line of cameramen on stepladders poured over us to take photos. In the commotion, I glimpsed my mountain buddies and elementary school friends who had travelled a far distance to welcome me home.

My husband had waited for me at the Tokyu Hotel, keeping at bay the press, there for a scheduled interview. "Welcome back. Good job," Masanobu said. I noticed that he and my mother and sister each appeared more tired than me. The burden of the past many months had taken its toll on everyone.

Ang Tsering and I spent two more days at the hotel for TV interviews and various greetings. My mother had left the airport having had only a brief peek at me; my daughter and husband returned to my sister's home until I could be there too. Meanwhile, I was invited to a lunch party with Japan's emperor and empress, prime minister, heritage and education minister, and minister of labour, all of whom I would never have met if not for the first women's ascent of Mount Everest.

Ang Tsering felt out of place in Japan once Hisano had returned to her home in Nara, so he accompanied me to my sister's house. Together we climbed Mount Fuji, ran experiments in the low-pressure lab at the University of Nagoya and visited Hokkaido. Our busy schedule had me drop 2 kilograms of body weight in Japan despite barely losing an ounce in the Himalayas.

Two months after my arrival back in Japan, I eventually returned to my home in Kawagoe. "Wasn't that more tiring than climbing Everest?" I said to Ang Tsering, still dazed by the whirlwind of activity that greeted our return from Nepal.

"Yes!" he said. By that point, he must have been longing for his own home. I helped pack his bags for his final leg of the journey.

To my surprise, the spotlight on our climb did not lessen. There was an invitation from Motorola, the telecommunications company; an offer from a German television show; speech requests at numerous mountaineering clubs, education boards and companies; and newspaper and magazine interviews. The list was endless, and in that first year after Everest, I had very little time to settle back into home life.

Our Everest did not culminate at the safe return to Base Camp as I expected it to, and the interest in our trip became more far-reaching than we could have imagined. In one way, the attention we garnered was positive. It allowed us to pay off the team's debt by way of a jointly written report book and photo exhibitions that were well received from miles around. In another way, it irreversibly changed my life.

By the end of 1975, almost one year after I had left for the Himalayas, I was finally able to send my husband on a trekking adventure in the Rolwaling area of Nepal, from where he would see Mount Everest himself. In booking his trip, I realized that we would once again miss spending New Year's holiday together, a record that would repeat itself throughout our long marriage. Such was our life as a couple of devoted mountaineers.

CHAPTER 11

Women on Everest

Near the time of our climb, the United Nations declared 1975 as International Women's Year at a world conference held in Mexico City. I heard afterwards that the audience at the conference surged with applause when news of the first female success on Everest was reported. Whether I wanted it to be or not, our climb became a symbol of women's social progress.

During the exact minute I was standing on top of Everest, another woman was also aiming for the mountain's summit, although from the Tibetan side of the mountain. Her name was Pan Duo, a member of the Chinese expedition, and she eventually reached the summit with male teammates on May 27, 1975, eleven days after my ascent.

The Tibetan landscape from the summit of Everest was striking to me. I had no idea the Chinese expedition of two hundred people was challenging the mountain from that side. The first I heard of it was when a reporter in Kathmandu asked me, "Can you believe that another woman was successful on Everest immediately after you? We've just received the news." I was surprised and then realized that the chatter we sometimes heard on the radio during our climb was that of the Chinese team.

In that era, China was a mysterious nation not forthcoming with information. The country was closed behind bamboo curtains, so to speak. Still, I aspired to meet Pan Duo, mainly because she was another woman who shared the same dream as me even though she was from such a veiled country. The eleven-day difference between her ascent and mine placed her as the second female climber on Everest, but Pan Duo was the first female to climb the Tibetan route. This intrigued me, as did our shared age of thirty-five.

My chance to meet her came unexpectedly one day. In January 1979, I received a telegram from Maurice Herzog, the first person to climb to more than 8000 metres. He was inviting me to be part of a film project in France that would include the history of women on Everest. Pan Duo was also invited, and we were to travel to Chamonix that coming August. I quickly replied yes, if Pan Duo would attend, and wasted no time in preparing for the trip.

By that time, three women had stood on the summit of Everest: me and Pan Duo in 1975, and Wanda Rutkiewicz from Poland in 1978. I was excited to meet them both, especially to hear their answers to Herzog's specific question: "Why Everest?" To which, each one of us had a unique response. "For myself and for my team," I said. "For the Republic of China," said Pan Duo. "For women's liberation," declared Rutkiewicz. I was shocked by their answers; their way of thinking was well beyond my basic reasons to climb.

Rutkiewicz led several women-only teams in her climbing career that included routes on the East Pillar of Norway's Trollryggen (1968), the North Pillar of the Eiger (1973) and North Face of the Matterhorn in winter (1978). She was a prominent light for women climbers in a time when men dominated the field. Sadly, she disappeared from the North Face of Kanchenjunga in 1992 during her amazing pursuit of all fourteen 8000-metre peaks, eight of which she summitted, including the first female ascent of K2 in 1986.

Pan Duo was sought after by the Chinese government to be part of the country's first attempt on Everest in 1960. She had a robust build and a successful climbing history that could not be ignored. Nonetheless, she was ordered to remain below 6400 metres on Everest. "Above that elevation is a man's world," she was told. Her frustration was evident.

In 1961 she was also successful on Kongur Tiube in China; however, due to sudden bad weather on the descent, one of her female teammates was killed and Pan Duo froze her feet (she had five toes amputated afterwards). When we met in Chamonix, she showed me the remnants of her lost toes and determinedly remarked, "My toes were given to the nation." I was shocked by her words, and as a person born in a country where people enjoy mountaineering for leisure, I was unable to relate to Pan Duo's easy acceptance of the matter.

The next Chinese Everest expedition, in 1975, was a nation-devoted project. The government recruited as many women candidates as possible for the first female ascent. At the time, Pan Duo, who was married to a Han tribesman, had three young children, including a baby still being breastfed. When she became an official member of the Everest team, she had to move to Beijing without her family to begin intense and difficult training for many years. She did not see her then five-month-old baby, who was adopted by her husband's parents, until nearly sixteen years later.

On Everest, the team was pushed extremely hard. "Climb ahead of Japanese women!" they were ordered. Pan Duo continued their story for me: "We had a tragic accident at about 8600 metres, and a member died. So, we retreated down to 8300 metres for a short while, with a heavy feeling in all of us. It was then we heard of your success and it greatly inspired us to resume our attack once more. Really good." I was impressed to know that our success raised their spirits. My friendship with Pan Duo was solid from our meeting in Chamonix until she passed away in 2014. She was seventy-five.

As it was for me, Everest was a huge game changer for Pan Duo. As a result of the climb, she was hired by the General Administration of Sport and became an active member in national politics. Her family became wealthy, too. She was chosen to represent China at the World Conference on Women held in Beijing in 1995, and in 2008, she gallantly carried the Olympic flag with fellow athletes for the opening ceremony of the Beijing Olympics. I tuned in to those games on television, and I felt a profound sense of pride when I watched her hold that flag.

Years after that trip to Chamonix in 1979, I thought about meeting all the women who had climbed Everest to date. I realized there were cultural and societal differences in our individual pursuits of the mountain, and I was interested to learn more about the female perspective, especially since the number of women on Everest was increasing year by year.

So, my long-acquainted climbing partner and friend Setsuko Kitamura and I created the opportunity to meet these women by hosting an event marking the twentieth anniversary of our success on Everest, titled Mount Everest Women's Summit 1995. I knew it was now or never; the number of women who had stood on Everest by then was thirty-two; it would be difficult to organize a greater number of women in the future.

In planning for June, we sent a questionnaire to each of the thirty-two climbers to narrow down who we would invite. Based on replies, people's availability, and what we could afford in terms of flights and accommodation, we invited nine climbers from six different countries. We also extended an invitation to Elizabeth Hawley, the American journalist specializing in mountaineering who had been living in Nepal for thirty-five years. Meanwhile, news arrived that on May 13, 1995, Alison Hargreaves, a thirty-three-year-old mother of two children from the United Kingdom, had been successful on Everest. She had completed a solo climb from the Tibetan side of the mountain without supplemental oxygen. "How wonderful," we said. "Let's invite her to Japan as well." Unfortunately, she had to decline the invitation. She was leaving for K2. She was sorry to miss the event and she wished us the best.

On August 13, less than three months after we had received her reply, Hargreaves died on K2. Her children were four and six years old. I had such regret for this loss; I wished so much that she would have come to Japan and that I could have met her. I found myself, even years later, trapped in the moment of thought she may have experienced in the split second of the accident that took her life. I completely understood the dread of such a moment.

When the day of the women's summit arrived in Tokyo, it had been sixteen years since I had first met Pan Duo in Chamonix. She looked remarkably different. Instead of the dark Mao-style suit she wore in France, Pan Duo was dressed in a blue suit patterned with large, colourful peony flowers; she carried a black handbag and wore pumps, and even her hair had changed from a plain short cut to a wavy style, with a few wisps of white peeking through to show her age.

"When I was just about at the top of Everest, not a thought of my children or family entered my mind. I was too afraid of not being able to make the summit at the last moment," Pan Duo said to me, suggesting she was not necessarily a warm family person. But her actions showed otherwise. She insisted that we must have our picture taken together, with my husband and children, too, because she had promised to share it with her family. She also spoke kindly with my son, Shinya. "Oh, you are the one born after *Chomulungma* [Everest]. All right, all right, you are a big boy now," and she repeatedly shook his hand. Shinya later remarked that the handshake almost crushed his bones. Behind her position as vice-chairman of the Chinese Mountaineering Association was a regular mother who deeply cared for children.

In her speech at the event, her diplomatic side shone brightly, too, exhibiting Pan Duo's pride in being a strong Tibetan woman. "In China, we have many mountains; nine peaks of more than 8000 metres share borders with either Nepal or Pakistan, just to list a few, and international mountaineers and explorers set their ambitions on them all the time. We welcome you folks to come over and climb the mountains in China, and I look forward to deepening our friendship and partnership. I cannot wish too much for a peace-and-equality flag to flutter high over those mountains in China."

Comments from other climbers offered even more of a cross-section of our collective experiences in the mountain world. We were a unique group, tied by our love for high places.

> It is very hard for women to get an education in India. I was one of five siblings but only one daughter, hence pressed to marry when I was fourteen. So, I left home at sixteen to avoid being married off and I went to university in Jaipur. My door to the Himalayas opened up when I joined an international camp held on Nun Kun massif in Kashmir in 1989, and eventually I was chosen for India's Everest team in 1992.
>
> – Santosh Yadav, India, two-time climber of Everest

▲

> South Korea has a strong tradition of Confucianism and it trends to male dominance. Having joined with the university's mountaineering club in 1979, I started realizing the absolute power gap between men and women through rock and ice climbing. There, I saw the general status between men and women begin to waver. My conclusion is that we have to upgrade women's status first before we climb mountains with ease.
>
> – Ji Hyun-ok, South Korea

▲

I have never been discriminated against as a female mountaineer. Having heard your stories, I feel lucky to have been
born in the United Kingdom, where outdoor activities are
encouraged no matter the gender. I started mountaineering
at age fifteen and naturally joined the mountaineering club
at university. I also chose to research the subject of altitude
sickness in order to connect my personal passion with my
work. My American husband and I met on a commercial expedition team for Everest and stood at the top of the world
together. So, Everest is a special place for me as well.

– Dr. Ginette Harrison, United Kingdom

On May 18, 1998, Dr. Harrison climbed the North Face of Kangchen-
junga and became the first woman to summit the world's third-high-
est peak; on May 22, 1999, she was the first British woman to summit
Makalu. In 1999 she died in an avalanche on Dhaulagiri, the world's
seventh-highest mountain. She was forty-one years old.

These stories traced a path through the generations and evolution of
big-mountain climbing, from the first four women on Everest in the
1970s who were responsible for all aspects of trip preparation, to a newer
era in the 1990s when commercial expeditions became available. I was
fascinated by the array of experiences we shared.

Lydia Bradey from New Zealand was the most distinctive of all the
female climbers at the women's summit. In October 1988, she became
the first female to climb Everest without supplemental oxygen. She
was tall and blonde and full of humour; her mischievous nature made
me feel like we had been friends for a long time. On the stage, she
spoke about her Everest climb while showing slides of the expedition.
She went there as a member of the joint team for New Zealand and
Czechoslovakia. Their original permit allowed them to climb the Southwest Face, but the weather was too poor to continue on that route. So,
alone, Bradey climbed the Southeast Ridge, without a proper permit,
thus making her success problematic. Three other Kiwi climbers, including the team leader, criticized her for continuing and returned to
Kathmandu while Bradey was still climbing to higher camps. They even

denounced her achievement when they heard she had summitted the mountain.

Unfortunately, she had no way to prove her victory. Her camera had frozen and she had lost her watch, and was therefore unable to record the precise time of reaching the summit. Furthermore, since she feared prohibition of entry back into Nepal for the next ten years for ignoring the Nepalese government's requirement for a permit, she played down her success. Her situation of true or false, real or fake, became dubbed Lydia-Gate, and as such, was highly controversial.

Time, however, proved to be on Bradey's side. A Spanish party paid homage to her account and provided testimony that they passed her near the summit on the day she claimed to be there. Under scrutiny, she was able to confirm specific details about summit conditions, to which the Spanish party agreed.

Open-minded and honest, she explained that the thought of using oxygen had never occurred to her. In fact, having not used bottled oxygen before, she was unfamiliar with how the apparatus even worked. She said that the sentiment of "I did it!" only caught up to her after she had summitted and then descended to the South Summit, where she felt safer, and could readily embrace her accomplishment.

I think the invitation to tell her story in Japan, while the debate was still ongoing, gave Bradey a welcome chance to officially report her climb. It was a pleasure to hear her version.

By the end of the women's summit, the atmosphere of the hall was vividly charged. We were an intense group of women. The next day, we would head to Mount Fuji to clean up the climbing area.

The next morning, the rainy days turned to blue sky. More than two hundred people showed up to participate, making it fun for everyone to contribute, public and climbers alike. Bradey chatted away as she gracefully stepped off route onto sketchy scree to pick up more garbage.

After the cleanup, the women Everest climbers regrouped and headed to an *onsen* resort in Hakone. Our Chinese, Indian and South Korean colleagues chose to not partake in the outside *iwa-onsen* (rocky hot springs). Likely, their cultural norms led them to feel a bit too exposed, naked in the outdoor pools. Bradey, on the other hand, jumped right in.

Before we knew it, Kitamura and I were in stitches, trying to talk the bare Bradey out of bouldering on the rocks that surrounded the pool.

Kitamura and I climbed the Eiger after the women's summit, and we sent a postcard to Bradey. When we returned home from Switzerland, a long letter from her greeted us.

> Thanks for the invitation. It was an amazing experience. Being accepted as a real summitter was like being purified. My image of Japanese people has been transformed as well. I used to think Japanese people were extremely serious with little room for humour; however, I was wrong. My conclusion is that Japanese have more of a sense of humour than the people in most of the countries I've been to so far, and that's why I was laughing for more than half the time I spent in Japan.
>
> Tell me how you arranged the good weather for Mt Fuji, as opposed to the rain we had every day up till then. It was a wonderful thing to climb Fuji with the keeners, in particular, the women. I also made good friends with the Everest summitters. I found it very interesting to know that, despite our different social backgrounds, all of us share certain ideas in terms of women's role in each society.
>
> I think the summitters in general are a group of cheerful people with a fun sense of humour. Research says that the women mountaineers who climb higher than 7,000 metres spend more than a quarter of their lifetime laughing, share domestic works with their partners and wear flashy-coloured clothes. Also, 89 per cent of women who have experienced climbing higher than 7,000 metres show more resolute attitudes toward everything....

I laughed having read Bradey's letter, and I especially enjoyed her parting offer: "Please come to New Zealand, Junko and Setsuko. I'll send the brochure for the routes I recommend." Climbing begets climbing, and in an unforeseen way, Everest opened the door even wider for many of us to continue following our dreams. These added friendships were a bonus to the many years of hard work and commitment that led us to Everest in the first place.

CHAPTER 12

Mount Tomur, Pobeda Peak

With the sight of the admired summit in front of us, we turned around and retreated down the mountain.

Mount Tomur, meaning "iron peak" in Chinese, has the highest summit in the Tian Shan Range that lies between the former Soviet Union and China. I was there on an all-women's expedition, a group of climbers that never gave up, until there was no other choice. We had to turn our backs on the summit. Prior to that decision, we climbed with all our might. There were four of us ahead of the rest of the team. We were climbing a bowl-shaped snow slope on a diagonal course towards a rock wall that, from below, looked like a ship's prow. We named it Battleship Rock and had set our sights there for Camp 3. Despite our constant efforts, the rocky feature was still a long way off, and Yuko Kuramatsu, the youngest member of the team, was suffering from altitude sickness. We were at 5550-plus metres of elevation, and her headache had progressed to severe. The other members, Fumie Kimura, Mayuri Yasuhara and I, were fine, but we had to act quickly for Yuko's sake.

As team leader, I decided that she would immediately descend to Camp 2, but she could not go alone. I weighed my choices. First, I asked her to empty her pack of the shared food and gear; the rest of us would divide the items up to carry. Next, I measured who was best to assist Yuko down the mountain. Yasuhara was at the top end of the rope, followed by me and Kimura, with Yuko tied in last. If Yasuhara left with Yuko, there would be too much extra rope at the front and tail, but if Kimura went down, Yasuhara and I could continue with the system we had in place, and I could manage the extra rope behind me. Decision made, I asked Kimura to join Yuko in the descent. "You bet," she said. "I'll go down with Yuko to Camp 2 and come back up once she is met there by the others, so I'll leave my backpack here. Our trail is clear and I'll be fine. I'll catch up with you soon." I nodded at her confident reply and sent them on their way.

"I'm sorry," said Yuko as she turned from our objective.

"Don't worry," I said. "Drink lots of water and rest well at Camp 2. If your headache remains tomorrow morning, go down to Camp 1. Please keep us updated by radio." She agreed to my words and began the descent with only personal gear in her backpack and Kimura two steps behind.

I coiled up the length of rope that lay behind me and secured it to the top of my pack. I knew we should continue to climb as high as possible while the snowpack conditions were safe. Yasuhara quickly repacked Yuko's share of gear and then began her strong steps up the untouched slope. The bowl was like a blank canvas, marked with the brushstroke of our ascent. Heads down and with no chit chat, we resumed the struggle in knee-deep snow. The two sounds that broke the cocoon of silence that enveloped me were my laboured breath and the bite of crampons as I kicked them into the slope.

It was 1986. We were an all-women's team of twelve, granted a permit from the Chinese Mountaineering Association for the first foreign-party ascent of Mount Tomur. We had also applied for a permit for the Soviet Union side of the mountain but were rejected; foreign expeditions were not yet being accepted there. Available information on the climb was slim, and all we had to rely on were reports from a 1960s Chinese expedition.

Greatly admired by climbers, the Tian Shan Mountains are a mountain range of dreams. To finally set foot there was almost unreal, but the environment posed challenges. Even reaching Base Camp was not straightforward. We used packhorses to carry loads of gear and food, hiked through areas with no trails or signage, relied on locals as guides and had to endure endless meetings with the liaison officer assigned to us by the Chinese Mountaineering Association. At first, we were hopeful since the liaison officer was said to have been a member on the earlier

Chinese expedition, but his memory was rusty and details were vague. We were on our own in this regard.

A maze of crevasses had us carefully navigate the glacier from Base Camp to Camp 1. A series of seracs were added to the puzzle en route to Camp 2, often forcing us to climb ice walls rather than contour around them. We were behind schedule and began to push things a bit, which meant that when the four of us left to establish a third camp below Battleship Rock, we had not allowed ourselves enough time to acclimatize. The result: we were down two climbers with Yuko suffering from altitude sickness and being accompanied by Kimura, while Yasuhara and I drove on.

We took turns breaking trail up the slope. Incredibly, Kimura caught up to us, yet Battleship Rock appeared no closer. Finally, as darkness began to settle, we arrived within an acceptable distance of the rock face. I checked my watch – 6 p.m. We dug a platform into the steep slope and pitched the tent. After brewing a hot soup, I stepped outside. There was heavy snowfall and the temperature was warm. I had a bad feeling about the combination of these factors. As we slipped into our down bags, we convinced ourselves to sleep that night regardless, and in the early morning we would re-evaluate the snow conditions.

In our cavelike hole, the tent was protected from the falling snow, but I could not put to rest the looming sense of danger I felt. My heart stirred in nonstop discontent. In the wee hours the next day, Kimura was the first out of the tent to gauge the situation. "Lots of fresh snow," she said, "about 70 centimetres." My heart sank further as I pictured that much new snow on such a steep slope. Avalanche. We were sitting ducks.

Stay there or move? We had to decide, so I stepped outside, too, for a better look. The steep drop of the slope beneath us was accentuated by the dark crevasses we could see lower down. If we moved, we would likely trigger the mountainside to release. First, I had to warn the members at Camp 2 and have them descend to Camp 1. Then we would climb higher once we knew everyone else was in a safe zone. This was the only reasonable solution I could formulate. Kimura and Yasuhara agreed. It was more dangerous for us to head downward than cover the final distance to Battleship Rock. A light snow continued to fall. The clouds hung low and visibility was poor.

As soon as we received a radio call to confirm that Camp 2 was va-
cated and our teammates were safe, we started to climb. I was in the
lead. Heavy packs, a steep slope and new snow dictated a gruelling pace.
We were at an elevation of more than 6000 metres, and I was breathing
hard. I felt rushed. Ultimately, I reached the bottom of the rocky prow
and hammered a 60-centimetre snow picket into the slope. "Climb up!"
I yelled once I was secured to the anchor. Kimura was next on the rope,
and then Yasuhara – they would climb in unison as I pulled up slack
in the line. I was braced on top of an overhang and was unable to see
their movement, but as the rope fed through my mitted hands I knew
they were on their way. Soon I saw the top of Kimura's helmet and was
relieved that she only had 5 metres left to climb. Then, a split second later,
she disappeared.

With a distinct and unforgiving sound, the snow cracked across the
slope between Kimura and Yasuhara, and the mountainside gave way.
The instantaneous force of the huge avalanche ripped out the snow
picket I had hammered in, and with it, yanked me from my perch. I
was thrown onto the slope below, somersaulting once, and then began to
turbo slide downhill atop the chunks of moving snow. A single thought
jolted my brain: React! I flailed my arms and legs as much as possible
while hard snow like sharp needles hit my eyes, nose and mouth. In no
time, I covered the distance that had taken us more than a day to ascend.
My thoughts expanded to this moment possibly being the end of my life.
"Shinya!" I called, the name of my young son, eight years old, at home
waiting for his mother to return. I felt helpless. What will happen next?
When will it stop? What can I do? These questions fiercely stormed my
mind as the avalanche pummelled me farther down the slope.

BAM! The massive pressure of the updraft slammed me against the
snow, and all movement stopped. The avalanche had dropped into a crevasse and the resulting updraft lodged me onto the surface above the lip
at the last minute. I was buried like a human corkscrew up to my hips.
Both my arms were free, but my legs were unable to budge, as if set in
concrete, and my body began to shake. Hastily, I pulled the rope that
lay in front of me on the snow, shouting, "Are you alive?" I desperately
looked for Yasuhara and Kimura, insistent that the rope was our life line,
that my friends would be all right. My mouth was completely dry.

More than 10 metres away, a pile of snow shifted, like a mole finding its way to the surface. It was Kimura. She, too, pulled on the rope, yelling, "Yasuhara-*san!*" There was another stir in the snow farther away, and Yasuhara appeared. Both were alive and uninjured. Miracle of miracles. They brushed themselves off and rushed over to help me, chopping with ice axes and digging with their hands through the debris that held me firmly in place. At last, my legs were freed.

Looking upslope, we saw the start of the fracture line close to where we were positioned before the slide. It was obvious another avalanche could be triggered in the bowl and that we had to get out of there. "Leave your packs and let's go down," I said, knowing that time was of the essence.

"Are we really throwing them away? A brand-new tent is in there. That's 70,000 yen," piped Kimura.

"Life is more precious than a tent, isn't it? We can work hard and buy a new tent again – if we go home alive. The priority now is to get down to a safe place as quickly as possible." Relieved of loads, we began our retreat.

We could hardly move fast enough in the deep snow, but we urgently pushed forward. Sure enough, another avalanche released, its white powder cloud chasing us like a giant wave. "Escape to the side!" I shouted, but we were too late. The edge of the avalanche hit us and we fell like dominos. We were covered with snow but not buried. We shook ourselves off and started to scurry down again. I looked back up the slope to reassess, and a third avalanche was on its way. "Coming on our left this time!" My heart pounded with alarm, but the debris stopped before it reached us. A depleted trio collapsed to their knees.

"So, avalanches happened as predicted."

"Good thing we came down."

"Had we stayed there any longer, we'd have all been buried alive in deep snow."

"We should be safe here for now."

Thus went the conversation we shared while trying to catch our wheezing breath. Truth is, we were terrified. Recalling the initial fall from the top scared us half to death.

Camp 1 came into view. The other team members milled around full of worry. They could only imagine what had occurred on the slope above and had no idea if we were dead or not. Fear abated as we approached the camp, and they hugged us with immense joy while we stood there, covered head to toe in snow. "Great to see you again, alive!" they cried as we gathered in a tent that night to celebrate our survival.

The merriment was short lived. At around midnight, much like at Camp 2 on Everest, another avalanche released and we were caught in its grip once more. With no warning, the rumbling noise like that of an oncoming train descended on camp. Although we were not hit head-on by the fourth avalanche, the force of the wind it created ploughed into our tent, pushing it away as if it were a feather. There were six of us asleep inside, and we were tossed around like marbles, banging into each other over and over. We were utterly useless in the fight against nature.

"What's happening?" we yelled, and then with the braking sound of a big truck, all movement ceased. I reached to unzip my sleeping bag, but fumbling in the darkness and overcome with confusion and shock, I was unable to locate the zipper. Trapped in my bag, I shouted, "Is everyone OK?"

Desperate pleas for help responded. "I can't move. I can't move," cried the voice of one of the younger members. I felt the fabric of the tent beside my head; I would have to cut it open to get us out. I finally unzipped my bag and grabbed the knife I always wore on a cord around my neck, and pulled open the blade with my teeth. I slit into the tent wall with abandon. "Save us now," I thought. "I'll deal with the tent later."

A rush of cold air struck my face, and in the black of night I could only see avalanche debris – it had scarcely passed us by. There were still two other tents to address, and frustrated by the difficulty I had in clambering out of my sleeping bag, I yelled, "Hey, are you safe?"

"We're all right," came a response, "cutting the tent open now." One by one, members crawled out of the enormous mess, hair strewn and faces bewildered, altogether shaken. Each person was accounted for, physically present in a setting of panic. I knew the cold temperature was our next enemy.

"Everyone, get dressed, put your boots on!" I demanded, despite my own overpowering sense of fear. I tried to ignore the playback in my mind of the events that had just occurred – *an avalanche blew by our tent in the middle of the night; inside, we were blown around like leaves in the wind.* I could barely articulate what to do next, but I kept delivering instructions. To a younger member who sat stunned and non-responsive, I spoke clearly: "Find your headlight first, put your down jacket on, find your boots and put them on." I realized my own boots were missing, but luckily, I had on down booties, an adequate substitute.

The camp looked like a battlefield, with the ongoing threat of attack from above. Petrified of further avalanches, we swallowed our fear while we grabbed whatever we could from the tents and organized ourselves to move.

We could not expose ourselves to a mountain where avalanches oc-curred at midnight. As soon as dawn was upon us, we would leave. In climbing, the purpose is to stand on the summit, but more important, there should be the same number of people in the party at the start of the climb and at the finish. I refused to turn my back on this conviction. "Come early morning, we'll go down," I concluded. "For now, let's prepare ourselves to not get cold and wait for the sunrise." The climb was over.

One teammate was too frightened to speak. I warmed my hands by rubbing them together and wrapped her cheeks with my palms. "It's OK," I said. "We'll go down together in the morning." I massaged circulation into her earlobes. With a big sigh, she began to cry, clinging to me. "It's all right," I repeated, "it's all right." I gently patted her back like a mother would her child.

The nighttime hours slowly passed as we waited in dread of our sur-roundings. All the gear was packed; as soon as any hint of morning light appeared, we would be on our way. As much as a hot tea would warm our spirits, we kept the stoves stuffed away, too scared of exposure to another avalanche. I wished I could have formulated a prayer for dawn to arrive faster than normal.

We huddled in two separate groups to avoid a mass burial should an-other avalanche hit. Those were long painful hours of waiting we en-dured, rubbing each other's backs and hands to encourage circulation, and stomping around to stay warm. My mind replayed the day's events, and I relived the panic I felt when I slid down the slope in the turmoil of the avalanche and thought my life was over. Yet no one died. And there we stood, the group of us, having survived a near burial at midnight. I wanted us back at Base Camp. I was as scared as the others, although no one would guess. They were pale and shaken; I felt responsible for cheering them up and getting us through this ordeal. "Remain patient and calm," I said to myself, "especially in the time of alarm."

I spoke with team doctor and assistant trip leader Kaori Hashimoto. "We'll split into two parties, mixing the Himalayan-experienced members with the novices. The ropes should be on the outside of the backpacks, ready to go, because even a small crevasse may be difficult to cross – our bodies don't work well in a state of panic," I said.

"Good idea," she said. "I'll do a medical checkup on everyone once we're at Base Camp." Her shared confidence offered me the hint of relief I needed.

My toes were numb. The temperature had dropped, and it was bitterly cold in the deepest of night. "Too cold for another avalanche," I thought, but I knew Mother Nature was unpredictable. Her unleashed power could demolish us in an instant. With that in mind, I had to humbly accept our situation while her stormy rage stabilized.

Silhouettes began to take shape. Dawn was upon us. The excitement from the night was over, giving me the chance to stop and think: "Don't hurry; look carefully around; check on everyone." We had to be methodical in our retreat, be certain that equipment was safe, that harnesses were correctly buckled up. There was no room for error. The party leaders were instructed to stay at least 20 metres apart at all times, providing some space between groups but not enough for us to lose sight of one another. Then we began our final descent from the mountain.

Base Camp was a brighter shade of green than when we were there last. To leave the glacier and stand on soil was a strange sensation, but a welcomed one. Three team members who had volunteered as base-camp managers held a banner written in Chinese characters, to greet us – 全員無事帰還、熱烈大歡迎, "A PASSIONATE WELCOME, EVERYBODY BACK HOME SAFE."

Once we were within a short distance of camp, we all began to run. There was an onslaught of hand shaking and hugging and patting of backs. The message was reiterated from our friends: "It's great, so glad to see you, coming back safe is the most important thing!" We were a team of distorted faces blurred with tears and runny noses, and for us there was no happier moment.

Although we were granted the first-ever permit for a foreign expedition on Mount Tomur, to continue the climb was beyond us. We chose survival over summit. It was a big change in plans to call off the ascent, but all members agreed that it was the right decision. Tomur was one of only a few mountains that I retreated from, forgoing the chance to stand on its peak. More than a decade passed before I had recovered from the fear that engulfed me on that trip.

Beyond Intellect

"It's strange. Something is wrong with my body. I can't even put my foot forward." In the second when I wondered what was happening, I spun around and felt a huge force push against me.

In 1990, four years after retreating from Mount Tomur at the 6200-metre mark, leaving the peak unclimbed by my team, I received a phone call from a fellow climber. "As the fiftieth anniversary event for my university's mountaineering club, we're planning to climb Mount Tomur. The only information available is the report from your expedition. Would it be possible to meet you and talk about it?" he asked. At the time, a Japanese team was yet to climb the highest peak in the Tian Shan Mountains.

So it was that three robust mountain men visited my home in Kawagoe. One of them I immediately recognized; he was the husband of a teammate of mine from Everest in 1975. I attended their wedding. No time was wasted before we delved into the contours of Mount Tomur. I was quick to admit that the route my team had taken was overly prone to avalanches, and I adamantly suggested they find another direction to climb. "I can't tell you if we could have found a route onto Battleship Rock," I said, something I would never know, "but I'll lend you all the photos we took. Study them well." Again, I strongly encouraged them to take a different route up the mountain than we did, and the three of them left my house.

My heart raced in August of that year when the news leapt at me that three climbers were missing on Mount Tomur. "It couldn't be," I thought, "not the three men I spoke with." I tried to convince myself it was impossible, the coincidence, but sure enough, in a deep state of concern for these men's lives, I traced the news to its source and yes, in fact, the three climbers, the strongest on the alumni team, were at the front end of the line when an avalanche struck. Same route as ours, same exact spot at 6200 metres in elevation. The man I knew, the one married to my Everest teammate, the father of three very young children, had been killed. It broke my heart to watch his kids run around, innocently at play, when I paid my respects to my friend.

I blamed myself for their accident, regretting that I had not told them more decisively that they should not climb the route I had been on, that avalanches were certain, that it was unsafe. I should have told them to look for another mountain.

Nine years later, from when I first saw those children play after their father had died, visions of their youth remained forefront in my mind. I still carried remorse when I thought of them, and I worried about their mother. From time to time, I sent small gifts, like gourmet treats or customary seasonal delicacies, as a way to express my ongoing sorrow.

Pobeda Peak

This fateful mountain, Mount Tomur, never quite escaped me. When the Soviet Union dissolved in 1991, climbing permits became available from the Kyrgyzstan side of the peak. It was time to try again. Once more, our party of twelve women, including two base-camp managers and hikers who planned to only go as far as the start of the climb, applied for and received the necessary documentation to set foot on Mount Tomur. Our expedition began in the small town of Almaty in Kazakhstan. A single day's drive from there led us to the unique tent-village of Kalkara in a setting of wildflowers. The location was ideal – there were restaurants and saunas, and the tent accommodations were sized for two people, with a front room attached. The ceilings were full height so we could enjoy standing upright. We settled in to acclimatize there while hiking the surrounding mountains. The remote destination was surprisingly busy with hikers and climbers from all over the world, but, as usual, we stood out among them as a group of Japanese women.

In Kyrgyzstan, the Chinese name for Mount Tomur is Pobeda Peak. Its neighbour, Khan Tengri, is a Matterhorn-like spire reaching 7010 metres, while Pobeda stands taller at 7439 metres but looks lower because it is within such a wide range that spreads like a massive horizontal wall.

Its extensive high-elevation ridgeline, 4 kilometres in length, makes Pobeda Peak one of the most difficult climbs among the five 7000-metre peaks in the former Soviet Union. The success rate on the mountain is low, while its death toll is the opposite. Quite simply, there is no other mountain that requires such a long ridge walk at an altitude of 7000 metres.

The span of a helicopter flight from Kalkara to Base Camp transported us from a village in full bloom to the sparseness of a glacier. Still, the sun shone bright. The mountain's obvious long, foreboding ridge skimmed the skyline, and high on its left stood Pobeda Peak. The view was different from that of the Chinese side, and the daunting ridge appeared difficult to reach.

Six of the women spent only one day with us, trekking in the area, before they flew back to Kalkara. Left behind were four climbers and two camp managers. More than once the Russian guides said to us, "Pobeda is a tough mountain. You need quite a bit of stamina for the long ridge." Its far-reaching silhouette proved their point.

To acclimatize, we ferried food and tents up to Camp 1. We repeated the trip three times, winding our way around the crevassed glacier. If anyone on the team failed to acclimatize well with this exercise, they would not climb any higher. It was strictly ice climbing above Camp 1, with fixed ropes and jumars. We had to move fast through that section and could not risk multiple climbs and rappels there. Hence, only those who were strong enough to continue would be chosen to do so.

We progressed well, yet one of the summit selects (I call her T) began to fall significantly behind. We helped T lighten her pack load, but she still could not maintain her pace. The remaining team of three had to stop and wait for her to catch up at the end of each pitch. Finally, one of the Russian guides stated that our teammate could not continue.

Obviously, expeditions involve investment – time, financial and personal commitment. We were simply a group of women who wanted to climb; we had neither a fancy title for our team nor outside monetary support. Each one of us paid the same amount to be on the trip. To tell someone she could no longer be part of the climb was detrimental to friendships and possible future expeditions. Nonetheless, as leader, I had to seriously consider the guide's input.

I reminded myself of how an expedition worked, that an individual's accomplishments, no matter what elevation they climbed to, contributed to the overall goal of reaching the mountaintop. In the case of Pobeda, we had a single chance for the summit. We would climb directly from Camp 1 to Camp 2 and Camp 3 to the top, with no ferrying of loads back and forth, and using supplemental oxygen above 7000 metres. We would carry the minimal number of oxygen bottles required to summit, meaning that our slower teammate would have to carry her own, which seemed unlikely given her state of weakness. Even if the four of us arrived at Camp 1 together, it had become obvious that she would not be able to continue past there; she was already stumbling on her crampons between Base Camp and Camp 1. My decision was clear. I would have to tell her the most disappointing news for a climber to hear, despite the trip's intent of being a fun, low-key expedition.

We reconvened at Base Camp and brewed tea, my mind heavy with the conversation I was about to engage in. I spoke honestly and openly with T, and expressed my concern for her current condition. I explained that the summit was no longer possible for her to consider. She disagreed and pressed me to reconsider. "I hear you," I said, "but that's not an option on *this* mountain."

A lingering silence filled the space around us. The tea had long since turned cold. The two other teammates remained as quiet as mice. They knew that if they voted for T to climb higher, then their chance for the summit would be compromised. We relied on T's complete understanding of the scenario. It was difficult for everybody.

"I see," she finally said. "I know I'm not in good shape. But it's such a regret to give up after getting all the way here. I really want to keep going – but I know it's not possible for me." Her voice broke off with the weight of her own sadness. But after another moment of silence passed, she spoke again. "I understand. I'll wait at Base Camp for you." Her positivity was welcomed but made it no easier for me. It was agonizing to tell a teammate that she could not make it to the summit while unsure of how my own body would perform higher on the mountain.

Two days later, three of us and the three Russian guides left Base Camp for Camp 1. Upon nearing our destination, a hanging glacier that sat about halfway down from the 4-kilometre-long ridge (but still significantly high above us) released and came plunging down. "To the right! Run to the right! Put your backpack like a shield and hide behind it!" yelled one of the guides. I ran a bit then dropped my belly to the ground and braced myself with my pack held firmly in front. Chunks of ice ricocheted off my pack as the avalanche came to a stop slightly ahead of us. We were safe. I must admit I was bold enough to take photographs from my hiding spot as I felt certain we were far enough away from the debris runout. Knowing my history on Tomur, I may have pushed my luck a bit.

It was agreed that we would move Camp 1 a little higher than originally planned. "Above here," our guides said, "there is no need to worry about avalanches." When had I thought that before? Needless to say, we moved the tent.

Early the next morning, we packed all the gear we would need for the summit, including food, gas and climbing equipment, and began our ascent on the ice wall. At 10 a.m. we again heard the sound of an avalanche. I turned to catch sight of it just as the tent we had slept in a few hours earlier was being blown away like a floppy rubber ball. We looked at each other, acknowledging that our only choice was to continue. Each movement was tediously hard work as we climbed the steep ice wall with heavy packs, but we were fuelled by the need to reach the start of the much-anticipated ridge. There, we would pitch Camp 2.

Finally, we were met with a narrow spot of snow and ice that we could call home for the night, with the Inylchek Glacier, the largest glacier in Kyrgyzstan, in the background. With barely enough room to move, we secured the tent to the ground, and when we sat down inside, our feet hung over the ledge into space. If we thought that was cramped, we should have waited until we had to use the toilet, which became a team effort. Essentially, a person had to be on belay for a free-hanging bathroom break. Coordination by all was essential to not tangle any ropes or trip anyone, an ordeal that required patience and calm and was not meant for the faint of heart.

The weather was good and seemed like it would stay that way for the next few days.

After a night's rest, we began to climb the final steep rock line that ran to the ridgetop, our route covered in continuous snow and ice. As a carryover from previous days, the sustained steepness and heavy load played on me. But I felt such relief to be out of harm's way that I was happy to focus on careful foot placements and ignore any discomfort. After nearly seven hours, we reached the ridgeline at 7000 metres, and the Chinese side of the mountain was exposed to the south. I asked my teammates to secure me on the rope so I could climb down there and have a look around. On belay, I saw the familiar landform, the one we had named Battleship Rock. Assuming the three missing male climbers from the university alumni team had fallen from there, trapped in an avalanche, I closed my eyes and placed my hands in prayer position. I asked for their eternal rest in peace. In that moment, I felt an unusual sensation overcome me, akin to a new presence in my body. I had hoped for lightness when I bid them farewell, but that was not to be. I literally felt a weight placed on my shoulders.

The dark of night was closing in, and we had to find a campsite. Two snow caves, likely from a previous party, presented themselves on a worthy patch of ground that was wider than our previous bivy site. Perfect. We made ourselves at home inside, cooked supper and ate. I had trouble falling asleep but persuaded myself to lie down, knowing that my body would benefit from rest even if I was wakeful. Quietly, I thought about the next day's summit assault.

By morning, I was ready to climb. I packed a bivouac sack with me in case we were delayed in returning to the snow caves, and we split the group gear amongst us. One of the guides set off, and I followed. "Here we go," I thought, "the first step of the day." Then I felt it again, that odd sensation I had the day before when I looked down at Battleship Rock. "It's strange," I said to myself. "Something is wrong with my body. I can't even put my foot forward." In the moment that I wondered what was happening, I spun around and felt the impact of a huge force against me.

I checked my surroundings; nothing had changed. My pack had less weight in it than the previous day but somehow felt heavier. Was it possible that those three missing men were telling me not to go? I was unsure, but I tried to understand the undeniable weight I felt on my shoulders. "Wait," I thought, "they also wanted to reach the summit." Suddenly, it made sense. They wanted to go with me. "OK, let's go together then," I quietly said. My legs continued to feel extremely heavy, and since I had never suffered from altitude sickness before, I questioned what else could be the cause of this distress if not the added weight of the souls of three missing climbers.

The flow of bottled oxygen, which we switched on for the summit assault, helped me feel a bit lighter in step, but I still positioned one foot in front of the other with great care. My breathing was strained, feeling the effects of elevation. The narrow ridge was juxtaposed between China to the south and Kyrgyzstan to the north, without an inch to spare in between. Each of us had to remain sharp on the rope until this section was over. I felt like there were several persons breathing via my lungs. How much could I sustain for those men to reach the top? I was determined to continue; I *had* to continue. My body was depleted, but my will to stand on the summit with these fallen climbers was too great.

We walked along the 4 kilometres of ridgeline at 7000 metres to reach the summit of Pobeda Peak. It was an endless stretch, but we succeeded in reaching the summit. The pressure of having to descend by nightfall had us quickly take photos and head back down, retracing our route. Darkness settled in once we were past the marathon ridgeline, and then the heavens opened up with thunder and hail. We found a small space in which to retreat; we would either wait out the storm then continue, or spend the night there. Tucked in our bivouac sacks in a seated position, we were comfortable enough for the duration, even though the bottles of oxygen measured empty. We shared the remaining food and water we had and were able to reassure Base Camp via radio that we were in decent shape.

The howling wind diminished the next morning and the sky was clear. A fast exit from the night's bivy had us reach the snow caves in good time, and we gathered the gear we had left behind only a day earlier and prepared to hike down to Base Camp. Before I left, I pressed my hands together in prayer once more towards the Chinese side of the mountain. In my heart, I spoke the words, "We were able to get to the summit. Thank you for protecting us. Please rest in peace." I bowed in respect and grabbed the rope for the descent.

Right away my body became so light that I thought I was flying. I had let the three men return to their final place of rest on Mount Tomur.

Feeling reassured that I could tell my friend that her husband had reached the summit with me, I began the long rappel. I was finished with this mountain.

Usually I am not one to recognize divine inspiration, let alone act on it; however, there have been several occasions when I have had a hunch to refrain from climbing on a particular day. On Everest, despite clear weather on a day when we were carving a route up the Khumbu Icefall, I had the feeling of not wanting to climb. While the rest of the team was adamant about continuing up the route, I was hesitant, for no obvious reason. I had a hard time speaking my mind but eventually suggested that we call off the day's plan. They said I let them down, that I was being too soft, but later that day a huge part of the icefall collapsed, burying our route. I was as surprised by the incident as anyone, and there was no viable connection between my feeling of reluctance to climb and what had happened, but there was also no denying it.

The experience on Pobeda was a far greater phenomenon for me; I had never felt anything as profound as that before. Although I did not share my story right away, my fellow teammates commented on the notable change they saw in me on the mountain. On our descent, I told them about the three Japanese climbers who had gone missing in 1990. They commended me for allowing the ghosts of those climbers to finally reach the summit. "They must have been waiting for you," one of them said, confirming my perception of the occurrence. At the end of the day, safely back at Base Camp, we pressed our hands together in a three-way prayer, and bowed once again, saying goodbye to those who were now at rest on the other side of Pobeda Peak.

I retold the entire episode to my Everest friend when I returned to Japan. For years to come, I enjoyed hiking with her in her retirement as she shared stories about her grown-up children.

With time, people's emotions change, and the intensity of sadness and suffering lessens – we heal. It was fourteen years before I was able to write about the wonder I experienced on Pobeda Peak. The splinter of pain and guilt I felt when I first learned of the alumni tragedy had finally lost its sharpness.

On May 13, 2016, after a speech I gave at a hotel near the Kannai Station in Kanagawa, south of Tokyo, I met with a Russian climber who was married to a Japanese woman. Earlier, he had sent me an email requesting a meeting, and he travelled a long distance to Kannai since it was the only spare time I had between speaking engagements during his visit to Japan. When I climbed Pobeda Peak, my team had hired a Russian climber named Alexei as one of our guides. He was a strong man, and very kind. Decades later, I still appreciated his efforts when I reflected on our summit success – it would have been unfeasible without Alexei's expert guiding skills. Sadly, the Russian man I met in Kannai informed me that Alexei had died on Everest in 2013. His parents composed an album of their son's mountain photos and diaries, in which Alexei wrote about climbing Pobeda Peak with a group of Japanese women. Photos from our climb were inserted in the book. Alexei's parents had asked their Russian friend to give this book as a gift to Junko Tabei in Japan, and hence, our meeting. I was saddened by the story but heart-warmed by the gesture.

The cause of his accident on Everest surprised me. The expedition party was a mix of two Russians, and an Italian and a Swiss climber. From the beginning, the Italian and Swiss team members did not get along with the Sherpas, and the party dissolved. The two Russians decided to attempt the mountain from a different route, and Alexei, one of the two, started to climb using a rope that was left behind by a previous party. The rope broke and down he fell.

This was unbelievable to me. We would never use another team's rope discarded on a route for fear of the weakness it would have sustained from exposure to extreme elements. I was shocked that Alexei, a professional climber, would resort to such a method. A moment of inattentiveness cost him his life. I appreciated the book I was given, and I thanked Alexei for it as I wished for him to rest in peace. How long would it take for the sadness of his story to wane from my being? Was that even possible?

Perhaps we climb for more than ourselves after all.

CHAPTER 13

Aconcagua

In January 1987 I summitted Aconcagua, the highest peak in South America. It was a memorable mountain for me, thanks to the people I met and – of all things – a dog.

Argentina is home to Aconcagua, the highest peak in the Andes of South America. People tend to think the mountain is based in both Chile and Argentina, as it stands a mere 15 kilometres from the Chilean border, but Aconcagua, in its entirety, is Argentinean. It is a unique summit because, despite its elevation of near 7000 metres, it can be climbed without an ice axe or crampons. Ski poles are sufficient to reach the top. But for me, the mountain might as well as have been on another planet. Located so far from Japan, I assumed it would never get ticked off my list of peaks to climb. Then an offer came that I was unable to refuse. I was invited to be the leader of a Japanese commercially organized climb on Aconcagua. The year was 1986; I was forty-six years old.

I was excited from the start and wasted no time in accepting the offer. Not only was Aconcagua my dream, I would have the chance to climb it with no expense to me – in fact, I would be paid. A friend advised me otherwise, stating it was risky to take clients up such a high peak. What if there was an emergency? How would I handle that on my own? At first, I shared the same concern, but another friend reassured me: "The most difficult parts about climbing Aconcagua are acclimatizing and crossing the river."

I could hardly imagine a river being the crux of the climb. That part was unexpected, but in terms of acclimatization, I had enough experience to feel like I could manage whatever presented itself. There would be a local guide with us, and if we remained conservative in our climbing, we should be able to safely succeed. Plus, I figured that clients who were accepted by the tour company had some degree of mountaineering experience. I accepted the job as tour leader for Aconcagua, one of many commercial trips I would guide for Saiyu Travel (the last one being in 2016 to Mount Kerinci in Sumatra, Indonesia).

At Narita Airport in Tokyo, seven women and four men, with the common goal of Aconcagua, met for the first time. Our instant team of eleven members ranged in age from thirty to sixty-five years. Everyone seemed well-prepared in terms of trip details and ready for an adventure. From Narita, we flew to Los Angeles, and then to Mexico, Lima, and Buenos Aires, followed by a domestic flight to Mendoza, Argentina, 100 kilometres from the border of Chile.

In total, it was two days of travel, leaving Japan at 4 p.m. on Christmas Eve, having one night's layover in Los Angeles, and arriving in Argentina in the late afternoon on December 26. I took advantage of the long flights and spoke with each client to develop a sense of their past climbing experience.

We met our local guide in Mendoza. There, we shopped for the climb – ten days' worth of food – loading up on potatoes, carrots, onions, cabbages, oranges, powdered juice crystals, raisins, crackers and more. Then we chartered a bus to Puente del Inca, the trailhead, where packhorses were readied to carry loads into Base Camp. The accommodation in Puente del Inca included four or five lodges, each housing approximately thirty people with rooms of bunk beds. The best part was the natural hot springs, which we enjoyed before (and after) the climb.

That first night, we sat submerged in the water surrounded by the layers of sandy and rocky mountain spires that stood between us and Aconcagua, the Southern Cross fixed in the sky above. As I embraced the view, I was impressed with myself: I had travelled a so very far to climb a mountain. The next day, our hike began.

The trail to Base Camp started at the side of the 6-metre-wide road that passed in front of the lodge and served as the highway to Chile. A final glance over our shoulders as cars disappeared in the distance was our goodbye to civilization. We began by threading our way through blooms of dandelions as the majestic view of the bright Andes valley spread in front of us. Fresh green leaves sprouted from the brown scree slopes, and short purple gentians swayed in the wind, already mourning the too-short summer. It was a harsh environment for plants, and every species hugged the ground, as if to hide from the intense sunlight, strong winds and cold temperatures of the mountains. A cocoa-coloured river ran through the valley, and even though its width was only 5 metres, it had a daunting presence – rapids that churned a tremendous volume of water. Aha, the crux of the climb. Staring at it, I completely understood why I had been forewarned.

Our South American horses looked small and weak. They were like a mix of horse and donkey. With less hesitation than I showed, they braced their strong legs and marched into the river, carrying us on their backs. There we were, crossing the threatening river, water up to our thighs as the current pushed waves as high as the horses' bellies. I tried to ignore the potential danger of the situation as I was numbed by the freezing cold glacial water that churned all around us. No sooner had I thought the crossing was over than a dog that had followed us from the lodge in Puente del Inca jumped in to join us. The rapids were fast and he was being swept downriver without a chance. "The dog is being washed away!" we yelled, upset by what we had witnessed. But, in the end, he popped out of the water onto land, having made it across on his own. We threw ourselves at him, this drenched dog, to make sure he was all right. Straightaway, somehow, he felt like part of the team, having succeeded the so-called crux of our approach, and we decided to keep him. We would return him to the lodge on our way home. Thus, Acon, after Aconcagua, marked my first mountain ascent with a dog at my heels.

The first night in our tents was at a site by the river at the bottom end of the valley, at 3300 metres. The stars dazzled in the dark as I looked up from our bivy in awe of the serene mountain setting. The next day, December 29, we packed our equipment and loaded it on horseback. Then we slowly but consistently gained 1000 metres of elevation on a wide trail alongside the cocoa-coloured river, crossing it at least another ten times. In the beginning, we removed our boots for each river crossing, but that was too tedious. Splashing through the water, boots on, was a much more efficient approach.

The Andes had a character all its own – imposing mountains of brown rocky peaks, some with dramatic rock shapes; others layered with various strata. The region had a dry brightness to it, vastly different from the white snow-capped peaks of the Himalayas. Then, between the towers of brown rock, snow spires began to show. Base Camp was close by. Acon must have sensed our excitement because he bounded ahead to lead the group, and we wondered if a dog could suffer from altitude sickness.

Base Camp sat at 4200 metres, right below the West Face of Aconcagua. It was unlike any of the base camps I had seen before – a small run-down cabin sat there, locked up and no use to us. On a large plateau, numerous tents of international mountaineers were pitched all over. I watched one group that had carried in tables and chairs, and were chilling their beer in the meltwater, commenting to myself that they sure knew how to have fun. A fellow from France, with the plan to paraglide from the summit down to Base Camp, was spreading out his equipment to double-check that everything was intact. We pitched three tents to house our team – one had the capacity for seven to eight people, and the two others were for four to five people each. I stayed in a smaller one.

"We'll start to ferry loads up to a higher camp tomorrow," I said. "No rush, though; we should take our time. Now I'll complete my last job of the day." I was referring to my evening ritual of cleansing my face.

"Oh, Tabei-*san*, why do such things?" said Hanako Majima, one of the women on our team.

"Why not?" I said. "When I was young, I didn't put anything on my face. I was too busy buying climbing gear rather than makeup, and I had no interest in the betterment of my skin. But, around the time of Everest, I started to realize how much damage the sun causes. It burns us. More so, any dark spots and freckles I get don't fade away like they used to when I was younger. So, at the very least, I wear sunscreen. And washing it off has become the routine that signifies the end of the day for me." I opened the blue quilted pouch my daughter, Noriko, had made me as part of her summer homework when she was in fifth grade. I pulled out a bottle of lotion, tipped the ingredients onto a cotton swab and wiped my face.

ABOVE Ishibashi family photo, circa 1943. From left to right, back row: Hisayoshi, Tsune, Fuchi; left to right, front row: Hisayuki, Morinobu, Kiyo, Junko, Chikako, Itsu.
COURTESY OF TABEI KIKAKU

LEFT Junko (third from left) with her university classmates at Mitake-yama, 1959.
COURTESY OF TABEI KIKAKU

LEFT Grade 4, Junko's first mountain hike, in the Nasu range, Grade 4, 1949. Junko in the lower right corner with Watanabe-*sensei* crouched behind her.
COURTESY OF TABEI KIKAKU

ABOVE Junko playing *koto* (Japanese harp), circa 1960.
COURTESY OF TABEI KIKAKU

BELOW Junko with Yariga-take in the background, Northern Alps of Japan, circa 1961.
COURTESY OF TABEI KIKAKU/LADIES CLIMBING CLUB

ABOVE Young climber Masanobu Tabei, circa 1963.
COURTESY OF TABEI KIKAKU

RIGHT Junko belays on a route at Tanigawa-dake, circa 1965.
COURTESY OF TABEI KIKAKU

OPPOSITE Junko and Masanobu at Tanigawa-dake, circa 1964.
COURTESY OF TABEI KIKAKU

THIS PAGE, ABOVE Best friends Rumie Sasou (left) and Junko, circa 1965.
COURTESY OF TABEI KIKAKU

THIS PAGE, LEFT Rumie Sasou (left) and Junko, winter climbing on the Central Ridge of Ichinokura-sawa, Tanigawa-dake, circa 1965.
COURTESY OF TABEI KIKAKU

ABOVE Yoko-o (left), Junko's climbing mentor, 1966.
COURTESY OF KOHEI TAKASHINA

RIGHT Rock climber Junko, circa 1966.
COURTESY OF TABEI KIKAKU

Junko (left) and Masanobu sharpen their rope skills, 1967.
COURTESY OF TABEI KIKAKU

Junko and Masanobu, to be married soon, 1967.

ABOVE Junko and Masanobu en route to their honeymoon, 1967.
COURTESY OF TABEI KIKAKU

RIGHT Masanobu on the summit of the North Face of the Matterhorn, 1968.
COURTESY OF TABEI KIKAKU

ABOVE Tabei peeking at Annapurna III with Miyazaki (left), Machapuchare in the background, 1970.
COURTESY OF TABEI KIKAKU/ LADIES CLIMBING CLUB

BELOW Tabei on Annapurna III; the peak on the back right is Machapuchare, 1970.
TABEI KIKAKU AND THE LADIES CLIMBING CLUB

RIGHT Climbers ferry loads from Camp 4 to Advanced Camp 4, Annapurna III, 1970.
COURTESY OF TABEI KIKAKU/ LADIES CLIMBING CLUB

LEFT Tabei (left) and Hirakawa on the summit of Annapurna III (7555 m), 1970.
COURTESY OF TABEI KIKAKU/ LADIES CLIMBING CLUB

ABOVE Annapurna III women's team, Annapurna III Base Camp, 1970. Back row, left to right: Hirano, Hirakawa, Manita, Tabei, Yamazaki; front row, left to right: Urushibara, Miyazaki, Sato, Dr. O-no,
COURTESY OF TABEI KIKAKU/ LADIES CLIMBING CLUB

OVERLEAF The beloved Mr. Gopal at Base Camp, handing out flags and flowers to Tabei after success on Annapurna III, 1970.
COURTESY OF TABEI KIKAKU/ LADIES CLIMBING CLUB

ABOVE Tabei (third from left), winter traverse with Ryoho Climbing Club members, 1971.
COURTESY OF TABEI KIKAKU

BELOW Masanobu with baby Noriko Tabei, 1972.
COURTESY OF TABEI KIKAKU

Everest team members in training, Tanigawa-dake, Japan, 1973. Back row, left to right: Shioura, Naganuma, Watanabe, Hisano, Fujiwara, Arayama, Hirashima; front row, left to right: Tabei, Manita, Taneya, Naka, Nasu, Mihara.

LEFT The Tabei family cerebrating Noriko's third birthday in advance, prior to leaving for Mount Everest, 1974.
COURTESY OF TABEI KIKAKU

ABOVE Mount Everest seen from Kala Patthar, March 25, 1975.
COURTESY OF *THE YOMIURI SHIMBUN*

BELOW Porters on duty, Mount Everest, 1975.
COURTESY OF *THE YOMIURI SHIMBUN*

ABOVE Mount Everest Base Camp, 1975. Tabei and Hisano (dark glasses, red socks) front and centre, in lower left corner of the team sign.
COURTESY OF *THE YOMIURI SHIMBUN*

BELOW Sherpas dig the tents out from avalanche debris, Mount Everest, Camp 2, May 4, 1975.
COURTESY OF *THE YOMIURI SHIMBUN*

ABOVE Tabei (left) and Watanabe sleeping with supplemental oxygen, Mount Everest, Camp 4 (7600 m), May 12, 1975.
COURTESY OF *THE YOMIURI SHIMBUN*

BELOW Tabei (left) and Watanabe (second) climbing the crux of the Lhotse Face on Mount Everest with oxygen masks, May 12, 1975.
COURTESY OF *THE YOMIURI SHIMBUN*

ABOVE Shaky steps on an airy ladder, Mount Everest, 1975.
COURTESY OF *THE YOMIURI SHIMBUN*

RIGHT Tabei on the summit to become the first female climber of Mt. Everest, 8848m, May 16, 1975.
COURTESY OF TABEI KIKAKU, PHOTO TAKEN BY ANG TSERING

ABOVE "We've arrived!" Junko Tabei on the summit of Mount Everest makes her historic radio call to Advanced Base Camp, May 16, 1975.
COURTESY OF TABEI KIKAKU/ PHOTO TAKEN BY ANG TSERING

RIGHT Ang Tsering on the summit of Everest, May 16, 1975.
COURTESY OF JUNKO TABEI

The sweet taste of success – coffee (after the summit), Mount Everest Camp 2, Tabei and Ang Tsering, May 17, 1975.

Tabei, on Ang Tsering's shoulders, celebrates their Mount Everest success, leader
Hisano stands beside them, Camp 2, May 17, 1975.
COURTESY OF *THE YOMIURI SHIMBUN*

Mother and daughter – Tabei holds Noriko close upon coming home from Mount
Everest, Haneda Airport, June 8, 1975.
COURTESY OF *THE YOMIURI SHIMBUN*

ABOVE Lady Everest summitters, clean up on Mount Fuji, 1975. From left to right, Ji Hyun-Ok, Kim Soon-Joo, Santosh Yadav, Rebecca Stephens, Lydia Bradey, Junko Tabei, Ginette Harrison, Bachendri Pal, Pan Duo and Gui Sang.
COURTESY OF TABEI KIKAKU

BELOW Junko, Noriko and baby Shinya, 1978.
COURTESY OF TABEI KIKAKU

ABOVE The first three women to succeed on Mount Everest. From left to righ, Pan Duo, Junko Tabei and Wanda Rutkiewicz, Chamonix, France, 1979.
COURTESY OF TABEI KIKAKU

RIGHT The Tabei family (Masanobu, Shinya, Noriko, Junko), circa 1983.
COURTESY OF TABEI KIKAKU

ABOVE Mount Tomur (7439 m), a deadly mountain for avalanches, 1986.
COURTESY OF TABEI KIKAKU/ LADIES CLIMBING CLUB

LEFT Tabei climbing Mount Tomur, 1986.
COURTESY OF TABEI KIKAKU/ LADIES CLIMBING CLUB

ABOVE On the route above Camp 2, Mount Tomur, 1986.
COURTESY OF TABEI KIKAKU/ LADIES CLIMBING CLUB

OVERLEAF Team of all women on Mount Tomur, 1986.
COURTESY OF TABEI KIKAKU/ LADIES CLIMBING CLUB

LEFT Masanobu and Shinya at a motocross race, circa 1986.
COURTESY OF TABEI KIKAKU

ABOVE Tabei with French cyclist who rode down Aconcagua, 1987.
COURTESY OF TABEI KIKAKU

ABOVE Tabei, Majima and Kitamura (with guide top right) climbing Vinson Massif in Antarctica, 1991.
COURTESY OF TABEI KIKAKU

LEFT On the summit of Vinson Massif, 1991. From left to right, Kitamura, Majima and Tabei.
COURTESY OF TABEI KIKAKU

ABOVE The Tabei family (from left to right, Noriko, Shinya, Junko, Masanobu) at the summit of Kosciuszko, Australia, 1991.
COURTESY OF TABEI KIKAKU

BELOW Tabei (pink shirt) and Kitamura (white shirt) with the locals, Carstensz Pyramid, 1992.
COURTESY OF TABEI KIKAKU

OVERLEAF Tabei with Illaga villagers, Carstensz Pyramid, 1992.
COURTESY OF TABEI KIKAKU

ABOVE Wet feet, Carstensz Pyramid, 1992.
COURTESY OF TABEI KIKAKU

BELOW Tabei (left) with one of her "young lads" on the summit of Carstensz Pyramid, 1992.
COURTESY OF TABEI KIKAKU

RIGHT Tabei climbing Khan Tengri (~6400 m), 1993.
COURTESY OF TABEI KIKAKU

ABOVE Tabei with Watanabe-*sensei*, Everest trekking, 1994.
COURTESY OF EIKO TABE

BELOW Tabei with Watanabe-*sensei*, Kathmandu, 1994.
COURTESY OF EIKO TABE

ABOVE Tabei (left) and Kitamura on summit of the Eiger, 101 years of age between the two of them, 1995.

COURTESY OF SETSUKO KITAMURA

LEFT Tabei with her mother, Kiyo Ishibashi, circa 1995.

COURTESY OF TABEI KIKAKU

ABOVE Mount Everest seen from Cho Oyu, 1996.
COURTESY OF TABEI KIKAKU

BELOW The Iranian team leader (second from left in patterned sweater) is invited for tea by the Japanese women's team, Pobeda Peak, 1999.
COURTESY OF TABEI KIKAKU

RIGHT Climbing Pobeda Peak, just below Camp 3, 1999.
COURTESY OF TABEI KIKAKU

ABOVE The 30th anniversary of the first women on Mount Everest, Kathmandu, 2005. Tabei (left) summitted on May, 16, 1975; Pan Duo summitted eleven days later.
COURTESY OF TABEI KIKAKU

BELOW Tabei on the way up to Pico Bolivar, 4978m, the highest mountain in Venezuela, January 2008.
COURTESY OF EIKO TABE

LEFT Tabei singing at Women of No Fear concert, for Cheer Up Tohoku, 2012. COURTESY OF TABEI KIKAKU

BELOW Cheer Up Tohoku concert by Women of No Fear, 2012. Tabei is third from left, in white patterned dress. COURTESY OF TABEI KIKAKU

294

ABOVE Tabei with her son Shinya, Western Australia, 2013.
COURTESY OF TABEI KIKAKU

BELOW Tabei offering reassurance to a tired student hiker on Mount Fuji, 2014.
COURTESY OF TABEI KIKAKU

ABOVE Tabei (second from left), hiking on Mount Fuji with the high-school students of Tohoku, 2014.
COURTESY OF TABEI KIKAKU

BELOW Tabei (bottom row, in pink shirt) on summit of Mount Fuji with high-school students from Tohoku, 2014.
COURTESY OF TABEI KIKAKU

LEFT Forty years after the summit of Mount Everest, Tabei reunites with former kitchen helper Lhakpa Norbu, who advanced to sirdar in his career, Everest trekking, 2015.
COURTESY OF YUMIKO HIRAKI

ABOVE Tabei inspecting a garbage incinerator (in need of replacement) provided by the Himalayan Adventure Trust of Japan, Lukla, 2015.
COURTESY OF YUMIKO HIRAKI

OVERLEAF The fortieth anniversary Mount Everest (in the cloud, to the right of visible peak) trek, 2015. From left to right, Yoshida, Tabei, Mori, Hiraki.
COURTESY OF YUMIKO HIRAKI

OPPOSITE, ABOVE The Tabei family (Masanobu, Junko, Shinya and Noriko) at the Everest fortieth-anniversary event, Kathmandu, 2015.
COURTESY OF TABEI KIKAKU

OPPOSITE, BELOW Tabei with former liaison officer Lhakpa Tenzing, forty years after her summit of Mount Everest, Kathmandu, 2015.
COURTESY OF YUMIKO HIRAKI

THIS PAGE, ABOVE Makeup time for Women of No Fear concert, June 2016.
COURTESY OF TABEI KIKAKU

LEFT Summit of Mount Kerinci (3805 m), Indonesia, Masanobu (left) and Junko (third from left), on her final overseas mountain trip, May 2016.
COURTESY OF TABEI KIKAKU

ABOVE Tabei ready to start the day on Mount Fuji with high-school students of Tohoku, her final mountain trip. She climbed to 3010 metres. July 2016.
COURTESY OF TABEI KIKAKU

Junko Tabei

"Wow, you aren't so different from us, the ordinary folk," said Majima. "What a relief. I was worried you might be an intimidating, strict *obasan* [auntie] who cares only for the mountains. To be honest, I usually don't like celebrities. I didn't enjoy a previous trip with a celebrity as the guide. But when I first met you at Narita, I was pleasantly surprised that you're not that way at all. I am so glad." I was relieved to have made a good first impression, because Majima and I went on to climb and ski together for years afterwards. Eventually, along with Setsuko Kitamura, we climbed Denali and Vinson Massif together. In 2003 Majima and I, along with two other female friends, also climbed Mount Assiniboine in the Canadian Rockies, with local mountain guides Barry Blanchard and Todd Craig.

Summit Dog

The plan was to establish Camp 1 and Camp 2, and then we would attack the summit from there. To start, we had to ferry gear from Base Camp to Camp 1. Only those members in good enough shape after spending the night at Base Camp's 4200 metres were allowed to continue. Nine of us fit the bill. Ten, counting Acon. Each climber carried 15 kilograms, for a total of 135 kilograms being transported per ferry load. The route we followed was a switchback trail of scree, similar to the mid-section of Mount Fuji.

Unified in thought, we hiked up the mountain. Acon either marched ahead or dropped behind the group, as if to ensure we were all together. He was low maintenance – we fed him and that was all – but he certainly had noticeable preferences (he chose meats and salami bought in Mendoza over leftover Japanese food). To answer our earlier question about dogs and altitude sickness, he certainly showed signs of wear as we continued to the higher camps. He moved more slowly and spent more time lying down compared to the start.

The reddish brown–coloured spires of Aconcagua rose to our right, and ahead of us was a large snow patch on an open scree field that would be Camp 1 (5200 metres). The wind was strong, and gusts blasted down from the mountainsides. The snow patch served as our source for meltwater. People in our group were already feeling the effects of altitude. The amount of available oxygen was about half that at valley bottom, and shortness of breath, headache, fatigue and loss of appetite were common complaints. The solution was to descend to lower elevations until symptoms subsided, and our team had to implement that strategy. Only four of us were able to stay at Camp 1; the other five returned to Base Camp to feel better.

Circumnavigating the snow patch of Camp 1, and hiking another 100 metres on the rocky trail, led to the big snowfield called Nido de Condores, or Condor Square. From that point, the mountains on the other side of Aconcagua came into view.

Two of the four team members who stayed at Camp 1 for the night immediately descended to Base Camp the next morning when they woke up with headaches. One of the remaining clients, another female, and I decided to ferry a load to Camp 2. From Nido de Condores, we continued up the switchback trail of rocks, scree and sand while inhaling the endless view of the purple-hued Andes Mountains, gaining elevation as we hiked. At 5800 metres, we arrived at Camp 2. The remnants of three small shacks were there, with neither glass panels in the windows nor roofs on top. The ground was dry sand – so different from the glaciated terrain of the Himalayas – and we had to utilize icicles that hung down from the shaded side of rocks for drinking water. It was a place of innovation.

Oddly, while resting there to catch our breath, we met an energetic young French man returning from the summit on his bicycle. He had carried his 13-kilogram made-in-Japan bike to the top of Aconcagua in three days, and would descend in one.

"Why on bicycle?" I asked.

"Because anyone can reach the summit if they climb it the regular way," he replied.

Happy to have met this interesting fellow, I then recognized the face of another man who appeared to be the cyclist's cameraman. He approached me and asked, "Aren't you Junko Tabei?"

Ah, yes, the French mountaineer who had climbed K2 in three days. We knew each other through various articles and photographs in mountain magazines, and it was funny to have met on Aconcagua, each of us so far from our homeland. Without further ado, we snapped a photo of us together, a picture that would unfortunately go missing, like many others, later in life.

Exhilarated by the pair's cheerfulness and positive energy, we returned to Camp 1. Concern set in though, when upon that night's 10 p.m. radio call with Base Camp, we learned that one of the male clients, Ono, who was supposed to have descended to Base Camp from Camp 1, was yet to arrive. The trail between camps was obvious and it was still light enough outside, but I felt uneasy, knowing Ono suffered from altitude sickness. I double-checked the number of people at Base Camp and realized a woman from our group was also missing.

I began to run through scenarios in my head. Perhaps she was tired on her ascent from Base Camp to Camp 1, and then ran into Ono, who was on his way down. Maybe they had joined forces and were staying together somewhere on the trail. Seriously worried, the local guide and I started our descent in the oncoming darkness to search for the missing team members.

At 10:15 p.m., we heard from Base Camp that Ono had safely arrived. We asked if he had seen our other teammate on the way. His answer was negative. How was that possible? There was only one trail. If two people failed to cross paths, then that meant one of two things: someone was off route or an accident had befallen them.

We kept the radio on and continued down the trail.

Half an hour later, we found our climber, crouched on the trail in the black of night. She was attempting to hike to Camp 1 on her own but was too tired and could no longer walk. It was lucky we found her. That close call taught me a profound lesson right there on the trail, and I knew from then on, I would strictly enforce a rule that should have already been in place: No one must act alone.

We returned to Base Camp, relieved that everyone was safe. As on Mount Fuji, there was one main trail to follow up Aconcagua, but a person could descend any of the path-like options that braided the route.

"Recalling it now, I was a bit confused," said Ono. "I thought I was following the trail, but suddenly the trail disappeared and I couldn't tell where I was. Knowing I could get lost if I kept descending, I decided to head back up. Then I saw the light from the tents and found my way. I didn't meet anyone on the trail because *I* must have been off route."

We were not a team that had been climbing together for years, yet everyone demonstrated concern and care for the lost hikers. Lights were turned on at Base Camp to draw the climbers downwards, and hot tea was ready for their return. Although it was not a technically difficult route, we still had to manage being at high altitude, and I reminded the team that we could never be too careful.

Since Camp 2 was established, we decided that the team members in good shape would continue up to Camp 1 then Camp 2 and on to the summit. Those with a slower ability to acclimatize would follow two days later.

I assumed the one thing we would not experience on the mountain in summer was a heavy snowfall, but we did. Even Base Camp was covered in a fresh layer of snow. And the wind was vicious. There was no way we could climb Aconcagua in such poor conditions, so we were forced to take a few rest days.

Eventually, the weather calmed down, and two days later, the snow disappeared as suddenly as it had arrived. The summit was ready for us to climb. On January 3 at 6 p.m., four team members with our local guide, and our loyal dog, Acon, reached the top of the mountain. We were delighted by the news and re-energized by the success of the dog.

At that time, we thought Acon was the only record holder for a high summit climbed by a dog. Later research by my canine-loving journalist friend, Kitamura, showed that the first record was set on Mont Blanc (4808 metres) in the European Alps by a dog named Tschingel in 1869. To celebrate Tschingel's success, the local mountain town of Chamonix performed a cannon salute. We had no means to honour Acon in that fashion on Aconcagua, and he had to settle for robust pats on the back.

Four months later, Acon's achievement was surpassed by two Bhotia dogs that reached the summit of India's Mount Chaukhamba (7138 metres) with a six-person Indian-Tibetan border-security team. In 1988, when Kitamura, Majima and I climbed Denali, a dog reached the summit with a French climber. What a sight it must have been years earlier in 1979 when Susan Butcher, the Alaskan musher, climbed Denali with a number of her sled dogs.

Acon aside, seven of our team members summitted Aconcagua, myself included. We endured several challenges that began with altitude sickness and expanded to strong winds, deep snowfall, −25°C temperatures and lost hikers. My sights for the summit had been set for January 7 from Camp 2.

A few members in the group, who were older, had no intention of hiking to the top, but their help was invaluable in ferrying loads from Base Camp to Camp 1. Ono, who had a rough start with altitude sickness, finally acclimatized and was able to summit. On his way down he even assisted a teammate who became too weak to continue past 6500 metres. In fact, I would not have summitted Aconcagua if it were not for Ono. At 500 metres from the peak, it was meant to be me who turned around with my client, but Ono stepped in. "Tabei-*san*, please go up to the summit. Another climber is still on their way up. I will go down, no worries," he said.

I was lost for words as Ono, the person who could barely reach Camp 1 at the start, turned to escort our tired teammate back down the mountain. I shared my heartfelt thanks with him, a true climbing partner, before I turned to face the summit trail. Having caught up with the other client, the two of us stood on the summit at 6:30 p.m. The sun still shone and the wide rocky summit plateau was an astounding burnt sienna.

A shiny silver cross stood on the peak. The custom we had heard pertaining to Aconcagua was that when a person summitted the mountain, they were to take an item that was left by the previous climber, and in return, leave something new. Thus, we unwrapped a strip of thin rope from the cross for our keeping and tied my bandana in its place.

For a team that came together as a commercial party, meeting for the first time at the Narita Airport, we had become integrated as one. Mountain trips have that ability. We worked together, everyone cooperating to ferry loads, set up camps and even take care of Acon. People looked out for one another and showed concern when warranted. My satisfaction with the trip was profound, and once again I felt certain that if a person is determined to pursue a dream, then, by all means, they have the ability to fulfill it. Although our ascent was not as unique as that of the man on the bicycle, it was an ascent after all.

Scanning the horizon of gradually darkening peaks that surrounded the summit, I wanted to yell, "Hey, your dad/your son/your daughter climbed Aconcagua!" After a final inhalation of the magnificent sunset, I stepped away from the summit, leaving it alone in the evening glow.

CHAPTER 14

Carstensz Pyramid

"Humans are made of pretty enduring stuff," I said.

"Why?" asked Tabei.

"We slept in minus 30 Celsius last year in Antarctica, and now it must be more than 50 degrees in the sun."

"Well, we'll be in a cool climate soon."

Here we go, aiming for Carstensz Pyramid (4884 metres), the highest mountain in the backbone range of New Guinea and the last of the Seven Summits for Tabei.

– Setsuko Kitamura

The chartered nine-passenger Cessna completed its bumpy landing on the grassy runway, and an audible sound of relief filled the body of the plane, as if we had all been holding our breath. We had safely arrived in Indonesia, one of my final mountain destinations. A variety of feelings filled my heart.

As I was about to step off the plane down a narrow ladder, I was caught off guard by our audience. We were surrounded by a group of almost-naked villagers from Ilaga. The men wore nothing but penis sheaths, and the women were dressed in straw skirts, their upper bodies bare except for knitted tube-like baskets that hung from their heads. A few wore T-shirts, but mainly, they were uncovered.

I was in awe that a culture thousands of years old remained intact. As a youngster, the descriptions of New Guinea I was familiar with were: jungle, unforgiving equatorial heat, a Second-World-War battlefield, malaria, and Indigenous naked tribes – all scary images made worse by the imagination of a child. Now, at the age of fifty-two, for my mountaineering trip, I felt better informed about the people of New Guinea. I had read the report of the 1964 joint expedition of the University of Kyoto and the Indonesian Army for West Irian, titled *Indigenous Tribes in New Guinea Highlands* by Katsuichi Honda, a prominent journalist of the era. I assumed the information from the thirty-year-old report was outdated, and thought the New Guinea society would have changed by the time I visited there. I was wrong. The same people I saw in the report's pictures stood in front of me as I descended from the airplane.

> Merrily, we marched through the fields to the village about one kilometre away, fully surrounded by the curious villagers. They were a step away in front of us, at our sides, and on our tail. I found it as amusing to observe Tabei in this type of situation as it was to watch the local people.
>
> To no one in particular, Tabei spoke in Japanese to the women who walked with us: "*Obasan, genki?*" (What's up, Auntie?) Then, "*Tou-chan wa?*" (How about your hubby?) And, "*Ei mino kiteru jyan?*" (You wear a nice straw skirt, don't you?) Tabei laughed at her own funny behaviour, which induced a giggle from the *obasan*. And so, the *Irian Jaya*–Japanese Women's Friendly Relations was established without effort. When the women mingle with cheer, the men approach, unable to resist their male curiosity despite an uncaring pretence. They wanted to know what was going on. To my knowledge, this is a common phenomenon all over the world.
>
> – Setsuko Kitamura

Members of the local Dani tribe, residing in Ilaga, were to be our porters, twenty-four in total, plus an extra eight just to carry their supply of potatoes. We were an international mix of climbers, a group of two Japanese women, two American men, one Mexican man and Tantio, the Indonesian guide by default (his predecessor failed to show up, so Tantio, with his polished appearance, took over the role somewhat ill-prepared).

Still becoming acquainted to the culture, it was our porters' names that next caught our attention. "Luther, Michael, Napoleon!" called the administrative officer who supervised the team's conduct. One after the other, the near-naked tribesmen stepped forward from the human hedge that formed the circle where we gathered.

It was the Dutch who discovered – though only through the perspective of Westerners – the Indigenous tribes that live in the New Guinea Highlands. Christian missionaries were said to have arrived there before the early explorers, and their ardent presence greatly influenced not only birth names but the existence of churches in nearly every village. Understanding this history, we were still surprised when our porters knelt in prayer to ask for the safety of our climb. We finally joined in their ritual and chanted amen on our knees with the palms of our hands pressed together.

Ilaga sits in a basin amidst low-elevation mountains that were fully green with trees and bushes up to their summits. It has an airport, a church and several markets. Although there was a well-maintained road for vehicles, just less than an hour's walk through thick grassland delivered us to a mountain trail. The first day of our trek was only three hours, as the next campsite was too far and there were no decent areas in which to pitch a tent once we were in the jungle. At camp, we learned how to prepare New Guinea's staple food, the potato. The tribesmen dug about a half metre into the ground and lined the dirt with banana leaves. Then a layer of potatoes, cabbage and some other leafy vegetables were covered by more banana leaves. They placed hot stones on top, and waited for forty to fifty minutes for the mixture to steam. Ta-da, and alas, dinner. Not to complain, but the meal was too bland for us without the addition of salt and spice.

The second day of trekking was more difficult. It rained every afternoon, sometimes continuing into the evening (but rarely all night), and the jungle was dark, insulated with thick and dense trees. Roots extended on the ground like an octopus's legs and were too slimy to walk on. The trail itself was extremely rough, full of muddy-boggy spots that were best to avoid. At first, we tried to protect our footwear from the soaking wet mud; but we eventually gave up – we were too tired to search for drier places to step. Thus, quickly, my brand-new hiking boots were a giant clump of mud, and my socks sodden as well. The jungle was vastly different from the pristine state of a glacier.

We hiked through the stretch of jungle in two days. The trees became scarce and the sky visible as we transitioned from steep jungle climb to mild grassland ridge. For me, a ridge had so often meant knife-point – sharp and narrow – but in this case, it was a vast area rising above the New Guinea jungle. I was surprised by the fresh breeze that welcomed us, an unexpected pleasure at the equator. My altimeter read 3900 metres.

My image of an extensive dry grassland quickly vanished. It was nothing more than a large marsh, with no dry place to sit, so we continued for six to seven hours each day until we reached a suitable place to camp.

By the end of the seventh day, the trail transitioned again, this time to an uneven path of sand and gravel. We scrambled over the steep rocky hills that stood like layers of screens between us and the emerald green lake far below. Rain became sleet and eventually turned to snow. The porters were dressed only in knitted grass raingear worn on top of their heads. They were barefoot and shaking with cold. Still, they maintained their amazing skill of grabbing tree roots with their toes while carrying heavy loads and continued without a fuss. They seemed to fly over the wet rocks rather than walk, much like mountain hobbits.

At New Zealand Pass, two trails branched from where we stood: to the right was Carstensz Pyramid and to the left, Jaya Peak. The highest summit in Indonesia was considered to have been Jaya Peak, formerly called Sukarno Peak. Historically, Jaya Peak was covered by a glacier, which melted over time and reduced its elevation to less than the neighbouring rocky spire, Carstensz Pyramid. I was interested in the fact that with a change of era came a change in mountain elevations.

From New Zealand Pass, which overlooked a valley of lakes scattered about like gems, another hour of walking had us at Base Camp at Yellow Pass.

> Before reaching Base Camp but after the jungle section, we walked along a ridgeline marked by rock, sand and alpine vegetation. The ridge was shrouded in fog and we breathed the authentic cool air of high alpine. Then, out of nowhere, from the other side of the scree ridge, three local guys dressed in rain ponchos appeared with a radio cassette player in hand, pop music blaring out loud. What the heck is this? They

explained that they had come up from Timika, a southern sea-shore city that required only a three-day ascent to Base Camp, with the convenience of partial car access. Our route from Ilaga needed a minimum of a one-week approach to Base Camp. The reason we chose the longer route was due to the mega mining operation in between Timika and Base Camp. The open-pit mine was mainly American-run and covered an area of 26 square kilometres. The Indonesian government did not permit mountaineers, except for local ones, to pass through it. Anyway, it took me a moment to pull myself together after having encountered the sudden onslaught of music on an isolated trail in the high alpine surrounded by glaciers and near the equator in New Guinea.

The first morning at Base Camp arrived early to a cacophony of loud snoring from the men's tents. I was up at 6 a.m. We had all gone to sleep early the night before, which showed how tired we felt, except for my buddy, Tabei. She looked like business as usual. The young American doctor, Bob, and the professional Mexican climber, Oscar, left to test the route without even eating breakfast. They returned at 7 p.m., totally spent but fully satisfied. Despite their physical exhaustion, they were happy to report success in reaching the summit. "It's a darn tough route!" Long and sketchy, they said. They told us that the slab section was manageable, but we would want a pair of Koflach boots and an ice axe when we reached the south side of the ridge as it was a mix of rock, snow and ice.

Then came the punch. "Junko, your reach is too short. Setsuko, even your height wouldn't make it. Us? We have no wish to climb a route like that again. Sorry, we can't help you."

"Tantio!" Tabei and I said, exasperated, sensing our trip was about to quickly disintegrate.

Our guide turned away and simply said, "Well, my ankles are in bad shape. I might as well go down."

To make a long story short, two days later, the team descended from Base Camp, leaving Tabei and me behind. As soon as Tantio said that he would do whatever it took to break past the mining operation to make their retreat quicker, the three other homesick men followed him without complaint.

"Come back with your friends who can climb with Junko, and with the necessary equipment, OK?" I asked Tantio, as Tabei and I organized ourselves to stay up there..

The friends I was referring to were members of University of Indonesia Mountaineering Club. The main reason I asked for them to join us was because they were just returning home from an Aconcagua expedition in Argentina. They would be arriving at Biak Airport anytime. If we could contact them, the top-notch climbers would likely come to help us with proper equipment. This was Tantio's suggestion in the first place, so perhaps it was not too late to implement it.

Just the two of us, Tabei and I did our own test climb. When we touched the slab that appeared smooth, it crumbled away. Alpine plants that clung to the thin mud of the rock face slid off too easily for us to rely on as holds. To add to the misery, my legs felt heavy, and I could barely lift them with willpower alone. We gave up at the end of the fifth pitch, leaving behind our shell jackets, a small-sized tent and 2 litres of water, to reduce the weight of our future ferrying up the route. We rappelled in the rain that started on cue and made the flakey rock and muddy surface much worse. So far, I was not as enthralled with the mixed climbing of rock and mud compared to the usual rock and ice combination.

Upon arrival back at camp, drenched, we fired up the stove to dry out. As we began to warm, a porter who had gone down with the men's party returned to us with a written message. "Two guides arranged. Come down to meet with them. Mining route available now if only with us."

In retrospect, we should have realized what it signified when we saw several more porters show up the next morning to carry all our gear down with them. Instead, we were so excited for the arrangement of two guides that, blindly, we

praised Tantio for such a great job. Time would tell us of our
folly.

▲

Navigating the mine was an adventure of its own. As we descended a very steep gully, the open pit came into view between narrow slights of rock buttresses. The land had been
desecrated by development; the footprint was like the skin of
an apple peeled into a giant spiral. It was a time warp, from
the fairy-tale highland full of lakes like jewels to the impact
of an industrial site right there in the mountains.

About 1500 vertical metres farther down, Tantio waited
for us in a marshland full of flowers, similar to Oze in Japan's
Fukushima Prefecture. "How are things with our guides?" we
asked, wasting no time when we met up with him.

"Well, you ladies wouldn't have come down had I not
talked you out of it this way. Going back via Ilaga would take
too much time and put our permit from the army overdue.
No good," he confessed in the midst of the beautiful flowery
marsh. We had been cheated of the summit, although in an
artful manner. Tabei and I looked at each other and saw disappointment, anger and fatigue.

"All right then, let's try again once this chap is relieved of
his duties," said Tabei.

"Fine," I said. "Whatever it takes, we'll get the permit
extended in Jakarta then arrange guides and equipment
afterwards." We reached the humid tropical city of Timika
at midnight by connecting a cable-car ride with a lift in a
Toyota Land Cruiser, having bypassed the mining operation.
But that night, Tantio was met with sad news. An accident
had occurred on Aconcagua and some of his friends had possibly been killed – the names were unknown at the time. Exhausted, Tantio's face distorted into sorrow. There was nothing we could do to help other than leave him alone. It was
already March 24 – we had six days left on our permit.

▲

The Japanese company Hitachi was also invested in the

mining operation we crossed earlier, a fact I uncovered through my own investigation. In Timika, I called the company's Jakarta office, asking for a favour. I also made use of my artistic talent from art club in junior high school as I experimented with polishing up the permit dates to be more accommodating to our needs. In truth, we did all we could to extend our stay in New Guinea and seek a way back up through the mining route, but our tropical dream did not turn out that sweet.

A proper-looking gentleman stopped us in our efforts. "Going through the mining area, in particular for foreigners, requires procedures of incredible steps. But you ladies have done a good job so far. Try harder in Jakarta. In terms of my boss's stamp of approval, he'll only say yes if you submit a proper application." So, we tore up our experimentally altered permit and packed our gear to leave, half with joy to go home, half with disappointment.

Thus, our, or more accurately, Tabei's attempt to complete the seventh summit ended in failure.

It was even more saddening to think that our jackets were forever waiting for our return, in the misty forlorn place on the rock route, Tabei's red and mine yellow.

– Setsuko Kitamura

Cold Night at the Equator

On June 25, 1992, three months after my first attempt on Carstensz Pyramid, I was back at Base Camp, having obtained a permit from the Indonesian Army and the much-needed pass to access the property of the Freeport mine. This time, Agus and Mulia, the alumni friends of Tantio from the University of Indonesia Mountaineering Club, were to climb with me.

In three days, we were at Base Camp via the Freeport route, compared to the ten days spent trekking from Ilaga the last time. It rained almost daily, the norm for a region that has an average of twenty-five days of rainfall per month. But for June 27, the day of our planned summit assault, the sky had cleared in the night and the stars shone above us, followed by a transparent blue that spread across the morning light.

Carstensz is a gigantic chunk of limestone. Right from the start, the route involved technical rock climbing with ropes. Since we had reached Base Camp at a quick pace, via the mining road and cable cars, we had not allotted enough time to acclimatize from sea level to the higher altitudes. At 4100 metres, my two young lads complained of headaches, which was understandable. Although they were locals, they usually spent most of their time at elevation zero. To alleviate the expectation for them to lead, I started to climb.

The rock wall that initially looked daunting from below actually had fairly good-sized cracks, and in various spots, the face was climbable, too, providing a range of options to choose our line. Also, a series of steep buttresses seen from the base had sections with a gentle grade, which further helped. The difficulty came in the length of time it took to reach the upper ridge that loomed above us.

Agus and Mulia, each about half my age in their twenties, were slow moving, likely due to altitude sickness. One of them said, "Let's go down to the camp today, and try again tomorrow."

"Well, let's just check a little farther to see what's over the col," I said. "Slow going is fine." I insisted on continuing and started leading the way up. They may not have been the best climbers, but they certainly filled a gap. Besides, who could expect such nice weather the next day?

We arrived at the spot where a 50-metre fixed rope was left hanging, a tiny bit frayed, but in good enough shape for me to set a jumar on it. It took my breath away to climb that 50 metres without a rest, even with the use of jumars. From the col we could see the south glacier in close proximity, and the mountains that extended indefinitely beyond, an endless mix of trees of rocks. It was 2 p.m. and the sun sat high in the sky without a cloud to be seen. I decided to attack the climbing; the lads sluggishly following behind. A ten-minute walk along the ridge from the col led us to a sudden drop-off that we had to rappel, and I found an anchor with an old sling hanging from it. We removed the faded tat and tied on a new sling, set up two ropes, and then rappelled down 40 metres. From there, we gingerly traversed the sandy face to then begin climbing again.

"That's the summit of Carstensz," said Agus, weakly lifting his arm to point to the rock spire in the far-off distance. It was slightly past 4 p.m., and it seemed unlikely we would reach the summit that day, considering the crux was yet to come – an overhanging wall in the form of a two-level stairway directly below the peak. The first level of the stairway was difficult and it was not until 5:30 p.m. that we finished climbing it.

"Continuing in the dark is dangerous. Let's find a good spot to bivouac," I said and rappelled down the pitch we had just climbed. By 6:15 p.m. we found a tiny hollow for the night, a spot with hardly enough room for the three of us to sit. We hammered pitons into the rock as an anchor to secure ourselves and the equipment to, and then sat there. Since we had no actual bivy gear with us, our camp was quite simplistic. Our water supply was down to 400 millilitres.

The radiant sun that had shone all day began to melt into the clouds, and by the time midnight came, streaks of lightning danced around a starry sky. The Milky Way stood out as a river of flowing wonder. I wished I could have shown this picturesque night to my children, but it would have been difficult for them to imagine me spending the entire time sitting stationary on the rock.

It was cold at 4700 metres. Repeatedly, I checked my watch, as if to hasten time. Eleven p.m., 1 a.m., 2:30, 4:00 – morning was slow to come. By 5:30, the sky brightened, providing us with the second sunny day in a row.

I stretched out my arms and legs, stiff from having sat in the same posture all night. Carefully, we put on our climbing equipment; it would have been disastrous if anything had dropped. At 6:30 a.m., we stood below the overhang that we had run out of time to complete the day before. It took another hour and half before we successfully climbed the intimidating staircase feature.

I assumed we had cleared the crux, but I was wrong. There were four more sections of the rock wall to the summit, which required repeated rappels and climbing. I reminded myself that the sand-covered rock surface was slippery – use caution – and I continued on my way.

As we neared the summit, with 5 metres to go, I handed my video camera to Agus and asked him to film our arrival there. The buttons on the camera – record and stand-by – were labelled in *kanji* characters, so

I briefly instructed him on how to use it as we were perched on the rock wall. A quick learner, he was able to shoot several frames of my final steps to the top. A finely engraved plate was embedded on the mountain's peak to welcome us.

"Congratulations!" said Agus, the lens of the video camera focused on me.

"Finally, I'm here," I thought. "I did it; it's the summit."

"*Terima kasih*," I said to Agus and Mulia in Indonesian. "Thank you." I poured my gratitude into the gesture of shaking their hands. I hoped it was enough to express my apology for having forced them to climb a difficult route beyond their fitness level.

As I looked around me, I realized this area was unique to the wilderness of New Guinea. The more common scene of indefinite forests was replaced with the glacier of Jaya Peak, the limestone of Carstensz Pyramid itself, and a scattering of gemlike lakes. The other outstanding feature, was of course, the Freeport mine, an obvious scar in the landscape. It befuddles me to think how mankind digs for gold and copper at the expense of the beauty of nature. The schemes of humans are a curious thing.

After summit photos were taken and video footage was complete, we began our return to home. Not even fifteen minutes later, the fog set in. Then the snow started to fall, and within minutes our route was transformed into a scary continuation of rocky spires. The ropes were wet and heavy, and knowing that most climbing accidents occur during the descent, I remained focused on being careful.

The 40-metre rappel down the side of a spire that was part of the up–down ascent to the summit became a challenging overhang climb on the way back. The strength in my arms had diminished and I had to rely on my jumars to help me ascend the soggy rope. The snow had turned to rain, and the fog had thickened. It was impossible to be certain of what lay ahead.

Night fell upon us when we thought it was still evening time. To make matters worse, all the headlamp batteries had run out, but none of us wanted to stay hugging the rock for another night. We yelled to each other and fumbled with the ropes to continue our rappel. Then I heard the much-anticipated word, "Finish!" escape from the pitch-dark night. I could breathe again. Still, with the rock wall behind us and shelter near by, I told myself again to remain cautious.

As predicted, I fell several times on the steep sandy trail, but the true danger of the route was over, and I could concentrate on searching for the tent in limited visibility. Since our timing on the summit would enable me to fly back to Japan on schedule, I was determined. "Well," I thought, "I'll just keep marching till morning if we don't find the tent."

At 0:05 a.m. on June 29, we arrived at our beloved tent.

A few months after our disappointing trip to New Guinea, a message came to me that changed history for women mountaineers. "Tabei-*san* just called to say she had success on Carstensz Pyramid and came down safely. She wanted me to let you know as soon as I could." This was the news a colleague of mine shared from the Jakarta branch of my Tokyo work place. As a journalist, I wasted no time in jumping on my computer to write the story.

Of all the articles I had written in the past, this was one of the most exhilarating stories to tell, although I would not be given credit for it – the text would be signed with my Jakarta colleague's name since the original story was his. Nonetheless, on July 2, 1992, the newspaper headlines read "First Woman to Complete the Seven Summits."

When we returned to Japan after our attempt on Carstensz, and were waiting for a new permit to be issued for another chance, Tabei and I had chatted about the climb. "In the lonely rainy night on the rock, the red jacket asks the yellow jacket, 'Hey, do you think they really will come back to get us?' Then the yellow jacket tries to offer solace, though half-sobbing, 'They will, because they are so cheap that they cannot give up old gear like us. They'll be back.'"

"Wait for us, you two lovely jackets. We will return." But, as I was already considered a person of miracles, having been granted the maximum allotted holiday time for Antarctica the previous year then Indonesia, my savings were down to zero and I could not afford to join Tabei on the second trial of Carstensz. That was reason enough for my fingers to type with feverish energy as I wrote the story of Tabei's success.

I thought back to another significant day, May 16, 1975, when Tabei's voice echoed above the bright white and blue Khumbu Glacier when she announced over the radio, "Just arrived at the summit!" It had been seventeen years since she stood on Mount Everest.

After that victory, we explored the world together, impressed by the good-looking mountaineers in the European Alps, excited by the flight to Denali, awed by the pure beauty of Antarctica, and deeply moved by the poor but happy spirited African locals of Mount Kilimanjaro.

It was as if I could hear Tabei's voice again, almost directly in my ear, reverberating in the midst of a tropical island, deep in the jungle, on top of the sheer spires surrounded by glaciated mountains, "Set-*chan*, I'm here!"

In typing the historic article, I found myself answering her: "Oh, my dear, I'm having such a fun life thanks to you." I praised her accomplishments; the woman was a hero.

Later, after Carstensz, Tabei said, "Hey, by the way, I brought back our good girls, too," and she handed me my old, much-loved yellow jacket upon her arrival in Tokyo.

– Setsuko Kitamura

THE SEVEN SUMMITS

by Setsuko Kitamura

The Seven Summits is an ambiguous term. While Junko Tabei was crowned the first female to ascend all seven summits, her achievement had several aspects to it.

The concept of climbing the highest peak of each of the seven continents of the world was first conceived by Richard Bass, a Texan millionaire and amateur mountaineer. He climbed six of the seven summits by the end of 1983, and in 1985, at age fifty-five, he completed the feat with success on Mount Everest (his fourth attempt). His book, titled

Seven Summits and co-authored with Frank Wells and Rick Ridgeway, was published in 1986.

Before the challenge of the Seven Summits was born, the eternal goal amongst prominent mountaineers was to complete the 8000-metre peaks of the world (fourteen in total). Now the Seven Summits has been added to the tag line of accomplishments.

At the time of Bass's success, and the elevations noted from the year of each ascent, the seven summits he climbed included:

> Mount Everest, Eurasia (Asia) (8848 metres)
> Aconcagua, South America (6959 metres)
> Denali, North America (6142 metres)
> Kilimanjaro, Africa (5895 metres)
> Elbrus, Europe (5542 metres)
> Vinson Massif, Antarctica (4892 metres)
> Kosciuszko, Australia (2228 metres)

However, Bass's definition of the Seven Summits was criticized, least not by renowned climber Reinhold Messner, the first person to ascend all fourteen 8000-metre peaks – without supplemental oxygen. Messner stated that the highest peak in Australia was not Kosciuszko but Carstensz Pyramid (4484 metres) in Irian Jaya of New Guinea. He based this argument on the fact that the Oceania Plate, on which Australia sits, extends north to include Indonesia, in which case, Carstensz Pyramid is the highest of that continent. Messner completed *his* new list of the Seven Summits, including Carstensz, in 1986.

Another mountain up for debate was the highest peak in Europe. Before the collapse of the Berlin Wall, Mont Blanc (4810 metres) had the honour. Circa 1990 Elbrus became known as the highest summit on the European continent. In Japan, the Seven Summits is still recognized without Carstensz or Elbrus on the list.

As for Junko Tabei, she climbed Mont Blanc with me in 1979, before the concept of the Seven Summits was in place. On a family trip to Australia in 1991, Tabei climbed Kosciuszko, noting, "A chair lift goes almost to the summit, and not-so-good-shape hikers enjoy a beer up there. It's a pretty good destination for tourists."

When Tabei became serious about her goal to climb the Seven Summits, she strove for perfection. Hence, even though when she climbed Carstensz in 1992 she was named the first female to climb the Seven Summits, in her mind the job was incomplete. A few months after Carstensz, she returned to her earlier-climbed Elbrus and summitted the West Peak (5642 metres). This settled her own internal conflict that the East Peak, her first summit on Elbrus, measured 5621 metres, thus was not precisely the highest mountain of New Europe.

In one way, word was that the Seven Summits were not a highly recognized prize. Why then would Tabei strive for this objective? Her answer: "By setting something as a goal, it always pushes me out of my box. For instance, I had an opportunity to see an absolutely different world in Antarctica thanks to pursuit of the Seven Summits."

Near the time of Tabei's completion of the Seven Summits, I had the impression that Tabei steered more towards climbing a greater number of mountain peaks in as many unfamiliar places as possible.

There is a book, One Hundred Mountains of Japan, written by late Japanese mountaineer-writer Kyuya Fukada in 1964, that introduces the concept of climbing lists to Japan. The title itself is unique in that there are only twenty-one peaks higher than 3000 metres within the country. The idea of all these mountains to climb gained such popularity in Japan that in the 1980s, countless middle-age-plus mountaineers pursued completion of the one hundred peaks, a feat that takes years, if not decades.

Behind the human desire to conquer such lists may be an older form of tradition, outside of mountaineering. For example, there is a list for people to visit the great number of temples and shrines in Japan – if the list is completed, one is promised to receive a divine favour. Really, the underlying purpose of that list is to "Share the goal with others and strive for it." This is the sense of spirit that may have been unwittingly embedded in Tabei's earnest pursuit of not only the Seven Summits but every mountain she climbed.

CHAPTER 15

Mountains of Later Life

When the word "cancer" was spoken by the doctor, who said, "...till June...,"
my immediate question was, "Does that mean I only have three months to
live?" Yet, calmly, I replied, "Is that so?"

In mid-February 2012, life took one of those turns that causes abrupt
change for a person. For me, it was signs and symptoms that spoke loud
and clear in the form of stinging pain that ran through my abdomen,
like sharp needles poking at my insides. Generally healthy and fit, I had
never felt anything like that before and I was concerned. But the pain
subsided, and I went on with my plans. It was the first day of an event for
Project Cheer Up Tohoku, a series of joint ventures designed to promote
and support Tohoku, the region of Japan affected by the country's most
devastating earthquake, which occurred on March 11, 2011. The event included an overnight stay at Nicchu *onsen* followed by a day of snowshoeing at Oguni-numa.

   In the aftermath of the Tohoku earthquake, Project Cheer Up Tohoku
was spearheaded by the Himalayan Adventure Trust of Japan, of which I
was chairperson. The project, still going at this writing, has two branches:
one is called Let's Go to Tohoku Mountains, with the catchphrase "Eat
local food, stay overnight and enjoy shopping"; and the other is Hiking
into Nature, which supports those people affected by the earthquake and
living in refugee shelters by taking them on hiking trips. The hiking aspect began in June 2011. By August 2013, twenty-eight hiking trips had
already been completed, with plans to continue the program for as long
as necessary.

Upon start-up, the reaction to the trips was extremely positive. The feeling was further confirmed by the words of the participants from the refugee shelters:

"Wow, it's been a long time since I hiked through forests. Beautiful green and nice breeze. It's energizing, isn't it? It feels very good to be out here!"

"My husband, who hasn't once stepped out of the refugee shelter, became interested if it was hiking. Here we are. First time hiking together since the earthquake. What a relief to see him smile!"

"I lost everything in the tsunami. But it's in the past. Now I feel like thinking about future. Thanks for giving me the chance to go forward."

People were refreshed after a hike, and they returned to the refugee shelters with renewed interest in life. I was encouraged by this response and continued to offer trips once a month.

A line from a conversation I had with local Member of Parliament Mr. Nagashima, for a television clip, highlighted the need for more hikes. He said, "Interestingly, what people in the refugee shelters suffer from the most is not really the shortage of material things, but from having nothing to do."

My concern for the great number of people who lived in the shelters grew when I read the addresses on the application forms submitted to the hiking program. Several were rooms at a high school (the science lab, the physical training room and a Grade 10 classroom). I asked fellow hikers how they lived in those conditions, and they remarked, "We put *tatamis* in the science lab and eleven people live in there together. There is no closet so we cannot put futons away. We just fold them in half and leave them there for the day." Essentially, the rooms were overcrowded dorms. In terms of eating, I was told they were unable to properly cook a meal because they had no stoves. Their three meals a day were fast-food lunch-box style.

"How about bathing?" I asked. The government built a make-shift public bath for the shelter dwellers, but as one of the hikers pointed out, imagine the state of the water after seven hundred people used it. My subconscious voice spoke up, and I suggested, "Well then, we'll go soak in an *onsen* after hiking next time." That was the impetus for an overnight trip. The phone calls poured in asking when the next hike was scheduled and what *onsen* would we stop at afterwards.

In January 2012 our first hike and hot-spring trip was arranged. We hiked to Shiono-yama on an easy trail that looked down on the town in Koshu Yamanashi. At the top, we were treated to *amazake*, a sweet thick sake, courtesy of the Yamanashi Mountaineering Association. After the hike and before dinner, people indulged in the outdoor *onsen* for an unusually long time. They could hardly bring themselves to leave the soothing water. I waited, and smiled, and asked the kitchen staff to be patient while blissful conversations about being in a dreamland flowed from the steamy pools. The view of snow-capped Mount Fuji in the distance sealed the atmosphere – this was indeed a bit of heaven for those displaced from their homes elsewhere in Japan.

Even before that January experience, in fact, since the fall of 2011, each time I caught a glimpse of Mount Fuji from the bullet train to or from Tokyo, I pictured high-school students from the earthquake-affected area climbing to its summit. While Hiking into Nature is primarily run for seniors, I wanted to expand the concept to include teenagers on their summer break from school. When I proposed the idea to Project Cheer Up Tokohu, everyone froze. I could hear their minds at work. Mount Fuji, at 3776 metres in elevation, would be a completely different excursion from hiking lower hills and mountains on gentle trails. Not to mention the staff members themselves were of an older age, making Mount Fuji a challenge to complete right there. And what about financing and transportation from Fukushima to Fujiyoshida and two nights' accommodation to include a soak in the huge *onsen* that skirted the mountain? I admitted there were a few creases to iron out, but the voice in my heart whispered, "Go for it."

Tadao Kanzaki, chief of the project, and, coincidentally, chief of the Japan Mountaineering Association, an organization responsible for training mountain guides and outdoor instructors, finally spoke. "All right, let's do it," he said. "We'll ask experienced mountaineers to guide the students and we'll take care of trip arrangements." From that meeting, a new project called Mount Fuji for the High-School Students of

Tohoku Earthquake was born, and July 2012 was set for its inaugural trip. First and foremost, though, we needed money. There were T-shirts to sell, companies to approach, donations to request. We held events like Project Cheer Up Tohoku Songs and Talks to encourage support of our mission, and it all paid off. The business world and public alike were drawn to our idea, and sufficient finances were raised.

Back to February 2012. A few days after the snowshoeing excursion to Nicchu *onsen* in Kitakata, I felt the unmistakable sting in my abdomen again. This time I knew something was wrong. I pursued an appointment with a doctor of internal medicine near my office in downtown Tokyo, had X-rays and was given a prescription drug for a potential intestinal obstruction. The worrier that I am, I also saw my family doctor, who had previously diagnosed me with early stage breast cancer. He added a Chinese medicine to my prescription that would activate my intestine, which needed a boost. I followed all instructions, but my belly tensed and I began to lose my appetite over the next several weeks.

I had a busy day scheduled for March 9. I had just finished a meeting with the bus company in support of the Mount Fuji project, and I was en route to the village of Otama, at the foot of Adatara-yama. It was the one-year anniversary of the earthquake, and I had been asked to deliver a speech there. I was also to attend another snowshoe outing with victims of the earthquake prior to the anniversary event. Having caught an earlier train than expected, I had a bit of extra time in Kouriyama. I could either go to the hair salon or phone my brother Hisayoshi, a urologist. I called my brother and he met me at the station. From there, things happened fast.

Although he could have examined me at the hospital where he worked, my brother immediately arranged for me to see his son-in-law, whose expertise was internal medicine. "You have to go to a better-equipped hospital," Hisayoshi said, and I was sent to the emergency department at another hospital. There, to my surprise, I was told I would be admitted; I was not to go home that day. My first thought was about the next day's snowshoe excursion, but I conceded to someone else stepping in as my replacement. The speech in Otama was a different matter. It had been planned for a long time and my presence was expected. Since I was not in pain, I pressed the doctor to let me leave. Reluctantly, he agreed under the condition that Hisayoshi and his son-in-law join me as escorts. Thus, I arrived in the village of Otama with two doctors as my guests.

By the time the sun began to set that evening, I had finished my seventy-minute speech, was settled back in the hospital and medical examinations were under way. I was connected to an intravenous drip and fluid from my abdomen was removed, both for testing and comfort as my belly had become taut again. When results were ready, it was my husband who was called into the doctor's office. "To be honest," said the doctor, "it's quite negative. Please be prepared."

Recognizing the seriousness in the doctor's eyes, Masanobu said, "My wife is ready to hear the results herself, so please let us listen to you together." I was brought into the room to join them.

In a quiet tone, my condition was explained to me. Cancer cells had been found in the fluid taken from my abdomen. X-rays showed that these cells had already spread over a large area, even the pelvis. It was obviously a situation not to be taken lightly. Should all the black spots on the film be cancer, my abdomen was full of it.

"What would you say about this condition?" I asked. What I really wanted to know was how long I had to live.

He remained silent for a while. Then, "Could be till June –" Three months? My life was suddenly confined to three months?

"That's not going to happen," I thought, but simply answered, "Is it so?"

And that split second, my take-action mode switched on and I knew I had to first decide if I would stay in the hospital or not. My family doctor called while we were discussing the options. The two doctors quickly conversed and I was told I could go home as an appointment had already been scheduled with Dr. Takizawa of the Cancer Institute at Ariake Hospital within the week.

By coincidence, my son, Shinya, was on his way to Tokyo from our family-run ski lodge in Numajiri. He picked me up from the hospital with a futon in the back of his van for me to lie on for the drive home. Meanwhile, Masanobu stayed at our Numajiri Lodge in order to lead the snowshoe trip for the people from the town of Okuma.

Although I loved outings in the mountains, I was happy to finally be at my own home in Kawagoe. All bases were covered with Cheer Up Tohoku, so in that regard I could relax, yet I truly felt heavy in belly and in mind. I had no appetite, and my muscles were diminished as I had only drunk water since my abrupt diagnosis. Packing to leave for the Cancer Institute at Ariake Hospital felt more sluggish than stages on a mountaineering trip.

On March 15 Shinya drove me to the cancer centre and I met with Dr. Takizawa. He was my past surgeon, who had conducted the procedure of preventive cervical cancer removal. When studying my recent X-ray, he remained completely at ease. In fact, he smiled. "We have great medication these days. By May or so, you might be asking 'What was that?' To start, you'll be admitted to the ward tomorrow." He announced this as though it was business as usual. Such a simple approach; no brooding air about my diagnosis. My secretary, Minako Yoshida, who had made the trip from my office in downtown Tokyo to be with me, stared blankly at the doctor as though to say, "That's it?"

While Yoshida's new job was to clear all my scheduled events for the next month, mine was to throw myself into battle with the cancer that had exploded in my body. In my opinion, I had no choice but to win.

No Fuss

The image depicted on the computer screen showed a black band stretched across the inside of my abdomen with black spots scattered all around it.

My new temporary home was the gynecology ward on the eighth floor of the cancer centre. After instructions on what to expect, the nurses came to and from my room countless times to measure my blood pressure and heart rate and to take samples for blood tests. My doctors, Dr. Iwase and Dr. Abe, were both leading female physicians, and Dr. Iwase was quite the sportswoman herself. She loved mountain climbing and ran marathons, and was lively and cheerful. Dr. Abe was soft spoken and easygoing. I could feel their passion for medicine and their drive for the betterment of it, which made it simple for me to trust them with my life. We were a good team.

In the days leading up to being admitted to Ariake, my diet consisted of either fluid fed intravenously at the previous hospital, or water. It had been nearly ten days since I had enjoyed a meal. My first lunch at the cancer centre was cooked rice with *gobo* (like parsnip, but stronger in flavour), onion soup, chicken sauté with carrot and cauliflower, potato salad and green beans stewed with mushrooms. Unbelievably, I ate it all. After lunch, a litre of fluid was drained from my belly once again.

That night, my two doctors explained the plan to me. I was to have a CT scan the coming Monday, the results of which would determine the appropriate treatment for my illness. The doctors spoke with a sense of brightness: "We don't know the cause of this cancer yet. Whether it's a return of your breast cancer, or, in a very unlikely case, a stretch from the potential cervical cancer that we operated for in 2009. Or, a totally new one. No matter what the cause, we'll do our best, and in the meantime, we'll treat any uncomfortable symptoms you may experience. Let's take on this fight together." I was greatly reassured by their optimism.

My encounter with cancer was in full force. In truth, I temporarily fell into a dark disposition when I interpreted my prognosis as a three-month life sentence with the clock ticking ever downward. Yet my inner voice assured me that I would not die in three months. To gain perspective, I purposely thought about what really scared me in life – was it this diagnosis? No. It was the moment of being hit by an avalanche all those years ago. I remembered the overbearing feeling of *this is it* as the blocks of snow crushed against me. By far, that moment of fear exceeded anything I felt as a patient in the cancer centre. So, I had one choice: to embrace the finest technology available at a hospital with the most expertise in cancer treatment, and face my future. I was seventy-two years old.

On March 22, the scan results were ready. I asked Yoshida to be with me to hear the outcome. "Not all these black spots are cancer; however, many of them are and it has spread to your abdomen. The test results suggest it's either a recurrence of breast cancer or the original peritoneal cancer. Fortunately, medication and treatment are the same for either case, and we'll follow that method." Then the stinger, "If it is peritoneal cancer, it's at stage III." My heart skipped a beat – stage III already? How was that possible when it had only been a month since I felt the first pangs of pain in my abdomen? Distracted, I quietly listened to the doctor continue.

"Here's what we do next. You'll be on an anti-cancer drug therapy starting tomorrow, and we'll use medications that are common with breast cancer treatment. Your dose will be administered on a once-a-week cycle for three weeks. Times that by four cycles, so twelve weeks of treatment in total. If this therapy works well and the cancer cells shrink, then you'll have an operation to remove any remaining tumours, followed by another twelve weeks of the anti-cancer drug therapy. Overall, the commitment is twenty-eight weeks. Seven months. You'll likely have anemia, and your white blood cells and platelets may decrease in number. If those numbers fail to increase back to a normal range, or other side effects persist, we may postpone the second round of therapy, extending the duration of treatment. Other complications may include nausea, vomiting, lack of appetite, hair loss, numbness and muscle pain. Take good care of yourself when your white blood cell count is lower, because your immunity will be weak. Don't go out into a crowd. Put a mask on, thoroughly wash your hands and gargle often. Once the increased fluid in your abdomen is gone, you can become an outpatient. There is a possibility of total recovery; however, there is also a potential of 70 per cent recurrence in two years, even once seemingly healed." The information hit me like a head-on storm, and it was all I could do to latch onto the doctor's closing reference that a five-year survival rate was 30 per cent. This was going to be tough.

As we made our way back to my hospital room, Masanobu repeatedly encouraged me to aim for that 30 per cent. "You can do it," he said. I was lost in thought, wishing I could base my recovery on effort alone. Despite my agreeable response to him, I was distant. Calm, but aloof.

I wondered if I would have remained as calm with my prognosis if I had not yet reached the milestone of my seventies. Not likely. Depression would certainly have set in if I had been told much earlier that my life would be cut short. Instead, my decades of a go-getter attitude and my history with good luck had me feel no regret and enabled me to gently accept my prognosis without a dramatic response. I admit, I wished I could have continued climbing mountains for another ten years, but I had a fulfilling past in that regard, too. I had lived a good life.

My main concern, of course, was leaving my family. I was apprehensive about my husband being alone after I died. We had been having such fun together since his retirement at age sixty. We shared the freedom of travelling and hiking more often, and it was nice to see Masanobu enjoy life after working so hard for all those years. Again, I concluded I was lucky to have reached my seventies, and I told myself to accept this next stage in life and do my best. No fuss, no mess.

On March 23, my first cycle of chemotherapy began. Anti-allergy, anti-nausea and anti-cancer medication inundated my body through IV, and I dozed off throughout the morning as a sleep-induced drug was also part of the mix. On days when I was free of therapy, I established my own routine of well-being. There was a private shower on my ward that I was welcome to use. There were also stocked bookshelves scattered about in the hallways, plus a mini library on each floor. I read as much as I could and enjoyed the endless supply of *manga* (Japanese comics) at my disposal. I could never quite adapt to the city view that surrounded Ariake; there was not enough trees and natural greenery for me. The saving grace was the cap of Mount Fuji and the expanse of Tokyo Bay visible through the gaps of the city's high-rise buildings. At night the Tokyo Tower lit up, creating a spectacular panoramic view of the cityscape, the nearly six hundred steps of the tower inviting people to climb it. But in the hospital, elevators were the only way up or down and I missed having access to stairways to keep myself fit. I was left to invent an exercise routine for myself, which was to walk to a distant bookshelf and take one book at a time back to my room. I found that my eyes quickly tired if I read for too long, but I was able to write, enough to stay on schedule with my book publisher and various projects while in the hospital.

The side effects of the chemotherapy drugs began to take their toll. Before I lost all my hair, I ordered a wig from a company whose president I had been acquainted with several years beforehand. Together, we were part of a panel discussion for a television show. Little did I know that my new wig would lead to a fashion statement at an evening Cheer Up Tohoku event that would take place in July. There I was, almost four months after I had started chemotherapy, performing with a group of singers called Women of No Fear, where all the women, in support of my illness, wore wigs like mine, laughing it up with their new-found hairstyles.

Mount Fuji

As I woke from general anesthesia, my throat hurt and I was aware of the numerous tubes connected to my body. I was on oxygen as well, something in mountaineering that one could only afford to use at 7500-plus metres of elevation.

As many as sixty students from Tohoku applied for the first planned trip to Mount Fuji, in addition to thirty local students from Fujiyoshida who also decided to join the fun. The Fujiyoshida Board of Education had expanded the original trip idea to include the phrase "Let's make it a friendship experience." Thus, our venture became larger than expected, and the sudden need for two busloads instead of one had us making last-minute changes with the local transportation company.

Seventy people responded to the request for volunteers with mountaineering experience. Grateful for people's will to contribute, we found jobs that suited everyone, including much-older volunteers who would have had trouble keeping pace with the teenagers in the group.

As in life, Mount Fuji was not the only mountain to climb in this enormous project – there were dozens of tasks to complete without even setting foot on the trail. Still, even with all the help we had, and although I knew arrangements for the hike would be perfectly taken care of by my good friend Tadao Kanzaki, my mind would not rest. I had concerns about the rental equipment and food, and the on-mountain instruction and guidance that would be provided to the students. I wanted the trip to run without a hitch.

Then came the morning of July 6, the day of the Women of No Fear concert. I reserved a hotel room near the Cancer Institute at Ariake Hospital because, the day after, I would be re-admitted to the hospital for surgery. Mine was the combined role of medical patient and event organizer, having packed the items necessary for a hospital stay and a singing performance. A dress, for example, and sweets and fruits to be served to event-goers filled my bags along with the more mundane toothbrush and dressing gown. My husband drove me to the places where I was expected, keeping me punctual.

Musician Muneyuki Sato arrived by bullet train and taxi, while the Kouriyama Women's Chorus had chartered a bus. I asked my son and his wife to greet and care for these stars who would grace the stage. Yoshida was in charge of selling tickets and guiding people to their seats (plus countless other duties that continually arose). My childhood friends from Miharu also showed up, although I had warned them I would have limited time to socialize. Unfazed, they settled into the theatre amongst strangers, and Shinya, not knowing that these were my dearest friends from long ago, approached them for a donation to the Tohoku cause.

Time flew and the curtain was raised.

Part one of the event was called Cheer Up Tohoku Talk One on One, hosted by non-fiction writer Michiko Yoshinaga and myself. Yoshinaga wrote a book titled *Women of No Fear*, which summarized the story of an amateur singing group that was born from a hiking club – MJ-Link – that I initiated in 2009 for professional women. The acronym MJ represents *mori* (forests) and *jyosei* (female), and from its early days, our group of singers evolved, called Women of No Fear. At the start, we were not very good performers, to the point of offering our audience ear plugs and eye masks, and serving snacks to make up for the fact that they had paid to see us. But over the years we improved, and up until 2016, we held concerts twice a year in Tokyo and various other local cities.

Part two was the Evening for Songs concert, which began with the Kouriyama Women's Chorus passionately singing *Memory of Summer*, a popular folk song that described the beauty of a subalpine meadow in Tohoku. Next up was Women of No Fear. On that night, my cohorts and I were adorned by makeup artists who had us looking like professional singers. Eyeliner, fake eyelashes that whooshed like fans with every blink, and the wig – I was transformed into a different person. I caught a glimpse of myself in the mirror, dressed in a vermilion red gown, and I was another form of Junko Tabei, layered in cosmetics and style. Since I was unable to see anyone from where I stood on the stage (I had relinquished my glasses in the name of fashion), I became unafraid of performing. We were introduced one by one with whimsical comments that made the audience laugh. By that point, everyone was at ease. I sang *"Plaisir d'Amour"* by Jean-Paul-Égide Martini and *"Le Marchand de Bonheur"* by Jean Broussolle and Jean-Pierre Calvet. During my second song, all the women from our group joined me on stage and the audience clapped in rhythm to the music. I could feel the connection in the theatre, the beat of the room in synch with the beat of my heart. The success of generating support and awareness for the people of Tohoku was well under way.

Muneyuki Sato sang next, with the audience enraptured by his music. After that, my friend Kanzaki wished the students safe pursuit on their Mount Fuji hike, and the crowd joined together for a rendition of "Fuji the Mountain." The evening was complete and marked a huge triumph when ticket, book and T-shirt sales, plus donations, added up to 850,000 yen (approximately CAD 10,000).

The next morning, I was re-admitted to the Cancer Institute at Ariake Hospital, a direct commute from the hotel. After the doctor explained the details of the surgery scheduled in two days, I asked if I could leave the hospital for one more day. I needed to travel to Matsuyama, a short airline flight away, to deliver another speech. Astounded, but knowing me well enough, the doctor granted me permission.

The trip to Matsuyama was based on a previous conviction of mine from my earlier experience with cancer, that my commitment to mountaineering and travel would still find its way in the midst of medical treatments. Thinking back to September 2007, I was on a climbing trip to Mount Aragats in Armenia and to Georgia. A day I remember as amusing, having watched our guide place specially designed crampons on the hooves of our packhorses for glacier travel, was also the day that marked my introduction to cancer. On that trip, in the shower, I felt an unfamiliar lump between my breasts. When I returned to Japan, the doctors were surprised by how early I was able to detect that tiny lump, which via biopsy proved to be malignant. "Breast cancer?" Masanobu was stunned at the diagnosis, but I lightly brushed it off by stating that removal of the lump was getting rid of the bad stuff.

My reaction was more along the lines of "Oh, cancer has come upon me, too. Darn." I dutifully followed the doctor's post-operative instructions for two days, then returned to life as usual. I attended a magazine interview, bought three dozen *sasa-dango* (rice cakes wrapped in bamboo leaves) as a thank you to the doctors and nurses, and readied myself for a trip to the Baltic countries that was approaching in ten days. What else could the medical staff add to my instructions other than recommendations like "Avoid hitting your chest with tree branches." I think I gave them reason to smile as I left the hospital.

As part of my goal to climb the highest peak in every country, I followed through with my planned trip. Thankfully, Lithuania's Aukštojas

Hill, Latvia's Gaising and Estonia's Suur Munamägi were not too demanding of me, even with stitches in my chest. More so, every time I changed the dressing on the incision, I felt grateful to mountains in general. It was because of climbing that I detected the lump in the slightest of spots. For that reason, I would uphold my commitment to mountaineering and travel no matter what else happened.

On July 9, 2012, at the Cancer Institute at Ariake Hospital, the day before surgery unfolded in textbook fashion: 11 a.m. shower; 11:30 IV attached; ongoing visits by surgeons and chief doctor for added reassurance. I felt cared for and set to proceed. Meanwhile, I could barely keep up with the volume of thank-you letters and emails that poured in after Evening for Cheer Up Tohoku. I had replied to most of them by 10 p.m. that night from my hospital bed with the IV stand by my side and my intestines having been cleansed all day. My stomach felt calmer than before any major summit assault, a good indicator that I was ready for 9 a.m. surgery the next day.

Masanobu arrived, then Noriko, early on July 10. I donned my favourite pashmina shawl from Nepal atop the customary, bland hospital gown and walked to the operating room. I was impressed by the number of rooms lined up, each one ready to, God willing, better a patient's life. As I stepped into the room of expertise, I was welcomed with a smile from the anesthetist, and the warm sheet on the operating table offered slightly more comfort. "*Onegai-shimasu*," I said. "Please, do your best," And within seconds, I was in a deep sleep.

Shortly after noon, I woke from the haze of anesthesia to the sound of the surgeon's voice: "Clean removal. It was almost unnoticeable." My throat was sore, and my body was connected to a myriad of tubes. I was on oxygen as well. Although my son and his wife came to visit, I was too drowsy to communicate. The urinal bag was an annoyance, but I decided to not let it bother me as I had just survived the removal of stage III cancer from my body.

I slept and woke every two hours for the next day and a half. When I tried raise my upper body from the bed, I was lightheaded from lack of sleep, but I felt no pain. The intravenous medication that swam through my blood system to keep discomfort at bay worked well. Feeling encouraged, I attempted to stand up, grabbing the bed frame for support. I was more stable than expected, so I took a few steps. I made it to the hallway, proving to myself that I could slowly walk on a flat surface. Victory!

By July 13 my diet branched out to include slightly more solid food (thicker rice porridge), and I was told I would be dismissed in two weeks' time. The update that intrigued me the most was when the doctor advised that walking was good for me, and that I could go at a pace relative to my conditioning and stamina. I only needed to hear that once, and within a short period I was growing bored of the continuous laps I walked back and forth in the hallway. The freshly sewn, 18-centimetre vertical incision down my abdomen was being put to the test. Meanwhile, the news on TV was warning people of an oncoming extreme heat wave. I felt like I had my own waves of complications to combat: a numbness in my hands and feet was getting noticeably worse.

As I recovered in the hospital, I watched a documentary film about Jamaican Usain Bolt, the fastest sprint runner in the world, as part of a television series called *Miracle Body*. The program focused on Bolt's ability to run fast despite his condition of scoliosis. I was impressed by this demonstration of the wonder and mystery of the human body, and it encouraged me to not cave in to the effects of the anti-cancer medication that I required. I realized then the doctors had prescribed strong medications for me because they agreed that my healthy cells could endure it. I was renewed in my thoughts about the necessary steps for a full recovery. I would tolerate the second round of chemotherapy that was to begin two weeks post-operative, even though I was forewarned that it would be hard on me after surgery. With a stern look from the doctor, I was also told, "Don't dare overdo things." I smiled to myself, thinking "These guys are getting to know me."

As promised, on July 19, hospital paperwork was signed in the morning and I was dismissed from the Ariake cancer centre. On the way home, I noticed my tendency to protect my abdomen by hunching forward and rounding my back. I knew I had to nip that reaction in the bud and concentrate on good posture to have half a hope of being strong and fit again.

The next day, I was back at work with media and my personal life was up and running. I participated in a live TV program entitled *Go to*

Summer Mountains! I could fulfill my role in the studio, and I completed the job without the film crew even knowing I had just been released from hospital.

On July 21, the premiere trip of the Mount Fuji for the High-School Students of Tohoku Earthquake project was under way. I still had to refrain from normal activity, which would have had me climb to the summit with the group. Instead, I was transported lying down in the back of Masanobu's car as he drove me to the event. I also relied on him to prepare my necessary gear for the part of the hike that I could join.

When we arrived at Fujiyoshida Youth Centre in the afternoon, I delved into tasks like sorting out rental equipment and bagging snacks for the trail. There was no shortage of jobs, even for me with having to sit so much. While some of us worked at the centre, students travelled by bus to Mount Fuji Gogome, the trailhead at the end of the road midway up Mount Fuji, to become familiar with the feel of 2305-metres of elevation. They returned exhausted from the excursion. That evening, after a meeting of logistics, staff introductions and double-checking everyone's equipment, bedtime came fast for the next morning's 4 a.m. departure, again by bus to Mount Fuji Gogome.

On the day of the official hike, July 22, transition from bus to foot travel was sluggish. The students looked tired and unfocused and in the need of great encouragement. The wee hours of the morning were too early for them, and the forested mist added a weight to their shoulders. At least the rain held off as I tried my best to offer each of them support: "A single step is 40 to 50 centimetres in length, but by continuing on, one step after another, you will absolutely reach the summit. Go for it!"

Our headquarters was based in the Sato Hut at Gogome. The place was chaotic with radio communication – thirty-five radios had been dispersed amongst the various groups and leaders, and transmissions back and forth had started. Three hours into the hike, more radio calls filtered in: "A student is squatted down, unable to continue – severe headache. Another student is trailing behind, unable to keep up, and yet another has completely given up." The list of defeat continued as the morning passed.

The trip leader, Kanzaki, managed to offer the right words of reassurance: "Let him have a break. Rehydrate him and have him take deep breaths. Find someone who can support him and keep him moving, even at a slower pace and apart from his original group." I completely agreed with his advice and sent as much positive energy as I could to all the climbers, knowing how much mental strength played a role in reaching the summit. "And remember, it's OK for the supporters to come down if they feel unwell," he said. "But try as much as you can to help these students reach the top." Kanzaki's words transmitted loud and clear over the radios, and everyone felt an optimistic shift in the entire group's capability.

At 10:06 a.m., the airwaves hailed with "Group 8, all the students got the summit." Applause filled the headquarters. Then, "Group 5 at the summit!" and "Group 2 as well!" One after the other, each leader relayed their news. By 11:33 a.m., every single student had stood on the top of Mount Fuji.

To add to the excitement of success, there was one participant on the mountain from the Fukushima School for the Blind. He had stated in his application, "As my disability is genetic, my vision range is narrow, and there is no question that some day I will become totally blind. I want to go up Mount Fuji, the highest peak in Japan, while I can still see things." My heart doubled in size when I knew the summit had been reached by all.

By 2 p.m. I was standing at the Gogome gate, welcoming students back from their ascent. High-fives were pronounced with their cries of joy: "I've done it!" "I did, too!" "I want to go up again someday." Their hair was soaked from the day's mist and inevitable rain, and drops of water streamed like gentle cascades down their young faces. Despite haggard appearances and obvious fatigue, the eyes and smiles of the hikers radiated excitement, and their spirits were clearly lifted. This marked a noticeable difference in character from before Mount Fuji. Trip leaders and assistants sifted in with the students, all of them having safely descended the mountain. Indeed, the first trial of Mount Fuji for the High-School Students of Tohoku Earthquake was a complete success.

Thank-you letters arrived within several days of the climb, and the written affirmations by students reconfirmed for me that the Mount Fuji event was a good idea.

Although I thought about giving up many times past 3400 metres, the staff people encouraged me every time when I felt weak, because of which I was barely able to stand at the top of Mount Fuji. It was great that I didn't give up. I have learned afresh the potency of humans; we're the creatures who can do almost anything if we strive to.

▲

It was like, "Ah, my headache is too bad to continue on. No way. I want to go down," that's how occupied I was by such a negative feeling. What helped me to keep going? The others. Everybody was trying his or her best. I didn't want to be the guy who only made it halfway, and I would have been if I had quit at that point. The word "appreciation" was circling around in my brain when I reached the summit. It was the first time in my life that I said thank you so spontaneously and with such good feeling. My wall, a blockage in my mind, collapsed. The idea of impossibility is actually one's own creation. Possibilities expand depending on one's own thoughts, so I realized.

▲

By going up to the top of Fuji, I gained some confidence in my daily life, too. I would like to go there again.

▲

One step followed by another surely makes it to the summit. Such a simple but precious lesson I learned. As well, don't give up, try your best.

▲

Mount Fuji, the previously thought absolute impossible for me, became possible, and I feel grateful for it from the bottom of my heart. Imagining how much energy was required by staff and how hard it was to get funding for this project, in addition to my own effort to succeed, I will never ever forget this mountain.

The trip home from that event was one of great satisfaction. Having been the recipient of other people's help many times in the long run of my life,

I was happy to be able to help these students, especially in light of my surgery. With cheerful goodbyes, we left. Masanobu and I drove to Hakone with the intention of a soak in the *onsen* and a visit to the Hakone Shrine, but the climber in me was awakened. The weather was picture perfect the next day and a hike up Kintoki-yama was in order. My legs felt heavy, but I knew I could reach the top at a slow pace. And there I was, two weeks after my operation and three days prior to the start of chemotherapy, on the summit.

Life Continues

Chemotherapy would be much easier if it came with no side effects. On the other hand, the symptoms it caused me to feel proved that I was alive, that I stood a chance to be cancer-free. In the midst of managing the side effects, I remained positive and looked forward to whatever opportunities were next.

Between weekly chemotherapy appointments, I walked mountain trails as often as possible. Those outings were my saviour during ten weeks of treatment. Rather than lie in bed, I continued to tick off my list of hikes: Kiso-Komagatake, Oze, Kurikoma-yama, Issaikyou-yama and Higashi Azuma-yama, only to name a few.

Admittedly, weighted legs and fatigued knees began to wear on me, and eventually even descent trails became exhausting. Four weeks into chemotherapy, my toenails turned purple and the numbness in my hands and feet became severe. Swelling and dizziness and an ulcer in my mouth began to develop. Worst of all, my balance became questionable as I struggled to put on pants or shoes while standing up. My gait was off, and I felt clumsy when I walked. Approaching the podium on a stage to deliver a speech became a nerve-wracking experience. I felt like a robot.

Test results told the real story. My white blood cell count was down, as was my immunity, and overall numbers did not reach the safe standard to continue with chemotherapy. "No IV today," reported the doctor at my six-week appointment. "Let's look for improvement in a week. Try to not eat raw food, and for now, please, scale down your hiking."

Still, I strived to live my normal life. My husband managed all the domestic work, like cooking and cleaning and laundry, while I became a master at verbal command. More than ever, I cherished the humour and fun we shared together.

My commitments to speeches never let up. From October 1 to 7 that year, I was a guest passenger on a ship run by Peace Boat, a global non-government organization whose headquarters are in Japan and promotes international awareness amongst groups that strive for peace, human rights, environmental protection and sustainable development, all things I believe in. I delivered three speeches on board as we sailed to Barcelona via London, and on to Morocco. This was my first overseas trip since my cancer diagnosis six months earlier, and I happily embraced the excursion to the fullest. Certainly, I would not have made it there without Masanobu by my side, assisting me up and down stairways and carrying anything I needed to have with me.

By the tenth treatment, the side effects took command of my body. I could no longer open jar lids or tear the seal on a snack bag, or put on earrings by myself, or pick up small pieces of food with chopsticks. It was difficult to pull bills from my wallet or unlock the door with a key. Even the most personal of tasks became impossible. I could hardly tell if I had pulled my underwear down far enough to use the toilet – I was like a floundering fish out of water, checking to see if I had succeeded.

Finally, on November 1, 2012, I finished my last chemotherapy treatment. From that day on, I felt free from sneaking out between appointments to hike. To celebrate, I decided I would climb the highest mountain in Bangladesh, Saka Haphong, which had been on my worldwide list for a long time. I planned my trip for the coming New Year holidays. To further my celebration, on December 6, the doctor announced that I was in remission. *Banzai!*

Unexpectedly though, the side effects lingered, putting a dent in my travel plans. I knew it would be too late to build up muscle strength if I waited for the side effects to disappear altogether, so I persevered with trip preparation. My mantra – "When would I work hard if not now?" – kept me focused and allowed me to develop some semblance of muscle strength. Although my physical body remained tired, my mental state was invigorated by having a goal, and so I stuck with it.

The Himalayan Adventure Trust of Japan had planned to be in Nepal in April and May 2013 to transfer the management of an apple orchard alongside the Everest trail from the trust organization to the local people. I wanted to join the project, plus climb Gokyo Peak afterwards to see if my body could endure a 5000er. I was ready to quit climbing if it had come to that, but I wanted to try one more time, and I dearly wanted to walk on glaciers again and see Mount Everest. It had been a long while.

At a later date, I planned to travel to South Korea and trek with members from MJ-Link. If necessary, I was prepared to wait at the trailhead and cheer people on if I was unable to hike with them. Quite simply, my overall goal was to remain motivated by trying as many different trips as possible, for years to come – that was me looking ever forward.

My son, Shinya, was the person who I think changed the most from my illness. Throughout his childhood, he had felt pressured to be a good boy as the child of Junko Tabei. His resistance to that pressure, and to Masanobu and me, continued into his thirties. But when I became ill, Shinya changed into a different person. "Sorry if I've annoyed you and had you worried for me," he wrote in an email upon my recovery. This was a huge step for a young man whose defiance towards his parents had become second nature. I was profoundly pleased by his words and felt that he finally understood all that parents hope for their child.

By October 2013 a year had passed since my final cancer treatment, and I was the tour leader on a commercial trip to Western Australia for wildflower enthusiasts. Shinya was my travel partner. He helped me in every way since I still struggled with a few remaining side effects from chemotherapy. His gentlemanly way extended to the rest of the group, mainly seniors, whom he had laughing in no time as he cheered them on during the trip. Watching him, I thought, "Things might have turned out better because of my illness."

The love of my family was easily expressed by my daughter, Noriko. When I was in the hospital, she came by my room every evening on her way home from work, just to massage my swollen feet. If ever I asked her to bring a specific shawl to me, she would deliver it that very day. I feel grateful for having such a person in my life. And my husband, Masanobu – such a diligent house-husband, who quickly transformed me into a princess as a result, one who may have been a bit too demanding. My "Do this and do that, please" was kindly met by his "Could you ask for things one at a time?" As a result of his good nature, I felt no stress in my daily life as I dealt with cancer, and for that I am thankful.

In remission, I went out almost every day, either for a work commitment or to practice singing with Women for No Fear. Back home, I would soak in a tub readied by Masanobu and bask in what I call happiness. I enjoyed the dinners he prepared, with a small glass of plum wine on the side, and then the foot massages he administered as he said, "Relax now." Whenever we were together, I put writing commitments to rest in order to purely enjoy his company. The icing on the cake was slipping into a futon Masanobu had warmed by a *yutanpo*, a hot water bottle, for a good night's sleep. My husband had perfected caring for me.

There is no doubt that Masanobu and I have spent more time together since my illness than in the decades of our marriage prior. We talk, we hike, we travel. Masanobu has joined me on almost every trip, whether in Japan or overseas, since 2012. To me, the added contentment I have discovered with my family and in life since my cancer diagnosis is the gift – the positive aspect – of this experience.

On a return trip to Nepal in September 2015, to celebrate forty years after I had reached the summit of Mount Everest, I stood on a hilltop at 3900 metres, with my friends and family around me, looking towards the giant peak. I said, "How could I have climbed *that* mountain? Young and bold I was...."

The End

About Junko

It was indeed shocking to see my wife take her last breath right in front of me; however, we felt more like "The time has come," as it had been four and half years since her cancer was found. In other words, we calmly accepted her death rather than fall into unstoppable lamenting, just to describe our reality.

When she was diagnosed with stage III peritoneal cancer, we discussed and decided to enjoy our life to the fullest without restraining much of what Junko wanted to do, either workwise or as a pastime, while simultaneously accessing the best medical treatments available to her. There had been a period of remission thanks to chemotherapy, so she was able to enjoy her daily life without serious problems. She took commuting trains herself and went abroad to climb mountains in more than twenty countries even after the cancer was diagnosed. But gradually, the side effects of chemotherapy made her limbs numb, and she regretted not being able to climb 5000 and 6000ers anymore.

In October 2014 cancer metastasis was detected, this time as a brain tumour. Junko continued with her normal life, mountaineering, hiking, delivering speeches and being interviewed for magazines and TV programs, without exposing the return of her cancer to anybody. Only five of us – myself, Noriko and Shinya, Junko's long-time secretary Minako Yoshida, and Setsuko Kitamura, who went to Everest – knew this secret. Junko asked us to zip our lips tight about this fact. She never liked to make people worry about her, and she continued to chat with them, like "I have plans to go to so and so mountains," always looking forward, business as usual.

Her inner strength and care for others had not changed at all since we met in our twenties. It was on the top of a mountain when we spoke to each other for the first time. Sometime around 1965, she happened to have followed the same route after I finished the South Ridge of Ichino-kura-sawa. I had brought a can of cooked sweet azuki, and I made instant azuki-sorbet with ice collected from a nearby snow patch and offered her some. I could tell by her face that she thought it was yummy. Having read Junko's book in later years, I found that she was actually impressed, saying, "I was surprised that he carried that heavy food in his backpack." *That* surprised me since it was simply my normal way to take something tasty as a part of mountaineering pleasure. I did not mean to woo her through this particular action.

To be precise, I had known her before we met. Female climbers are a regular part of the scene today; however, it was an outstanding feature to see women climbing rock at that time. In particular, the cutting-edge ones were extremely few. Imagine an era when many mountaineering clubs openly advertised "No women allowed." So, I had been aware of Junko, naturally watching her, like, "Yeah, she's out there, climbing hard again."

Being in my early twenties, I was yet to be interested in women as I was totally into climbing – nothing else distracted me, neither cars nor cool-looking clothes. Junko was just like that, too, she said to me later, to the degree that she considered people who did not go to the mountains as not human; she also chose not to vote at elections just to save the time for climbing. Thus, in retrospect, we, the like-minded, met.

Still, we did not shorten the distance in our relationship with the snap of a finger. Instead, time fermented our closeness, along with the range of our conversations that varied from climbing to more diverse subjects like families and life; in a couple of years we had no need to confess our feelings or propose. We knew that both of us were thinking "Life together with her/ him would be as good as being natural."

We thought of our marriage as positive and beneficial, not simply a legal obligation. Many of my married buddies whined about their marriages as failures, with comments such as, "I can't go climbing as much as before," or "I used to go to *yakitori*-bar three times a week, now reduced to one," or "I can't ride my motorcycle anymore." Those stories disappointed me because I had the idea that marriage should be a new way of life in which the two help each other achieve something a bachelor life could not offer.

When I was sixteen years old, I had spinal caries that pushed me to the edge of life or death. Tuberculosis patients were abundant then, and a patient in the next bed could suddenly die. That was not a rare case. I was horrified at this phenomenon, and I felt powerless and desolate. At the end of the day, however, it occurred to me that I should survive and live with some established goals in my life.

Junko was also a person who became so into climbing that she must have had the spirit for challenge. As a matter of course, I had never dreamt of her being a housewife, not even for a second. We had a two-year-old daughter, Noriko, when Junko went to Everest. And it was me who requested, "Have a child first, then go to Everest."

Mountaineering inherently comes with risks, so the person who climbs and the ones who send them off both need to understand and be steadfast about whatever could happen. And people who have family they care for and protect become cautious about taking risks. I, too, used to take chances, hopping past the crux on a rock-climbing route with one heck of a daring move, as it would have been me alone to suffer the result of a fall. But once I had family, this attitude was excluded from my options.

By then, Junko had been successfully pushing more difficult routes with male climbers on Tanigawa-dake and in the Northern Alps of Japan. It was not hard for me to believe in the possibility of her climbing Everest based on her skill and judgment, but I still wanted her to stay conservative on top of her high-quality ability.

I was often questioned if I, too, wished to go to Everest, as I was also a climber, but that was not the case. By then, a man on Everest was not that unusual, so I thought that for Junko to challenge being the first female to climb Everest was far more interesting than me going, especially in terms of spending the family's limited money.

When she returned home after the success, she was treated like a rock star overnight. Her face was frequently in the media, and she was running around all over Japan with the sirdar Ang Tsering for speeches and other invitations; she did not come back to our house for more than a month after landing on Japanese soil. I still recall my puzzled feeling that society was making such a big deal about her having just climbed a mountain, albeit the big one, so much so that people would whisper, "Oh, Tabei-*san* is out there," or "Wow, she bought eggs."

At that time, Junko often said, "We shouldn't get stuck up. Don't let our feet be carried away by the fame and flattering words. Keep standing solid on the ground – it's the same as in mountaineering." But the reality of life was not that simple. Journalists swarmed our home, and Noriko came to hate people who carried cameras. Our son, Shinya, who was born after Everest, also tried to avoid the label "Junko Tabei's son." In his rebellious years, one day he came home and announced that he had quit high school.

I, however, never minded being seen as Junko Tabei's husband. Interestingly, people might have thought that it was out of my control to do anything I would like to do; they often sympathized with me, like, "You have a hard life taking care of home and family while she is away, don't you?" Thanks, but no, those were totally unnecessary worries.

Probably due to my work for Honda, I took interest in motocross in my private life, and attended competitions a couple of times a year. I even went as far as Mexico to join a car rally race, and I also enjoyed piloting a dinghy yacht, and so on. In other words, I played hard in the mountains and at sea as well. As Junko's expeditions usually lasted a couple of months, one summer I took advantage of the time and travelled with Shinya to the United States to ride a motorcycle across America, with him in the sidecar.

It was most likely that my wife felt she could go to the mountains without conflict since I was doing my own things, too. Usually the wives who leave their husbands behind for their hobbies worry about things like, "Is he cooking all right and eating well every day?" or "What if he just stays lazy at home doing nothing?" We had no such concern. When Junko announced her goal to climb a 7000er, I would send her off cheerfully, "Go ahead and enjoy!" and then set myself up for the States to ride my motorcycle.

When I suggested that Junko cut down on some of her work after her cancer relapse, she resisted. "What are you talking about? Are you trying to take my pleasure away?" Despite her determined spirit, she started to show fatigue at home as time passed by. It became more frequent that no sooner had she said hello when she arrived home than she lay down on the couch to rest. She confessed her fear of being hurt by bumping into people when she walked through a crowd, so I began to drive her to wherever necessary, making the back seat more restful as discomfort increased with water-retention in her chest.

In July 2016, when the pain of her side effects from chemotherapy began to outdo the cure, we decided to stop the therapy after discussion with the doctor. It was the time to make a choice.

Junko was admitted to hospital on July 25, with the event Mount Fuji for the High School Students of Tohoku Earthquake scheduled for the next day. After having 800 millilitres of fluid withdrawn from her chest in the hospital the next day, we headed to the Fujinomiya trailhead.

It was in this state that Junko spoke to the teenaged students: "You will certainly get to the summit if you keep going up one step at a time. *Ganbaro!* (Let's have a good fight!)" And there she went, Junko resuming her hike, though at a slow pace. Regrettably, her condition was far worse than she expected, so the 3010-metre mark was the highest she could reach, and that was her last mountain. Not being able to move around as she had hoped, and having worried the people around her, she appeared quite shocked. Nevertheless, she still concerned herself incessantly with the future summers of this event in order to fulfill the original goal of getting one thousand students to stand on the summit of Mount Fuji.

That was when Shinya, who is in the outdoor activities business, encouragingly said to her, "Rely on me!" Although I have never heard my wife make demands for certain things on our children, this project was an exception. She openly verbalized, "I want this project continued." I jumped in to tell Shinya not to take his mother's words too seriously, as in "inherit the legacy," but rather to think more lightly. My wish is for him to simply continue after his mom, in hopes that he finds his own meaning or enjoyment in the project.

At about that time, Junko was mad at me for trying to reassure her any longer with the phrase "*Ganbaro.*" She was beyond the point of fighting her cancer. "Why do I have to do more while I have been doing my best?!" she said. Those were her honest feelings, and from then on, our tone of conversation changed to "Let's enjoy...." So, we increased the feeling of enjoyment in our life and let the fight subside.

On October 4 Junko moved to a hospice in Kawagoe after she did a radio talk show interview on the way there. "Eat well. Be kind to each other, family is better off that way," and so on, she kept advising us even from the hospice bed. Nearing her last week of life, her vocal system was impaired and she could not speak well anymore. Six days before passing, she wrote a letter to me, "*Otousan* ("Daddy," a Japanese way of calling one's husband, especially after having had children), *forgive me if I wasn't able to speak anymore as I'm getting weaker. Don't be upset, sorry. Although I also wish to talk to you kindly, I cannot do that anymore. Your gentle face makes me happy.*" She used to say like a mantra, "Illness doesn't necessarily make me a sick person." This was not the case anymore in my eyes; at this stage, she looked very sick.

Two days before her death, Junko took a piece of paper and scribbled, "I am not a sick person" in letters almost too difficult to read. Half jokingly, I replied, "Not a delusion?" against which she talked back, "NO!" And she drew something like a picture of a mountain in the upper space of the paper. I asked, "Everest, is it?" and she nodded. She must have badly craved to jump out of the bed and run up the mountains she loved.

A few days before drawing the mountain, about five days before she died, Junko also wrote something like this, even with her signature: "*Everyone, thank you so much! Thank you! Thank you a million times! Junko Tabei, 2016-10-15.*"

While these words may also include her family, I believe she meant to straightforwardly express her gratitude to all the people who supported her to live a full life as a mountaineer, who enjoyed and embraced the mountains to the best of her ability.

A Son's Tribute

by Shinya Tabei

October 20, 2016, 10 a.m. – my mother stopped walking. She had climbed mountains and hiked around countless places of the world until that moment. Although we knew for certain "the day" would come, as she had been fighting cancer, we were not ready to say goodbye. In the end, her condition worsened and she could no longer even sit up on the bed. So, we, my father, sister and I, took turns caring for her around the clock.

I had a very precious time in the last days of her life.

Since I was born to "Junko Tabei" as the baby of the family, there was little time to share affection; in fact, I likely bothered my mother more often than not. However, in her final days, I was able to show her that I cared, and I did so to the best of my ability. I helped her brush her teeth; I rubbed her skin with a warm cloth – these things made me extremely happy. In a way, I had her all to myself.

A few days before my mother passed away, she and I, alone in a private room of the hospital, spoke about the many things I could not say before, everything I had wanted to tell her for so long.

Among them were the words, "I love you so much, Mom," to which she replied, "Very much the same from me. I love you way more than I like the mountains."

That was my last meaningful chat with her.

How badly I had upset her in the past, and worried her about my behaviour. I am really grateful for our final conversations, to have reached beyond the earlier years.

About a week before my mother died, I was by her side, using the hospital room as my office. I thought she was asleep, then all of a sudden she raised both her arms and bellowed, *"Banzai! Banzai! Banzai!"* She must have been dreaming. "All right, everybody," she continued, "gather here, please, and let's eat *onigiri* (rice ball)." Her conversation continued, as though with her friends, "No way we'll split the group into different routes. We'll absolutely go together." She was hiking even in her dreams. That was my mother, a person who truly loved mountains.

In July 2016, she climbed as high as 3010 metres on Mount Fuji for the event called Mount Fuji for the High School Students of Tohoku Earthquake. She wholeheartedly encouraged the students as she sent them off for the summit. That was her last outing in her long career as a mountaineer.

"Mountaineering is not a competition. For your mom who has no athletic talent, the first mountain I went on was great fun, and inspiring, too," my mother said.

On October 19, I had a work commitment that could not be cancelled, so I left for Fukushima. I dropped by to her ward first thing in the morning and I said to her, "I'm going to Fukushima just for a night." She squeezed my hand so hard and nodded as she was not able to speak by that point.

After my work, I stopped briefly at our Numajiri Lodge in Fukushima then left there early the next morning. I arrived at the hospital at 9:40 a.m. My mother passed away twenty minutes later. She had been waiting for me to send her off.

I am very grateful to have been there when she left for her final trip. Though her physical presence is not on this earth anymore, my mother is still, and will always be, alive within me.

She asked me to do three things, so I will pursue them as I promised her I would.

1. Let as many people as possible know the wonder of Mother Nature.
2. Continue the program Mount Fuji for the High School Students of Tohoku Earthquake until it surpasses the original goal of one thousand participants.
3. Protect and take care of my father and sister.

I also wish for people to know about the full life of Junko Tabei and that she was part of the early group of women who challenged the high peaks of the Himalayas many decades ago.

Thank you for the countless heartwarming emails and messages we have received regarding my mother's passing. Please continue connecting with us the same as before.

Lastly, thank you, Mom.

October 23, 2016

Snow falling more and more.
Sky getting darker and darker.

    Let's pitch a small tent
        And have a hot meal
    Let's sing a favorite song.
        And have a good sleep

Tomorrow morning
        We shall be on the sunny summit!

Do you know.
The joy of a woman
To climb with
        women.

Why don't you
        join us!

Beyond Mountains

by Setsuko Kitamura

At the end of 2016, during this book's making, we had a memorial to say goodbye to Junko Tabei at the Showa Women's University Hall in Tokyo, where she had graduated fifty-five years earlier. Tabei passed away on the morning of October 20, 2016, after four and half years of fighting with cancer. She was seventy-seven. The memorial ceremony was arranged by friends, and a total of 1,400 people showed up to offer flowers. This shows just how popular Tabei was, right to the end of her life.

As an add-on to the Introduction in this book, I wish to highlight Tabei's activities after 2000, which were even more remarkable than before then. She turned from energetic climber to social activist and began to disclose more of her family-woman profile than she did when she was younger. From midsummer (the peak of her climbing career), to cool autumn (when she transitioned to being a mentor), to the too-early winter (her final stages), Tabei's life was immensely fulfilling. It is the later part, in particular, I focus on here.

When I met Tabei in 1973, in preparation for Everest, I was quickly drawn to her, the petite woman who spoke clearly to the end of each sentence with a cheerful voice, the woman who was the assistant leader and climbing leader for the expedition team. Since that time, I was not only accepted as a team member but personally shared decades of fun mountain trips with Tabei. Meanwhile, I unwittingly played a role, as a journalist, in observing her growth as a person and in her relationship with Japanese society.

Illustration by Setsuko Kitamura
COURTESY OF SETSUKO KITAMURA

"Well, I have to look for a part-time job as I've spent all my money...," Tabei said on our trek home from Everest.

Astonished, I raised my voice, "What the heck are you talking about? You'll be rounded up by media gangs for a while, no time for work or such a thing, I warn you." Tabei's idea of her mountaineering being "just a housewife's hobby" was so fixed in her mind that she never expected her achievement as the first woman to climb Mount Everest to be worthy of such praise.

The year she came to be truly aware of her social responsibility, I think, was 1979. There were only three women summitters on Everest at that time, and the famous French climber Maurice Herzog invited the three women to Chamonix. "Why Everest?" he asked them as part of a documentary film he was making on "Everest for Women."

I was there with them, and having listened to their remarks, I strongly felt the different social reasons for climbing Everest, one singular mountain. And I assume Tabei must have felt the same; her acceptance of media exposure became greater after this event, and it was obvious that she made up her mind to do her job for society. Meanwhile, she completed pursuit of the Seven Summits in 1992, the first female to do so, and again she became a popular figure, even amongst the non-mountaineers in Japan.

In her fifties, Tabei started to work as a commercial tour leader on high (but not so technical) mountains, like Aconcagua. And her personal destinations seemed to veer towards more unfamiliar places than just hard climbing on high mountains.

At this point, she was also frequently presented on television programs, not only as a mountaineer but as a mother of two. Although her son's teenaged rebelliousness was at its peak, Tabei never tried to cover up that fact, and commented, "A woman cannot keep her son in her pocket, right?" People loved her straightforwardness.

In the summer of 2008, NHK, Japan's national public broadcasting organization, launched a program that featured a young male newscaster hiking the country's most popular, but not the most hard-core, alpine traverse, guided by Tabei. It is along a ridge from Tateyama to Hodaka, a 60-kilometre route in Japan's Northern Alps that varies in elevation between 2500 and 3000 metres. The trip took three weeks (usually an eight-day hike) since it was filmed by the camera crew. The audience saw the beautiful mountains and the tough routes they went on, and more so, the much older Tabei (sixty-eight then) cheering up and reassuring her young male partner as he completed the ridge.

This show was a major hit that made Tabei a much beloved person, even more than before, as her fans started to favour her because of her kind personality, not just admiring her for being the first woman on Everest.

Besides TV appearances, Tabei started to write more of her stories, a skill she was naturally good at. Notes for daily personal occasions, or postcards with place information that she discovered, or a thank-you letter written in her powerful handwriting were found often in my mailbox. Many of her mountain friends benefitted from her documentation-buff trait – comments like, "Brittle rock, here (with arrow mark)," and "Right side of this is precipitous," showed up on maps and such. So, the publication of her writing almost made the sound of the friction of rope running through gloves, and the eye-stinging light that reflected from fresh snow, seem very real.

However, her writings never had tones of bragging about hardships or showing off, but were consistent throughout with "Yes, you can!" Thus, her "can-do" bottom line became accepted by a broad range of ordinary people outside the mountain community.

Furthering Tabei's contribution to society, she and I established two hiking clubs for working women. The first one, just before the year 2000, was for older women past the child-rearing stage. When that club dissolved, we started another one in 2009 called MJ-Link, aimed at young female professionals. Its focus was to convey how we, the older generation of women mountaineers, got over the hurdles (being women, raising children and working outside home). By then, Tabei knew that she had "to contribute to women's mountaineering history of Japan." Her awareness and transformation from being an active climber to a leader-mentor, in particular for women, was complete.

For Tabei, a significant turning point occurred with the disastrous Tohoku Earthquake on March 11, 2011. Tabei's birthplace, Fukushima, suffered incredible, triple-fold devastation: the earthquake, the tsunami and the nuclear plant accident.

She must have thought through the aftermath with great detail to eventually suggest the unique project titled Mount Fuji for the High-School Students of Tohoku Earthquake. The objective was to stir up youthful energy while everything else lay in ruins.

To be honest, Fuji is not considered difficult to climb, except in winter; it is a long, monotonous hike mostly on a scree slope with no vegetation around. But it requires toughness to achieve, and it has been a sacred symbol for Japanese for millennia due to its plain, beautiful figure. Tabei must have seen the spirit in this, Japan's number one symbol, for the youth to overcome difficulties in the earthquake-affected areas.

Another turning point arose, ironically on the same day (March 11) the following year, in 2012 – late-stage cancer for Tabei. We were waiting for her at her family ski lodge, and she did not show up, having been admitted to hospital on the spot upon diagnosis.

Having socially been represented as the "energetic auntie" that she was, Tabei's cancer was kept from the public. A small group of close friends were informed of her illness, with her wish, "Don't make a fuss over this. I'll be treated and come back." I suppose her willpower and well-trained physical shape worked like a near miracle during her recovery, even though the prognosis was dire. As she predicted, she returned to her active social life in less than half a year, at which point she declared publicly for the first time, "I am not going to be beaten by cancer," and continued to make Mount Fuji for the High-School Students of Tohoku Earthquake happen. She even had a concrete plan: "Let a total of 1,000 students climb Fuji. This will take 100 students a year times 10 years," and she started running around to raise 6,000,000 yen per year for this project.

Tabei was determined not to end up as just a "sitting" organizer. She continued hiking with the students year after year while she battled with cancer in her mid-seventies. One might have seen her on TV, encouraging beginner teenaged hikers, "Here you go, keep going up one step at a time and you'll be at the summit," and "Hey, we rely on you guys for the Tohoku recovery! Are you ready!?" Her cheerful and powerful signature voice, her "can-do" attitude was seen and heard across Japan through multiple media sources.

Regrettably, from around the time of summer 2016, the therapeutic effects began to fade and the side effects of cancer treatment became dominant. Without complaint, Tabei had led the trips and delivered the speeches lined up on her schedule, one after the other. "Whining doesn't make things better at all, as I'm receiving the best treatment. What else I can do?" she said. Her attitude reminded me of how she dealt with numerous difficulties in mountaineering. "Don't lose your nerve; whining won't help," was her consistent style of thinking whatever the situation, be it avalanche hazard, impossible ferrying of loads or traversing chancy gullies.

On September 22, 2016, Tabei invited 140 friends to celebrate her seventy-seventh birthday party, a noted event in Japanese culture. She could barely stand straight. Concealing the seriousness of her condition, she dared to sing songs and even cracked a few jokes with me. Her signature smile and cheerful voice was heard throughout the event; however, many of us, noticing her leaner-than-normal figure, realized that this was it. It was a bright-spirited but sad party as people silently felt the seriousness behind the scene. Tabei was admitted to the hospital immediately after the party and never came home. Even then she kept private her reality except around her family and the closest few. "Don't bother busy active people when it's time to leave," was her bottom line.

She must have also wanted to spend profound time with her immediate family after decades peppered with her absence. Her husband, Masanobu, had done an awesome job supporting her by being with her around the clock after her cancer was diagnosed.

Her late mother used to wish Junko, then a rare female university graduate from a well-educated family, to marry somebody with a similar background and degree. Junko's decision to marry Masanobu, a high-school graduate, nevertheless proved right for her.

"It's much better and way more interesting that she climbs bigger ones than I, a man, would try. And she has the ability to do so," Masanobu reasoned. Thus, he continued sending her on countless expeditions, including Everest, despite him being a top-notch climber. He also completed a solid work life as an engineer for an automobile corporation without being caught in the common trap of the expedition-*ronin* (a permanent part-timer who hops around to different jobs without a firm boss), which many keen climbers fall into. I cannot forget the impression that *she* was the one who relied on him spiritually rather than vice versa. "It feels so good to have a place to come back to. 'Let's go home safely where I can relax' is always my base motivation," she once uttered in front of me.

After the cancer, she began to more openly rely on her husband, if not to cling to him. Their relationship was more like close peers or comrades, calling each other *ojisan* (uncle, old man) and *obasan* (auntie, old woman), which felt good to witness. I suppose other people around them must have been surprised by, while admiring, the rare scene of a Japanese couple in which the husband helped his wife with daily chores and movements, becoming her limbs when she could no longer rely on her own. Tabei was unwittingly letting us learn that there *are* men like him *and* it is possible to have a relationship like theirs.

Whenever I see hikers and mountaineers, irrespective of age and gender, wrapped in bright-coloured outfits here and there in Japan, I cannot help taking it as the new scenery made possible by Junko Tabei, as that sight was not present or even thought of prior to her Everest. By demonstrating what we, the women, can do, and then we, the middle-senior aged, can do as Tabei did when she reached that age group, she continued opening the door to nature for all.

Self-satisfaction was her original motivation for climbing mountains, which turned to a social aspect after she gained fame and became aware of her responsibility. She exemplified her life philosophies of "can do" by always practicing them herself. She also presented us with another legacy of courage, about how a person can leave this world when the time comes.

Junko Tabei, my master of mountaineering and genuine friend, was a people's person who could initiate chatting, even with villagers in remote countries, in her bright voice and in Japanese, "Hey, Mom, how's your hubby?" or "Oh, Daddy, taking care of your woman well?" Then smiles and laughs happened without reason, as she reached out to shake hands with them.

She also had the irresistible habit of making sure her friends ate good food by carrying heavy fruits and snacks in her already heavy backpack, and serving them with exquisite timing. No wonder her fixed spot at camp was always in front of the cook stove.

"I would like to die saying it's been a good life; I had so much fun," she often said. Let me ask her now, "Was it so?" Yes, that rich life of hers must have been wonderful. I believe this as I bid farewell to my dearest friend, Junko Tabei.

LIFE CHRONOLOGY

Year	Mountains and Special Events	Elevation	Country	Note
1939	Born September 22 (the youngest of seven siblings), in Miharu-cho, Fukushima, Japan			
1949	First mountain Tabei ever climbed, Nasu-dake (1915 m), led by school teacher			
1962	Graduated university; started winter mountaineering			
1967	Married to Masanobu Tabei; female climbing partner Rumie Sasou killed on Tanigawa-dake			
1968	Masanobu Tabei climbed the North Faces of Matterhorn and Grandes Jorasses			
1969	Established the Ladies Climbing Club (LCC) with the goal "to climb overseas by women alone"			
1970	Annapurna III	7555 m	Nepal	First woman to climb. First Japanese to climb.
1970	*Mount Damavand	5610 m	Iran	
1972	Daughter, Noriko, born in February			
1975	*Mount Everest*	8848 m	Nepal	Highest in the world. First woman to climb.
1977	Yala Peak	5732 m	Nepal	

1978	Son, Shinya, born in August			
1979	*Mont Blanc	4807 m	France	
1981	*Mont Kilimanjaro	5895 m	Tanzania	Highest in Africa.
1981	Shishapangma	8027 m	China	First woman to climb. First Japanese to climb. LCC team leader
1983	Sepchu Kang	5200 m	Bhutan	First foreigner to climb.
1983	Mount Hanuman Tibba	5984 m	India	
1985	*Mount Communism	7495 m	Tajikistan	Now called Ismoil Somoni Peak.
	Korzhenevskaya Peak	710 5m	Tajikistan	Now called Ibn Sina Peak.
	Lenin Peak	7134 m	Tajikistan	First women's expedition to climb three 7000-m peaks in one season.
1986	*Mount Kinabalu	4095 m	Malaysia	Climbed up to 6200 m.
	Tomur (Jengish Chokusu)	7439 m	China	Also called Pobeda Peak, Victory Peak.
1987	*Aconcagua	6960 m	Argentina	Highest in South America.
	Tuqllarahu/Tocllaraju	6032 m	Peru	
	Pisco	5752 m	Peru	

	Urus	5495 m	Peru	Also called Yanarahu.
	Ishinca	5530 m	Peru	
	Popocatépetl	5452 m	Mexico	
	Iztaccihuatl	5230 m	Mexico	
1988	Yushan	3952 m	Taiwan	Highest in Taiwan.
	Denali (Mount McKinley)	6194 m	USA	Highest in North America.
	Mount Shiva	6142 m	India	
	*Mount Wilhelm	4509 m	Papua New Guinea	
1989	*Chimborazo	6268 m	Ecuador	
	Mera Peak	6476 m	Nepal	
	Tuagn Degli	4200 m	Mongolia	
	Mount Elbrus (East Summit)	5621 m	Russia	
1990	*Mount Cook	3724 m	New Zealand	
	Cosmic	4000 m	France	
	Matterhorn	4478 m	Switzerland	
	Breithorn	4164 m	Switzerland	
	*Monte Roza	4634 m	Switzerland	
	Dent Blanche	4357 m	Switzerland	

	Mount Rindjani	3726 m	Indonesia (Lombok)	
	Mount Agung	3142 m	Indonesia (Bali)	

Himalayan Adventure Trust of Japan (HAT-J) established, Tabei was chairperson from 1990 to 2014

1991	*Vinson Massif	4892 m	Antarctica	Highest in Antarctica.
	*Toubkal	4167 m	Morocco	
	*Mount Kosciusko	2228 m	Australia	With family.
	Erciyes-Dagi	3916 m	Turkey	In addition to three other peaks in Turkey.

The International Symposium on Conservation of Mountain Environments, Tokyo (HAT-J operation), with Sir Edmund Hillary and Reinhold Messner

1992	*Carstensz Pyramid	4884 m	Indonesia	Highest in Oceania.
	*Mount Elbrus (West Summit)	5642 m	Russia	Highest in Europe; the first woman to complete the Seven Summits.

1993	Volcán Tajumulco	4220 m	Guatemala	
	Volcán Tacaná	4060 m	Guatemala	
	Semeru	3676m	Indonesia	
	Hang Tengri	7010m	Kazakhstan	Climbed to 6950 m.

1994	*Fansipanan	3143 m	Vietnam	
	*Ras Dashen	4550m	Ethiopia	

Bayan Kol	5791 m	Kazakhstan	
*Hang Tengri	7010 m	Kazakhstan	
Auyán-tepui	2560 m	Venezuela	

1995 Held the Women's Summit 1995, Tokyo, invited the nine female Everest summitters

Eiger	3970 m	Switzerland
Mönch	4099 m	Switzerland

1996

Cerro Chirripó	3820 m	Costa Rica	
Volcán Barú	3475 m	Panama	
Mauna Kea	4206 m	USA (Hawaii)	
Mauna Loa	4170 m	USA (Hawaii)	
Mount Siguniang DaFeng	5025 m	China	
Cho Oyu	8201 m	China	Third 8000-m peak.

1997 The Oze Forum (HAT-J operation), invited Sir. Edmund Hillary and youth from several Asian countries

*Qurnat as Sawda'	3083 m	Lebanon
*Jabal an Nabi Shu'ayb	3666 m	Yemen
Mount Kumgang	1638 m	North Korea

1998

Gasherbrum II	8035 m	Pakistan	Climbed to 7800 m.
Mont Blanc du Tacul	4248 m	France	

1999	*Mount Olympus	1952 m	Cyprus	Not to the top (as a Royal Air Force radar station is located there).
1999	*Pobeda Peak (Tomur)	7439 m	Kyrgyz	Received Snow Leopard Award.
	*Mount Cameroon	4070 m	Cameroon	

Visited Mount Everest Base Camp to research the garbage issue for Master's degree

2000	Master of Arts degree completed, Kyushu University			
	Mount Sinai	2285 m	Egypt	
	*Huascarán (South Peak)	6768 m	Peru	
2001	Mount Roraima	2810 m	Venezuela	Highest peak in Guyana's Highland Range.
	Mount Ossa	1617 m	Australia	Highest in Tasmania.
	*Pico de Orizaba	5636 m	Mexico	
	Muztagh Ata	7546 m	China	
2002	Pico Ruivo	1861 m	Portugal	Highest on the Madeira Islands.
	Torre (Serra da Estrela)	1993m	Portugal	Highest of mainland Portugal.
	Mount Assiniboine	3618 m	Canada	
	Mount Athabasca	3491 m	Canada	

	Mount Gower	875 m	Australia	Lord Howe Island.
2003	Mount Aorai	2066 m	French Polynesia	Tahiti Island.
	*Pico Turquino	1974 m	Cuba	
	Kaçkar Mountains	3932 m	Turkey	
	*Mount Ararat	5137 m	Turkey	
2004	Mount Victoria (Nat Ma Taung)	3053 m	Myanmar	
2005	Cerro Pastillitos	5090 m	Chile	
	Volcan del Laguna	4900 m	Chile	
	*Ojos del Salado	6893 m	Chile	
	*Mount Teide	3718 m	Spain	
	*Yding Skovhoj	173 m	Denmark	
	*Kebnekaise	2097 m	Sweden	
	*Halti	1328 m	Finland	
	*Galdhopiggen	2469 m	Norway	
	Mount Whitney	4421 m	USA	
	*Mount Apo	2954 m	Philippines	
	*Jebel Chambi	1544 m	Tunisia	

First concert by the Women of No Fear; the project continued until 2016, total of 12 concerts held

2006	Mount Etna	3323 m	Italy	Tallest active volcano on the European continent; climbed to 3252 m.
	Mount Ruapehu	2797 m	New Zealand	Climbed to 2600 m
	Manaslu	8163 m	Nepal	Climbed to 7000 m.
	*Musala	2925 m	Bulgaria	
	*Moldoveanu Peak	2544 m	Romania	
	*Kékes	1014 m	Hungary	
	*Gerlachovský štít	2655 m	Slovakia	
	*Rysy	2499 m	Poland	Also climbed two other peaks on the Slovakian side.
2007	Mount Lamlam	406 m	USA (Guam)	Highest in Guam.
	*Mafadi	3450 m	South Africa	
	Hodgson's Peak (North)	3251 m	South Africa	
	*Thabana Ntlenyana	3482 m	Lesotho	
	Nanhu Mountain (North Peak)	3592 m	Taiwan	In addition to three other 3000-m peaks in Taiwan.
	*Mount Aragats	4090 m	Armenia	Also climbed the West Peak and South Peak.
	Mount Ortsuveri	4365 m	Georgia	

*Aukštojas Hill	294 m	Lithuania	
*Gaizinkalns Hill	312 m	Latvia	
*Suur Munamägi	318 m	Estonia	
2008 *Pico Bolivar	4978 m	Venezuela	
Malchin Peak	4050 m	Mongolia	
*Khüiten Peak	4374 m	Mongolia	
Stok Kangri	6153 m	India	
2009 Mount Pulag	2922 m	Philippines	Highest in Luzon.
Taal Volcano	311 m	Philippines	Smallest volcano on Earth.
Monte Cinto	2710 m	France	Highest in Corsica.
Punta La Marmora	1834 m	Italy	Highest in Sardegna.
Jagattsk	5332 m	India	
*Pico da Neblina	2994 m	Brazil	
*Phnom Aural	1813 m	Cambodia	
2010 *Mount Tahat	2908 m	Algeria	

2011   Established the Cheer Up Tohoku project (HAT-J operation) following the Tohoku Earthquake

*Hvannadalshnjúkur	2110 m	Iceland	
Aiguille du Tour	3540 m	France	

2012	Started the program Mount Fuji for the High School Students of Tohoku Earthquake (run by the Himalayan Adventure Trust of Japan); has continued annually.		
	*Keokradong	986 m	Bangladeshi
2013	Ben Nevis	1344 m	United Kingdom — Highest peak in Scotland.
	*Zugspitze	2962 m	Germany
	*Sněžka	1602 m	Czech Republic
	*Cerro El Pital	2730 m	El Salvador — Climbed to 2500 m; highest point of El Salvador.
	*Pico Mogotón	2106 m	Nicaragua
2014	*Bukit Timah Hill	164 m	Singapore
	*Jabal Umm ad Dami	1854 m	Jordan
	*Dinara	1831 m	Croatia
	*Coma Pedrosa	2943 m	Andorra
	*Mount Ramelau	2986 m	East Timor
2015	*Mont Idoukal-n-Taghès	2022 m	Niger — Also called Mont Bagzane.
	Piz Languard	3262 m	Switzerland
	*Kneiff	560 m	Luxembourg
	*Signal de Botrange	694 m	Belgium

	*Jebel Shams (South Peak)	2997 m	Oman	The North Peak was unavailable to climb due to military restrictions.
2016	Saddle Peak	732 m	India	Highest of Andaman and Nicobar Islands.
	Mount Kerinci	3805 m	Indonesia	Highest of Sumatra; the last mountain Tabei climbed overseas.
	Mount Fuji	3776 m	Japan	Climbed to 3010 m; the last mountain of Tabei's life.

Passed away on October 20, at the age of 77

* Listed are the highest peaks of continents, countries and regions, and other mountains of interest; elevations according to most updated records.

GLOSSARY

Japanese and Nepali Terms

banzai
Direct translation means "10,000 years!" Nowadays, a simple cheer in daily life.

-chan
Commonly used as an honorific addition to a person's name (e.g., Jun-*chan*). Among several similar designations (-san or -sama), *chan* is the friendliest style and more commonly used for children or a person younger than the speaker.

-cho, -machi
Affixed to a name to indicate a town or an area within a town (e.g., Shinano-machi or Miharu-Cho).

chawan-mushi
A Japanese egg-custard dish; unlike other custards, it is usually eaten along with the main course.

daijyobu
"All right" or "OK."

daikon
A white root vegetable that resembles a carrot, often seen in Japanese and Chinese cuisine; spicy and tart, similar to a radish.

-dake, -take, -san, -zan, -yama
Mountain or peak; sometimes used as a part of a place name even without mountains.

furoshiki
A square piece of fabric used to wrap things, like gift wrap, but also used as a bag for groceries, etc.

ganbare
Means basically the same thing as *ganbatte* (see below), but more of a command.

ganbaro
"Let's do our best!" or "Let's all hang tough!"

ganbatte
A saying used to encourage people to try hard, or used before a performance to say, "Good luck!" or "Do your best."

hatsu-gatsuo
Means "first bonito of the season" (a type of fish that usually shows up in the market in early summer).

hiya-yakko
A Japanese dish made with chilled tofu and toppings.

hontoni omedeto
Omedeto means "congratulations." Adding "hontoni" (truly) makes the offer sincerer.

-kai / kai
An organization or club.

kanji
A system of Japanese writing that uses Chinese characters.

kasuri
Refers to blurry, feather-edge patterns that look as if they were splashed onto fabric; used to decorate textiles and clothing (like on a *kimono*).

kibi-dango
A bygone Japanese food, famous for being the ration of the folktale hero Momotarō; a specialty sweet of Okayama Prefecture.

kimono
Japanese traditional clothing.

koinobori
Carp windsocks, streamers or banners that decorate Japan's landscape from April to early May, in honour of Children's Day (May 5).

kotatsu
A low wooden table frame covered by a futon, or heavy blanket, with a tabletop. Underneath is a heat source, formerly a charcoal brazier but now electric, often built into the table itself.

koto
Japanese instrument similar to a harp; lies on the floor, not upright; musician uses pick attached to fingers.

kura
Warehouse, storehouse, shed.

kurotome
Most formal style of kimono for married or older women; black with brilliant patterns on the bottom half only, and with small family crest on the back; usually worn at weddings by the female family members of the couple.

memsahib
Used as a form of address for a European woman in South Asia or colonial India.
Also used for a female mountaineer employing Sherpas or porters in the Himalayas.

nori
An edible seaweed, eaten either fresh or dried in sheets.

oblaat
Thin, edible paper made of starch that melts easily in water; used to wrap powdered medicine that is difficult to swallow; also used to wrap candies.

oishi mono
Tasty things; food, delicacy.

omedeto
Congratulations.

Om mani padme hum
Buddhist mantra that Tibetans believe invokes the blessing of Chenrezig, who embodies compassion.

onegai-shimasu
Difficult to translate to English; roughly, "Please take care of me," or "I am in your care."

orizuru(s)
Paper crane(s); Japanese tradition denotes that people make numerous (most commonly, 1,000) paper cranes to pray for recovery from illness.

otsukaresama deshita
An expression used in the work place that shows appreciation for the hard work of a colleague.

ramen
Quick-cooking noodles (in oriental cuisine), typically served in a broth with meat and vegetables.

-san
Most commonly used honorific added to a person's name. Not altered by gender.

sanma
Japanese name of Pacific saury.

sashimi
A Japanese dish of bite-sized pieces of raw fish eaten with soy sauce and wasabi paste.

-shima
Island; when included as a part of a place name, such as Hiroshima or Fukushima, it does not necessarily denote an actual island.

Soran-bushi
Accompanies the bon dance in many parts of Japan, with its own dancing styles that date back many generations; depicts ocean waves, fishermen dragging nets, pulling ropes and lifting luggage over the shoulders.

tanden
A popular Japanese word in martial arts, Zen practice and far-Eastern medical tradition. It is an energy centre or area, about the size of a grapefruit, located deep inside the *hara*, roughly midway between the top of the pubic bone and the navel.

tarcho
Means "prayer flag" in Tibetan

tatami
Japanese straw mat used for flooring. Japanese measure the size of rooms by counting the number of tatami mats on the floor. Tatami mat size varies by style or area; the most common size is 182 centimetres by 91 centimetres.

yen
The official currency of Japan.

Mountaineering Terms

altitude sickness
Illness that results from lack of oxygen in the air (thin air) at higher elevations. Symptoms include headache, loss of appetite and sleep disruption. It can progress to high altitude pulmonary edema (HAPE), or high altitude cerebral edema (HACE), which are potentially fatal conditions.

belay
A rope safety system that runs a rope through a climbing device to provide a secure line to a climber.

bivouac
A temporary camp without tents or cover used especially by soldiers or mountaineers.

bivouac sack
An extremely small, lightweight, waterproof shelter used by climbers, mountaineers, soldiers and minimalist hikers; also known as a bivy, bivvy, or bivi.

buttress
A prominent feature that juts out from a mountainside.

carabiner
An oval metal loop with a spring-loaded gate used as a connecting device by climbers and mountaineers.

col
The low point of a ridge or saddle between two peaks.

cornice
An overhanging mass of hardened snow at the edge of a mountaintop or ridge.

crevasse
A deep, open crack in the snow and ice of a glacier.

fixed rope
A rope that is anchored to a point of protection.

high porter
A high-altitude porter.

ice axe
A metal tool with an adze and pick at one end of a shaft and a spike at the other; used by mountaineers to ascend and descend snow- and/or ice-covered routes.

Jumar
A mechanical device used for ascending on a rope (also called an ascender).

Kissling
A type of classic rucksack, made from canvas; one of the top brands in earlier mountaineering.

onsen
Hot springs.

piton
A peg or spike driven into a rock or crack to support a climber or a rope.

rappel
To descend a rock face by way of an anchored rope system.

self-belay
A self-directed system of rope safety for a single climber, rather than a two-person belay.

sirdar
A Sherpa mountain guide who manages the other Sherpas in a climbing expedition or trekking group.

snow picket
An anchor designed for snow and used for climbing, securing tents, etc.

Acknowledgements

Thank you to Junko Tabei for sharing her stories about mountains climbed, lessons learned and a life well lived, and to the Tabei family for their support in the completion of this book. Additional gratitude to all the friends, teammates and climbing partners of Tabei-*san*.

Thanks to the entire team at Rocky Mountain Books, with special recognition of Don Gorman who supported the idea of *Honouring High Places* without hesitation and Meaghan Craven for her diligent editing work and positive approach in the final stages of the project. Added thanks to Barry Blanchard, Lydia Bradey, Jennifer Carlson, Patricia Cullimore, Tetsushige Doyama, Derek Holtved, Taichi Ishizuka, Rieko Ito, Setsuko Kitamura, Tomo Kosaki, Marc Lavoie-Moisan, Lynn Martel, Shin Matsumoto, Naoki Matsushita, Makoto Miyazaki (*The Yomiuri Shimbun*), Hiroshi Namba, Mariko Namba, Dr. Monica O'Gorman, Chic Scott, Eiko Tabe, Kohei Takashina, Brian Webster, Vita Yamamoto and Minako Yoshida. Extended thanks to the many people included in these memoirs.

References

Ladies Climbing Club. *Annapurna: Women's Battle.* Tokyo: Tokyo Shimbun Publishing Bureau, 1973.

Kitamura, Setsuko. *Lipstick and Ice Axe.* Tokyo: Tokyo Shimbun Publishing Bureau, 1997.

Tabei, Junko. *Leave the Apron, Off to the Dream Mountains.* Tokyo: Tokyo Shimbun Publishing Bureau, 1996.

———. *Loving High Places.* Tokyo: Shogakukan Inc., 2007.

———. *Tabei-san, It's the Summit.* (Second- and third-edition title of original *Mom on Everest*, 2000) Tokyo: Yama-kei Publishers Co., Ltd., 2012.

———. *Climbing Mountains, Nevertheless.* Tokyo: Bungeishunjyu Ltd., 2013.

———. *The Mountains for Me.* Tokyo: PHP Institute, Inc., 2015.

———. *Relapse!* Tokyo: Bungeishunjyu Ltd., 2016.

Tabei, Junko, ed. *Women on Everest.* Tokyo: Yama-kei Publishers Co., Ltd., 1998.

The Yomiuri Shimbun. Everest: The Women's Glory. Tokyo Shimbun Publishing: 1975.

INDEX